CHRISTINA LAMB is one of Britain's leading foreign correspondents and a bestselling author. Currently Chief Foreign Correspondent of the *Sunday Times*, she has won fourteen major awards including five times being named Foreign Correspondent of the Year and winning Europe's top war-reporting prize, the Prix Bayeux. She is the author of numerous books including *Farewell Kabul, The Africa House, Waiting for Allah, The Sewing Circles of Herat* and *House of Stone*. She co-wrote the international bestseller *I Am Malala* with Malala Yousafzai and *The Girl from Aleppo* with Nujeen Mustafa. She is an honorary fellow of University College, Oxford and was awarded an OBE in 2013.

'A wake-up call to the magnitude and horrors of rape in war – the world's most neglected war crime. These women's stories will make you weep, and then rage at the world's indifference'

AMAL CLOONEY

'In her new book, *Our Bodies, Their Battlefield: What War Does to Women,* she tells the untold stories of war rape survivors and their lonely battle for justice. Her book is a wakeup call to the magnitude and horror of rape for women throughout history and the world. Sharing these stories is necessary and incredibly brave'

SHERYL SANDBERG

'Christina Lamb has done the impossible – and written women into history … An extraordinary achievement of in-depth journalism, powerful storytelling, grit and heart. A wake-up call to the magnitude and horror of rape of women throughout history and the world. If you read one b̶̶̶

'Lamb is a gifted writer ... A timely reminder that better outcomes will come only when we start insisting that these stories are heard'
Daily Telegraph

'A harrowing but vital book ... The litany of pain she recounts is all too believable. I know because I have heard it too ... silence is women's worst enemy, and that's why, while some may be tempted to turn away from the horror, this is such an important book'
LINDSEY HILSUM, *Guardian*

'This harrowing account of the thousands of rape victims airbrushed from history is required reading ... [A] deeply traumatic and important book ... Provides a corrective that is by turns horrific and profoundly moving ... Lamb is an extraordinary writer. Her compassion for those she talks to and deep understanding of how to tell their stories makes this a book that should be required reading for all – even though (and perhaps because) it is not an enjoyable experience ... This is a powerful book that not only underlines how women have been written out of history, but how victims of rape have had their suffering enabled, ignored and perpetuated'
PETER FRANKOPAN, *Guardian*

'Superb exposé ... To tell some of these stories, Lamb clearly has put herself in peril, and it's difficult to overpraise her courage or a book that – for the breadth and moral force of its arguments – is perhaps the most important work of nonfiction about rape since Susan Brownmiller's *Against Our Will* (1975). A searing, absolutely necessary exposé of the uses of rape in recent wars and of global injustices to the survivors'
Kirkus

ALSO BY CHRISTINA LAMB

Waiting for Allah: Benazir Bhutto and Pakistan

The Africa House: The True Story of an English Gentleman and His African Dream

The Sewing Circles of Herat: My Afghan Years

House of Stone: The True Story of a Family Divided in War-Torn Zimbabwe

Small Wars Permitting: Dispatches from Foreign Lands

Farewell Kabul: From Afghanistan to a More Dangerous World

I Am Malala (with Malala Yousafzai)

The Girl from Aleppo (with Nujeen Mustafa)

CHRISTINA LAMB

Our Bodies Their Battlefield

What War Does to Women

WILLIAM
COLLINS

William Collins
An imprint of HarperCollins*Publishers*
1 London Bridge Street
London SE1 9GF

WilliamCollinsBooks.com

HarperCollins*Publishers*
1st Floor, Watermarque Building, Ringsend Road
Dublin 4, Ireland

First published in Great Britain in 2020 by William Collins
This William Collins paperback edition published in 2021

1

ISBN 978-0-0-0830004-3

Maps by Martin Brown

Set in Bell MT
Printed and bound in Great Britain by
CPI Group (UK) Ltd, Croydon

We have given our most precious thing and have died inside many times but you won't find our names engraved on any monument or war memorial.

Aisha, survivor of rape in the 1971 Bangladesh war

Contents

Maps

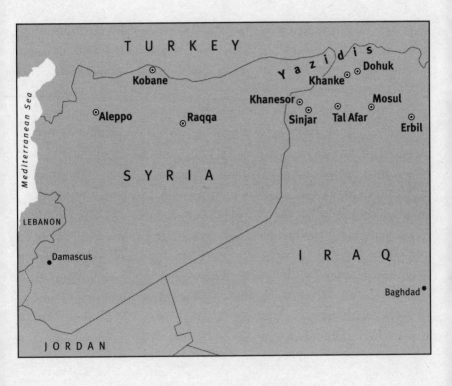

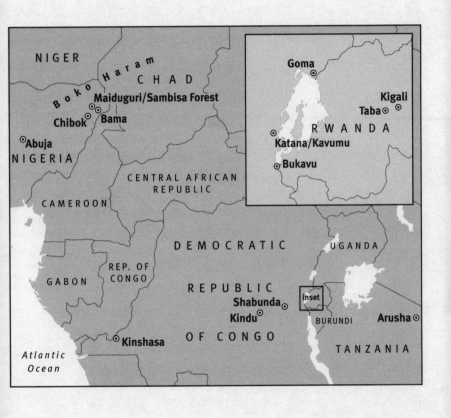

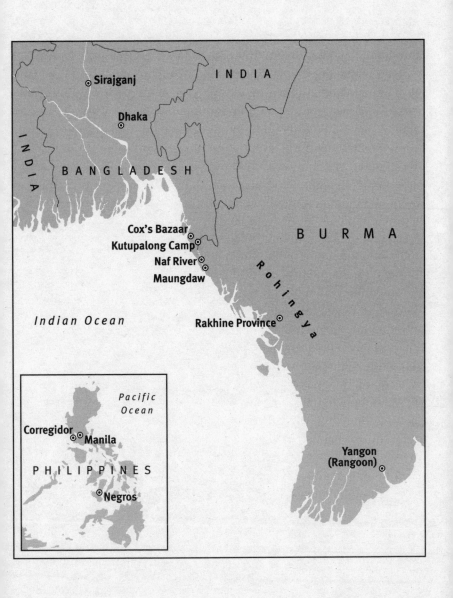

Prologue

The Girl I Once Was

They put the names in the bowl and began to draw them out. Ten names, ten girls. The girls quivered like kittens caught under a dripping tap. For them this was no lucky dip. The men pulling out the slips of paper were fighters from Islamic State and each would take a girl as a slave.

Naima stared at her hands, blood pounding in her ears. The girl next to her was younger than her, about fourteen, and mewling with fear, but when Naima tried to hold her hand, one of the men whipped off his belt and lashed them apart.

That man was older and larger than the others, around sixty, she guessed, with a belly cascading over his trousers and a vicious curl to his lips. By then she had been nine months in ISIS captivity. She knew none of them were kind but she prayed that one didn't pick her name.

'Naima.' The man who read out her name was Abu Danoon. He looked younger, almost like her brother, the hair on his chin still fluff; maybe he would have less cruelty in his heart.

The draw continued. The fat man picked out the young girl next to her. But then he said something to the others in Arabic, pulled out two crisp hundred-dollar notes and slapped them on the table. Abu Danoon shrugged, pocketed the money, and handed over his slip of paper.

Minutes later the fat man was shoving her into his black Land Cruiser and driving through the streets of Mosul, a city she had once dreamed of visiting but which was now the capital of these monsters who had swept into her homeland and abducted her and six of her brothers and sisters, among thousands of others.

She stared through the tinted windows. An old man sitting on a cart was whipping a donkey to jerk it forward, and people were out shopping, though the only women in the streets were in black hijab. It was strange to see everyday life still going on for other people, almost like watching a movie.

Her captor was an Iraqi called Abdul Hasib and he was a mullah. The religious ones were the worst.

'He did everything to me,' she later recounted. 'Hitting, sex, pulling my hair, sex, everything … I was refusing so he forced me and hit me. He said, "You are my *sabaya*" – my slave.

'After that I just lay there and tried to float my mind above my body as if it was happening to someone else so he couldn't steal all of me.

'He had two wives and a daughter but they did nothing to help me. In between pleasing him I would have to do all the housework. Once I was washing dishes and one of the wives came and made me take a tablet – some kind of Viagra. They also gave me contraceptives.'

Her only respite came every ten days when the mullah went to Syria to visit the other part of their Caliphate.

After a month or so, Abdul Hasib sold her for $4500 to another Iraqi called Abu Ahla, a healthy profit. 'Abu Ahla ran a cement factory and had two wives and nine children. Two of his sons were fighters with ISIS. It was the same thing, forcing me to have sex but then he took me to the house of his friend Abu Suleiman, and sold me for $8000. Abu Suleiman sold me to Abu Daud who kept me for a week then he sold me to Abu Faisal, who was a bomb maker in Mosul. He kept me for twenty days of raping then sold me to Abu Badr.'

In the end she was sold to twelve different men. She lists them one by one, their *nom de guerre* and real names, even their children's names, all of which she had committed to memory, for she was determined they would pay.

'To be sold like that from one to another as if we were goats was the worst,' she said. 'I tried to kill myself, to throw myself out of a car. Another time I found some tablets and took the lot. But still I woke up. I felt even death didn't want me.'

I am writing a book about rape in war. It's the cheapest weapon known to man. It devastates families and empties villages. It turns young girls into outcasts who wish their lives over when they are hardly begun. It begets children who are daily reminders to their mothers of their ordeal and are often rejected by their community as 'bad blood'. And it's almost always ignored in the history books.

Every time I think I have heard the worst I can hear, I meet someone like Naima. In jeans and a checked shirt with black trainers, her hazel-brown hair drawn back in a ponytail from a pale scrubbed face, she looked like a teenager, though she was twenty-two and had just turned eighteen when she was captured. We sat on cushions in her neatly swept tent in Khanke camp near the northern Iraqi city of Dohuk, one of row upon row of white tents that had become a home of sorts to thousands of Yazidis. We talked for hours. Once she'd started, she did not want to stop. And though sometimes she laughed, telling me of small acts of revenge she managed to inflict on her captors, she never smiled.

Before I left she turned her phone over to show me a passport photo inside the back cover. It was her as a smiling schoolgirl and the only thing she had left from a childhood in which she had never heard of the word rape. 'I need to believe I am still that girl,' she said.

*   *   *

Maybe you think of rape as something that has 'always happened in war', that goes along with pillage. Ever since man has gone to war he has helped himself to the women, whether to humiliate his enemy, wreak revenge, satisfy his lust, or just because he can – indeed rape is so common in war that we speak of the rape of a city to describe its wanton destruction.

As one of few women in a field that was still mostly male, I came into war reporting by accident and it was not the bang-bang that interested me but what went on behind the lines – how people keep life together and feed, educate and shelter their children and protect their elderly while around them all hell is breaking loose.

The Afghan mother telling me how she scraped moss from rocks to sustain her children as she shepherded them through the hills to escape bombing. The mothers under siege in the old city of East Aleppo who conjured up sandwiches for their children from fried flour and foraged leaves, and kept the children warm by burning furniture or window frames while streets around them were bombed into grey dust. The Rohingya women who carried their children through forests and across rivers to safety after Burmese soldiers massacred the men and burned down their huts.

You won't find these women's names in the history books or on the war memorials that we pass in our railway stations and town centres but to me they are the real heroes.

The longer I have done this job, the more disquieted I have become, not just at the horrors I have seen, but at the feeling we often only hear half the story, perhaps because those collating the accounts are generally male. Even now, histories of these conflicts are mostly told by men. Men writing about men. And then sometimes women writing about men. Women's voices are too often left out. During the first part of the war in Iraq in 2003, up to the toppling of Saddam Hussein, I was one of six correspondents on the ground for my newspaper, the *Sunday Times*. When I read the reports afterwards, my three male colleagues and one of my two fellow women had not quoted a single Iraqi woman. It was as if they weren't there.

It is not just the writers who see these lands of war as lands of men. Women are often excluded from negotiations to end wars even though study after study have shown that peace agreements are more likely to endure if women are involved.

I used to think we were safer as women in a war zone, that there was a certain honour toward women. But there is no honour among terrorist groups and merchants of evil. It seems clear that in many of today's conflict zones it is more dangerous to be a woman. Over the last five years, I have seen more shocking brutality against women, in country after country, than I have witnessed in more than three decades as a foreign correspondent.

*   *   *

One only need visit the great galleries of the world or leaf through the classics to see that rape in war is nothing new. The very first history book in western history, by Herodotus, opens with a series of abductions of women by the Phoenicians then the Greeks and eventually the Trojans snatching Helen, setting off the Greek invasion of Asia and the Persian retaliation. 'Plainly the women would never have been carried away, had not they themselves wished it,' quotes Herodotus, in an early indication of how men would write history. In Homer's *Iliad*, the Greek general Agamemnon promises Achilles women in abundance if he captures Troy: '… if the gods permit us to sack the great city of Priam, let him pick out twenty Trojan women for himself.' Indeed the feud between the two men is caused by Agamemnon being forced to give up the woman he took as a 'prize' and trying to help himself to that of Achilles. The Roman writer Tacitus writes how Britain's iconic Iron Age warrior queen Boudicca rose up against Nero's Romans after the death of her husband Prasutagus when they not only looted her palace and publicly beat her, but gang-raped her two daughters.

Rape and pillage were ways of rewarding unpaid recruits and for a conqueror to emphasise victory by punishing and subjugating opponents, what the Romans termed *Vae victis* (Woe to the conquered).

Nor was it just in ancient times. If we follow the ancient Greeks, Persians and Romans, Alexander the Great and the string of fair-haired blue-eyed children left across Central Asia, to the 'comfort women' of the Imperial Japanese Army and the mass rapes of German women by the Red Army in World War Two, we see that women have long been seen as spoils of war.

'Man's discovery that his genitalia could serve as a weapon to generate fear must rank as one of the most important discoveries of prehistoric times along with the use of fire and the first crude stone axe,' concluded the American writer Susan Brownmiller in her ground-breaking account of rape, *Against Our Will*, published in 1975.

Rape is as much of a weapon of war as the machete, club or Kalashnikov. In recent years, ethnic and sectarian groups from Bosnia to Rwanda, Iraq to Nigeria, Colombia to Central African Republic, have used rape as a deliberate strategy, almost a weapon of mass destruction, not just to destroy dignity and terrorise communities but to wipe out what they see as rival ethnicities or non-believers.

'We will conquer your Rome, break your crosses and enslave your women,' warned Abu Mohammad al-Adnani, spokesman for the Islamic State, in a message to the West as ISIS fighters swept into northern Iraq and Syria in 2014, abducting thousands of girls like Naima.

A similar threat came from Boko Haram, an even more deadly terror group, as it stormed villages in northern Nigeria, killing the men and rounding up girls as 'bush wives' to be kept in camps to produce offspring, a new generation of jihadis in a chilling real-life version of Margaret Atwood's *The Handmaid's Tale*.

'I abducted your girls … I will sell them in the market, by Allah,' declared Abubakar Shekau, after kidnapping hundreds of schoolgirls. 'I will marry off a woman at the age of twelve. I will marry off a girl at the age of nine.'

I listened to women with unimaginable stories and as I poured my heart into trying to do justice in recounting them for the readers of my newspaper, I asked myself, over and over, How does this keep happening?

The intimate nature of rape means it is under-reported generally and even more so in conflict zones where reprisals are likely, stigmatisation common, and evidence hard to gather. Unlike killings, there are no corpses and numbers are hard to quantify.

But even where we do know, where courageous women come forward to describe their ordeals, rarely is action taken. It almost seemed as if rape was somehow trivialised and regarded acceptable when it occurred in war, particularly in far-off places. Or that we didn't want to know. Sometimes after I tapped the last full stop and sent off my stories, editors told me they were too shocking for readers, or slapped 'Disturbing Content' warnings across the top.

To my astonishment the first prosecution of rape as a war crime was only in 1998.

Surely rape during war had been illegal for centuries? The first trial I could find was in the German town of Breisach in 1474 when Sir Peter von Hagenbach, a knight working for the Duke of Burgundy, was convicted for violation 'of the laws of God and man', a five-year reign of terror in which he raped and killed civilians as governor in the upper Rhine valley. His defence that he was 'only following orders' was rejected and he was executed. Some describe the twenty-eight-man panel set up by the Archduke of Austria as the very first international criminal tribunal; others argue that this wasn't war rape as there was no conflict at the time.

One of the very first comprehensive efforts to codify the laws of war rejected the long-held view of rape as an inevitable consequence of conflict. President Abraham Lincoln's General Orders No. 100, also known as the Lieber Code, issued in 1863 for the conduct of Union soldiers in the US Civil War, strictly prohibited rape 'under penalty of death'.

In 1919, in response to the atrocities of the First World War, including the massacre of hundreds of thousands of Armenians by the Turks, a Commission of Responsibilities was set up. Rape and forced prostitution were near the top of a list of thirty-two war crimes.

That didn't stop it in the Second World War. Outrage at the horrors of that war, when all parties to the conflict were accused of rape, led to the victors establishing the first international tribunals in Nuremberg and Tokyo to prosecute war crimes. Yet there was not a single prosecution for sexual violence.

Not even an apology. Instead silence. Silence on the sexual slavery of the comfort women. Silence on the thousands of German women raped by Stalin's troops whom I read nothing about in my school history books. Silence too in Spain where General Franco's Falangists had raped women and branded their breasts.

For too long this has been the reaction. War rape was met with tacit acceptance and committed with impunity, military and political leaders shrugging it off as if it were a sideshow. Or it was denied to have ever happened.

The second paragraph of Article 27 of the Geneva Convention adopted in 1949 states: 'Women shall be especially protected against any attack on their honour, in particular against rape, enforced prostitution, or any form of indecent assault.'

For decades it has been the world's most neglected war crime. It took rape camps being set up again in the heart of Europe for the issue to get international attention. Like many people, the first time I heard of sexual violence in conflict was in the 1990s during the war in Bosnia.

The resulting outrage suggested the end of the tacit acceptance of rape in war that had existed historically. In 1998, the same year as the first conviction, rape as a war crime was enshrined in the Rome Statute which established the International Criminal Court.

On 19 June 2008, the United Nations Security Council unanimously passed Resolution 1820 on the use of sexual violence in war, indicating that 'rape and other forms of sexual violence can constitute a war crime, a crime against humanity, or a constitutive act with respect to genocide'.

A year later, the Office of the Special Representative of the UN Secretary General on Sexual Violence in Conflict was established.

In twenty years the International Criminal Court had not made a single conviction for sexual violence until November 2019, when it convicted Congolese warlord Bosco Ntaganda, nickname 'Terminator', on eighteen counts, including murder, rape, sexual slavery and using child soldiers. If anything there seems less international appetite than ever to act against atrocities such as those in Syria, Burma and Yemen.

Having these crimes on the statute books is a start, but clearly no guarantee of enforcement or even proper investigation. By their very nature these crimes are often not witnessed and direct orders not written down, and hard for victims to prove or admit to. The situation has not been helped by the fact that investigators are often male and not always adept at eliciting testimony on such sensitive matters. Decision-making positions are often held by male prosecutors or judges who do not see sexual violence as a high priority compared to mass killings, sometimes even suggesting the women 'asked for it'.

Sadly, the fact that the international community now recognises that sexual violence is often used as a deliberate military strategy, which can be prosecuted, has ended nothing in many places across the world. The 2019 report of the UN Special Representative on Sexual Violence in Conflict listed nineteen countries where women were being raped in war and named twelve national military and police forces and forty-one non-state actors. This was by no means a comprehensive list, it noted, but 'where credible information was available'.

And then there was #MeToo. For many of us 2017 may be remembered as a turning point for speaking out about sexual violence. The emergence of the #MeToo movement following the allegations by a string of actresses and production assistants against Hollywood producer Harvey Weinstein lifted the guilt and shame so many assaulted women felt and emboldened them to speak out.

Like many women I followed the #MeToo movement with a mixture of delight and horror. Delight that so many women were speaking out and refusing to take more of the harassment many of us middle-aged women once took for granted. Horror that sexual violence was so prevalent – one in three women experience sexual violence in their lifetime. It knows no race, no class, no borders: it happens everywhere.

But I also felt a certain unease. What about the women who do not have resources for lawyers or access to media? What about those in countries where rape is used as a weapon?

As we saw with those who spoke about Harvey Weinstein, even strong independent women in the liberal west who speak out about sexual predators do so with extreme difficulty and dread. Often they are pilloried in the press and have to go into hiding, as happened to Dr Christine Blasey Ford, the lawyer who alleged she had been sexually assaulted as a teenager by Brett Kavanaugh, nominee for Supreme Court judge.

Imagine then women with no money or education in lands where those with the gun or machete exert the power. Not for them rape counselling or compensation. Instead they are often the ones condemned. Condemned to a lifetime of trauma and disturbed nights, problems in forming relationships, not to mention physical damage, perhaps a childless existence – they may even be ostracised from their communities, what one referred to as 'slow murder'.

Around the world a woman's body is still very much a battlefield, and hundreds of thousands of women bear the invisible wounds of war.

And so I set out to tell some of these women's stories in their own words. It would be the start of a shocking journey through Africa, Asia, Europe and South America to explore some of the darkest deeds known to man. The more places I went to the more prevalent I found rape was, because of the repeated failure of the international community and domestic courts to bring perpetrators to justice.

These are not easy stories to tell or to listen to. But they are often ones of astonishing bravery and heroism.

Women are not just bystanders of history. It's time to stop only telling half the story.

1

On Mussolini's Island

Leros, August 2016

When I look back to that summer on the tiny Greek island of Leros, to the derelict mental asylum littered with pigeon droppings and rusting iron bedsteads, where I first met the Yazidis, I still see the girl's eyes, so deep and troubled and pleading.

She is thrusting her phone at me to show me a video. I can see an iron cage with perhaps a dozen young women inside and Arabic men crowded around jeering, Kalashnikovs on their shoulders. At first, I don't understand. The women look petrified. Then the men step back, flames engulf the cage, there are screams and the video ends.

'That is my sister,' said the girl. 'They are burning virgins alive.'

Everything seems to stop and spin. It is a vision of Hell. I don't know if the sound in my head is the sea outside or blood rushing to my ears. Sun is pouring through a hole in the roof and sweat is running down our faces. A small Yazidi child is trailing through the rubble and broken glass and downed rafters, singing to herself, a waif of a thing with strands of hair stuck to her cheek like fronds. She is getting closer and closer to a large crater in the floorboards until, in panic, I yank her away. Her mother, resting against a stone wall next to the girl whose sister was burnt alive, stares blankly ahead. What has happened to these people?

I want to get out of that asylum with its barred windows and stained walls. Before coming here I'd watched an old documentary called 'Island of Outcasts' and images crowd into my head from that film of shaven-headed men and women, some of them naked and chained to their beds, limbs jerking at strange angles, others in shapeless smocks, crammed on the floor of a room staring into the camera.

Through the window's bars, I can see down below, row upon row of white prefab containers surrounded by wire concertina fence, and beyond that the Aegean Sea, jarring in its deep blue perfection.

The camp where these Yazidis are living is more than a thousand miles from their homeland under the tall sacred mountain between Iraq and Syria on which they believe Noah's Ark came to rest.

I had never before met Yazidis. Their religion is one of the world's most ancient but, like most people, the first I had heard of

Living in containers in the shadow of the derelict asylum

them was at the end of summer in 2014 when I saw the pictures of thousands of Yazidis trapped on that mountain where they had fled convoy after convoy of black-clad ISIS fighters intent on exterminating them.

In the ruins of that asylum that sweltering August day, one after another came forward from the shadows to tell me their stories, stories that shook my very core, were worse than anything I had heard in three decades as a foreign correspondent.

Broken people, the women with thin wavy bodies and long purplish hair framing faces drained of light, it seemed to me they were neither living nor dead. All had lost parents, brothers, sisters. In whispery voices like wafts of wind, they told of their beloved homeland of Sinjar, which they pronounced as Shingal, and the mountain of the same name which they thought would give sanctuary but where many perished of hunger and thirst. They told of a small town called Kocho, which ISIS had kept under siege for thirteen days then slaughtered all the men and older women and captured the virgins. And of the Galaxy Cinema, on the east bank of the Tigris river, where girls – some of them their sisters – were divided into ugly and beautiful then paraded to ISIS fighters in a market to be bought as their sex slaves.

The mother of the little girl who almost walked into the hole was from Kocho. She was thirty-five, her name was Asma Bashar and her voice was staccato like a machine gun. The others called her Asma Loco because they said she had lost her mind. She told me that forty members of her family had been slaughtered, including her mother, father and brothers. Four sisters and twelve nieces had been taken as sex slaves. 'I have no one left but one sister who managed to escape from captivity and is now in Germany,' she said. 'I take pills to try and blot out what happened.'

A younger woman who until then had stood still as a portrait against the cracked blue wall, started speaking. 'I am twenty but I feel more than forty,' she said. Her name was Ayesha and she told

Ayesha, whose parents and brothers were killed by ISIS

me her parents and brothers were killed in Kocho. 'I saw my grandmother die, I saw children die and now I just remember bad things. Four of my friends were sold for just twenty euros.'

She had managed to flee to the mountain with her husband then they had somehow made their way across war-torn Syria into Turkey. There they had paid $5000 to people smugglers to cross the Aegean to Greece, making several abortive attempts in patched-up overcrowded dinghies before finally landing on the island.

'After all this we find we are still not free,' she said. She held out her left wrist. Raised red scars criss-cross the pale skin like angry worms. 'I tried to kill myself with a knife,' she shrugged. The last time had been just two weeks earlier.

* * *

Leros has always been an island of outcasts – a leper colony, an internment camp for political prisoners and an asylum for so-called 'untreatables'. In 2015 it became one of many Greek islands that had been swamped by refugees, fleeing war in Syria, Iraq and Afghanistan.

It was the refugee crisis that had brought me as a journalist to the island. Leros was one of five Greek islands that had been declared 'hotspots' after the European Union struck a deal with Turkey in 2016, paying them three billion euros to stop any new arrivals crossing the Aegean. Ten thousand refugees left stranded on the islands were concentrated in these five processing centres but the process was so slow they were in effect island prisons. I'd been to others in Lesbos, Chios and Kos and witnessed the uneasy juxtaposition of these desperate refugees fenced in camps, stadiums and former factories, so preyed on by sex-traffickers that women wore nappies at night in order not to have to leave their tents, while nearby carefree holidaymakers were enjoying the sun, sea and moussaka washed down by ouzo.

Leros was different. I'd never been anywhere quite like it. It had the blinding white fishing villages of higgledy-piggledy houses, windmills, tavernas and sparkling blue seas typical of the Greek islands. But its main town Lakki was a study in Stalinist art deco, all wide avenues and sharp-angled villas in stark concrete, with a colonnaded cinema, a circular marketplace, a school that resembled an agricultural silo, a minimalist clock tower, as well as buildings that looked like a UFO and an old-fashioned transistor radio. It was like stumbling across a forgotten film set.

The island had once been central to Mussolini's plans to create a second Roman Empire. Leros, along with all the Dodecanese, had been seized from the Ottoman Turks in 1912, becoming part of an Italian colonial empire that included Libya, Somalia and Eritrea. When Mussolini took power in the 1920s, he decided its deep natural harbour made the ideal naval base from which to establish control over the entire eastern Mediterranean. So he sent in naval forces and administrators, as well as architects to plan a modern city in the fascist style the Italians call *razionalismo.*

After Italy was defeated in the Second World War, control of the islands passed to Greece, and Lakki (or Portolago as the Italians had called it) was largely abandoned. When the colonels later seized power in Greece in 1967, they used Mussolini's naval barracks to lock up political prisoners, then as a place to banish the mentally ill. Thousands of patients were shipped from the mainland and kept in medieval conditions until this was exposed in the press and the 1990 documentary I had seen, which prompted outrage across the EU and led to its closure in 1997. Then came the refugees.

To get to the refugee camp I drove past a series of abandoned brick buildings and rusted ambulances. A few people came out to stare including a wild-eyed man pushing a wheelbarrow and waving a fist – some patients had remained.

It was an eerie place for a camp. Inside were about 700 Syrians, Iraqis, Afghans and Pakistanis, a third of whom were children. There were around a hundred Yazidis. These refugees made up 10 per cent of the population of the small island.

Up close the white containers turned out to be Iso-Boxes designed for transporting food, now turned into homes, with lines of laundry strung between them and old men crouched outside playing improvised backgammon with bottle tops. Conditions were not bad compared to some camps I had visited but, as its administrator Yiannis Hrisafitis pointed out, 'This wasn't their dream.' They were not allowed to leave the island and so were stranded in limbo while EU countries failed to agree who would take them. Meanwhile they had nothing to do, nothing to think about but their terrible memories, and no hope for the future.

I wandered between the laundry lines followed by a small boy clutching a large teddy bear, who ran away when I tried to speak to him. A gaggle of Syrian women sat on a bed smoking, their faces deeply lined. The local hospital had told me that there were regular suicide attempts.

The camp was surrounded by a double fence topped with whorls of razor wire like a prison. 'It's to stop those from outside coming in,' explained Yiannis. 'Maybe somebody wants to steal children or young women or buy organs or sell drugs.'

The Yazidi section had another fence round it to make a camp within a camp. Yiannis explained that a couple of weeks before my visit the Yazidis had been attacked by other refugees, Sunni Muslims, who denounced them as devil worshippers just as ISIS had done, so he had cordoned them off for their own protection. They had gone to the asylum to talk to me because they considered it safer.

I noticed the Yazidis all had red and white cords twisted round their wrists. When I asked what these signified, they explained that the white symbolised the peace they yearn for, and the red the blood of their people killed in previous genocides – by Muslims, Persians, Mongols, Ottomans, Iraqis … all their neighbours. They told me the latest genocide, by ISIS, was the seventy-fourth. There had been so much violence against Yazidis that they had a word for attempted extermination – *ferman* – long before its English equivalent, genocide, which was coined only in 1944 by Polish lawyer Raphael Lemkin.

'Here is like a prison, everyone fighting each other,' said Ayesha, the very still girl who seemed to have stepped out of a painting. 'We have nothing left, no money, we spent everything to get here and the world does not care about us.'

On my last day on the island the Yazidis told me of a secret village in Germany where they said more than a thousand of the girls kept as sex slaves were being sheltered after having escaped or been rescued. I was intrigued.

2

The Girls in the Forest

Baden-Württemburg

Turko looked down at her wrist on which she wore a bracelet of blue glass-eye beads common in the Middle East as protection against the evil eye, as well as one of the twisted red-and-white genocide cords, and she fiddled with them. 'How does it help me to tell my story?' she asked.

That was a difficult question. Turko was from Kocho, the village where ISIS massacred 600 people and abducted many girls. She told me she was thirty-five but with her dark hair scrunched back from a face that looked as if it had had all the light drawn out, she looked ten years older.

I was torn between the journalistic desire to know, the fear of what she might have to say, and above all the concern that telling me her story would bring her more grief. I looked around the small room she had been living in for the last year, sparsely furnished with a single bed, small wardrobe and a few photographs of children taped on the wall, almost like a student's room. Outside the window was nothing but dark forest.

'Maybe so it never happens again to other women,' I ventured. 'But don't say anything you don't want to.'

Turko fixed her eyes on me as if staring into my soul. Then she started speaking. 'Everything began that first Sunday in August two years ago when Daesh moved into Sinjar,' she said. 'We thought the peshmerga [Kurdish militia] who manned the checkpoints would protect us but they had fled.

'I used to work doing odd jobs in the fields and was with my mother and three-year-old niece early that morning when three cars roared up and armed men in black jumped out. They rounded up about forty people and shoved us into a chicken shed where they said "Give us your phones, gold and money!" They took everything we had.

'Then they separated the men from the women and children. My uncle and cousin were with us and they took them to the fields. Then we could hear the bullets, rat-a-tat-tat, one after another.

'We started shaking. They put us in a truck and drove us past the dead bodies of the men to Badosh prison. The prisoners had been released and they had filled it with women, hundreds of women. It was a kind of Hell. We were given no food or water, just a piece of dry bread each day. We were so desperate we were forced to drink from the latrines.

'On the first day the fighters brought a long-bearded man with three Korans who told us he would teach us Islam. We said no, we don't want your religion, we want our families back. That made them angry. They pointed their guns at us and said "We'll kill you if you don't convert!" Then they pushed us against the wall and beat us with wooden sticks.

'We marked a notch on the wall for each night. After fifteen days we were loaded in buses to Tal Afar, and taken to a hotel where we were penned with hundreds of women. First they separated children under twelve then they divided us into married women and virgins. I pretended to be the mother of my three-year-old niece to avoid being taken with the virgins.

'We were kept in that hotel for two months. Sometimes ISIS fighters came and beat everyone and took a woman or young girl for two days then brought them back. For a while I was taken with some of the older women and mothers to the next village to work in a bakery and make food. But then they realised the children were not ours and said they would take us to Syria.'

She stopped for a cigarette and drew on it heavily, her hand shaking.

'We got to Raqqa about 11 p.m.,' she continued. 'They took us to a two-storey building with about 350 women and girls. Every day people were coming and looking at us then women would be taken and handed out to ISIS men.'

Turko was kept in that market for forty days, fearful every day. In the end it was her turn. She and her little niece were taken to the Syrian town of Deir Azzour and handed over to a Saudi man, a judge in the Sharia courts that ISIS had set up. The first night he summoned her to his bedroom. 'I bought you so you are my *sabaya* and it's written in the Koran I can rape you,' he told her.

He was referring to a pamphlet issued by 'the Isis resurgence fatwa department' in October 2014 with guidelines on how to keep, capture and sexually abuse slaves. The pamphlet stated that Yazidis were infidels whose enslavement was a 'firmly established aspect of sharia' so they could be systematically raped. They could be given as gifts and sold on the whim of the owner for they were 'merely property'.

'I tried to resist him but he beat me until blood streamed from my nose,' she said. 'The next morning, he grabbed me by my hair, cuffed my arms to the bed [she mimicked being outstretched like a crucifix] then forced himself on me. For four months it was like this, he raped me three times every day and never let me out.

'When he went to work, he locked me inside. He beat my niece but didn't rape her.

'One day he came home with a British woman he had married. She was 22 and went by the name "Muslim". Whenever he raped me this woman went crazy, she was very jealous. Eventually he got fed up, put me in a black hijab, drove me to ISIS headquarters in the town and locked me in the car. After ten minutes he came back and said "I sold you for 350 dollars."

'They were trading us on the internet,' she said. Fighters had a forum called Caliphate Market where they advertised women along with PlayStation consoles and second-hand cars.

'My new "owner" was a prison warder from Syria. He took me and my niece to stay with an ISIS woman. It was the same as before. Every evening the Syrian came and raped me then went away in the morning. When the ISIS woman went out she handcuffed my arms to something so I couldn't escape.

'Any time any Yazidi girl fled captivity and went on TV, they would beat us more, saying they are badmouthing ISIS so we will teach you a lesson. I often thought of killing myself. The only reason I didn't was because my brother's little girl was with me and then she would die too.'

Turko

Turko was kept by the prison warder for two months until one of her uncles eventually paid $2500 to get her and her niece freed. On 25 May 2015, after more than nine months in captivity, she was taken to a refugee camp in northern Iraq.

On her hand was a small tattoo which she told me was the name of her brother. 'I have no one else,' she said. 'My father died years ago and the last time I saw my mum was in the ISIS prison when we were first captured. From my whole family so many died.

'That's why when I heard about the air bridge to Germany, I applied to come with my sister-in-law and niece. What could we do in Iraq anymore, we who had been raped and dirtied?'

Germany had long had a sizeable Yazidi community and the idea of giving women like Turko shelter surfaced in September 2014 when local Yazidi leaders approached Winfried Kretschmann, premier of the southern state of Baden-Württemburg. 'Please do something!' they begged as they showed him pictures of mass killings of their people in Sinjar, including beheadings and crucifixions, and told him of girls kept as sex slaves.

Krestchmann was a committed Christian and member of the Green Party and he was horrified. He spoke to Dr Michael Blume, an academic who was responsible for religious minorities for the state and married to a Turkish Muslim. They found that under German law it was possible for a province to intervene in a humanitarian crisis overseas, though it had never been done before.

That October the state government organised a refugee summit to bring together members of political parties, church leaders and mayors. All agreed they should help and arrange an air bridge from Iraq to bring out 1100 women and children who they would give three-year visas. Ninety million euros were apportioned to what they called the Special Quota Project and Dr Blume was appointed to run it.

'The federal government said we, the state, would have to do everything ourselves,' he said. 'We didn't know how – we had no army, no boots on the ground.'

Blume contacted Professor Jan Kizilhan, a psychologist specialising in trauma whose own family were Yazidi Kurds, and, in February 2015, they and a medical doctor set off for Iraq.

By then many of the enslaved women had escaped or, like Turko, had had their freedom bought and were in camps in Kurdistan in northern Iraq. Around 1600 women were referred to the German doctors. Each underwent an hour-long psychological assessment, a medical examination and a discussion of how they might benefit from the programme.

The stories were beyond imagination for the three German men. 'After listening you don't sleep,' said Dr Blume.

There was the mother who told him how she had been forced to convert and read the Koran but stumbled over a passage so they tortured and killed her baby in front of her. An eight-year-old girl who had been sold from one man to another and raped hundreds of times. Or the young woman with the deeply scarred face and neck because she was so desperate she had set fire to herself.

'As a man I feel ashamed and so does my wife as she is a Muslim,' he said. 'And as a German I know that less than a century ago our own European civilisation did such terrible things and we don't seem to learn.'

It was perhaps no coincidence that Germany had been the country to take in the Yazidi women just as its leader Angela Merkel had been the one to say '*wir schaffen das*' – 'we can do this' – as she opened the borders to one million refugees as the rest of Europe was closing theirs.

'The hardest thing was deciding who to take and who not to take,' Dr Blume said. 'How do you decide between a woman who has lost two children and another who only lost one but it was killed in front of her?'

The first priority was emergencies. 'Some were suicidal,' he said, 'or would have died because they were sick – gynaecological damage or terrible burns from self-immolation.'

For those remaining there were three key criteria – whether they had suffered traumatising violence; if they were without family support (if their husbands were alive they tended not to take them); and whether taking them to Germany would help them.

'It was awful not to take all,' said Dr Blume. 'But every life is worth the effort.'

In March 2015 the first women were flown from Erbil to Stuttgart. Over the next year Blume made twelve trips to Iraq and brought over 500 women and 600 children. Of these around 1000 had been taken to Baden-Württenburg, 60 to Lower Saxony and 32 in Schleswig-Holstein.

It was an astonishing gesture by a single province. However, more than 5000 women were thought to have been enslaved, so Blume estimated that they had given refuge to only a third of those in need. 'In the end around 2000 were referred and in the meantime the numbers grew because more girls managed to flee or bought their way out. So we believe there are still more than 2000 women needing help in camps in Iraq.'

Among the children rescued were young boys who had been beaten and forced to be child soldiers. These were all under thirteen as those fourteen or over were killed. 'They were killed if they had hair on their ankles,' said Blume.

As a father of two boys and a girl, he found the children's stories particularly distressing. 'Once I entered my office in Iraq and a thirteen-year-old Yazidi girl was standing there with her back to me and looked exactly like my daughter,' he said. 'She looked so similar, hair, everything … It made me realise it could have been ours. These children are like our children.'

* * *

It took me a series of phone calls and a few weeks after leaving Leros to establish that there was not a secret village of rescued Yazidi girls as the refugees had told me, but rather an entire German province. They had been housed in twenty-three secret shelters in twenty-one different towns, mostly remote areas, hidden from view to shield them from unwanted attention.

Dr Blume agreed to let me visit and meet some of the women who were open to sharing their stories. The first indication of how difficult this journey would be came when Shaker Jeffrey, the young Yazidi refugee living in Germany who had agreed to be my interpreter, stopped answering his phone in the days leading up to my flight to Stuttgart.

'He's going through a personal crisis,' said the Yazidi doctor who had put us in touch. When we finally meet, I mutter to Shaker about his elusiveness. Later, in the car, he told me quietly that his own fiancée Dil-Mir was one of the girls enslaved by ISIS and taken to Raqqa, their capital in Syria. 'Everything was set with my life,' he said. He spoke excellent English having worked as an interpreter for the US troops in Iraq. 'I was studying pharmacy at Mosul University, had saved money from my job, and was supposed to marry the girl I loved on my birthday, 4 September 2014. But one month before that, ISIS came and took her.'

Like tens of thousands of Yazidis, Shaker, his mother and five siblings fled to the mountain, scrambling up the rocks in blistering heat. 'There was no water, no food, no shade – it was an inferno,' he said. Shaker was desperately searching for apples and water for his family when Dil-Mir called and told him she had been abducted. Oddly ISIS had not taken the girls' phones so they were able to contact anguished relatives from captivity.

'The first day they raped her three times,' he said. 'Then she was handed on to two brothers who were fighters and made her cook and dance for them … as well as other things.'

In between escorting his sick mum to Turkey, Shaker desperately tried to find ways to get Dil-Mir out. Twice she tried to escape and failed. He even tried disguising himself as ISIS and going to a slave market near Aleppo, hoping to buy her. 'The last time she managed to call me she told me "I wish I was dead",' he said. 'She sounded so tired.'

Her last text read 'Come find me Shaker. Hurry.' Then the calls stopped. Eventually he learnt that she had committed suicide. He showed me the screensaver on his phone of a beautiful girl with long auburn hair, a wide smile and dancing eyes. 'I couldn't save her,' he said. 'She would have been twenty-one.'

His eyes were wet with tears. 'That's why I am here,' he said after a while. 'What I saw on the mountain and what they did to my fiancée made my heart like a rock – I no longer cared if I lived or died. First I wanted to fight the people who had done this. But then I decided the best revenge was to get to Europe and help those girls who did survive and to tell the world.'

He bade farewell to his mother and left the camp where they were living in Turkey, then crossed a river into Bulgaria and on through Serbia, Hungary and Austria to Germany, using the $4000 he had saved for his wedding to pay a people smuggler. The journey took twenty-two days during which he was detained several times. In Germany he had been granted asylum and ran a Facebook group of Yazidi activists to try and save other girls, but it was not the life he had envisaged.

The first shelter was a long drive from Stuttgart so on the way I asked Shaker about Yazidism which I had been reading up on since meeting the refugees on Leros. 'If you Google Yazidism, only one per cent is right,' he said.

Yazidism is an ancient and mysterious religion originally from Mesopotamia and older than Islam that comprises elements of Christianity, Sufism and Zoroastrianism. They spell it Yezidi, a name which comes from their word Ezid for God and literally means followers of God.

Some say it is not a real religion because unlike Christianity, Islam and Judaism, it has no book. But Shaker insisted this was not true. 'We had a book called the Black Book with everything written in it but this was stolen,' he said.

I told him I was surprised to see him wearing a blue shirt – I had read that they have an aversion to blue, as well as to lettuce. He laughed. 'That's the older generation like my mum – she won't eat salad!'

He could not explain the dislike of lettuce but believed the aversion to blue originated from the days of the Ottoman ruler Ahmed Pasha, whose forces carried out one of the many genocides against the Yazidis, as they wore blue hats.

There are around one million Yazidis around the world, of whom 450,000 were in Sinjar. Aside from Germany, many Yazidis lived in the US. Followers worship the sun and a peacock angel who they believe God created before man and then sent to Earth to paint it with the colours of its feathers to create the most beautiful planet. Yazidis do not shower on Wednesdays because they believe this was the day the Peacock Angel came to Earth.

Members of ISIS were told that this peacock angel was Iblis, the Satanic figure which appears in the Koran. Yazidis, they said, were devil worshippers. They seemed to me the most gentle people I had ever met.

We stopped to buy cakes for the women in Schwäbisch Hall, a medieval village of pink and yellow timbered houses and cobbled streets, which looked as if it belonged in a fairy tale. The shelter was nearby but so discreet it took a while to find. Eventually, we drew up in a car park for a series of residential buildings, rather like student hostels, dotted around leafy lanes. To my surprise it was another mental institution. We tracked down the three-storey block where thirty-nine Yazidis were living. A few children were playing on bicycles near the door though not venturing far.

We were shown into a long bare room where the only decoration was a line of children's colourings of birds, flowers and butterflies pinned on one wall. A group of women drifted in with haunted eyes like figures in an Edvard Munch painting. A number of doors led off to bedrooms in one of which we met Turko.

Afterwards we went upstairs to meet a much younger woman called Rojian, aged just eighteen, who greeted us with an uncertain smile from behind a curtain of mahogany hair.

She was sitting cross-legged on her bed, clad in a black T-shirt and black sweat pants, her only adornment a gold peacock angel round her neck. Like Turko's, her room was small and bare. The only decoration was a Yazidi calendar. Next to her on the bed was her mobile phone. The word Hope was spelled out in sparkly pink letters on the case.

Rojian's peacock angel pendant

Rojian told me she was the niece of Nadia Murad who had become the international face of the Yazidi tragedy. Murad had been captured at nineteen by ISIS fighters who killed six of her brothers and her mother and when she escaped, was the first to tell her story on the world stage. She had recently been appointed UN ambassador for the Dignity of Survivors of Human Trafficking.

'Nadia and I were captured together,' she said. 'My father who was killed by ISIS was her brother.'

'This is his name,' she added, touching the inscription on her peacock pendant.

Rojian was just sixteen on 3 August 2014 when ISIS invaded her village near Kocho. Like most Yazidis in Sinjar, the family were poor and she had left school two years earlier to work in the fields growing potatoes and onions.

'Some villagers escaped to Mount Sinjar. They thought our sacred mountain would shelter them. But it was far away and we heard that ISIS fighters would kill those who tried so we fled to the neighbouring village where my grandmother [Nadia's mother] lived.

'We were kept under siege for almost two weeks,' she said. 'All ways out were blocked by ISIS fighters, we could hear their call for prayer from their checkpoints. We stayed in the house, scared to go out. Whenever the power came on, we watched TV and could see the people on the mountain desperately trying to get on the Iraqi army helicopters sent to rescue them or grab the aid packages they dropped.

'We didn't know what would happen to us. After nine days an ISIS commander came and gave us an ultimatum – either convert and become a member of the Caliphate or face the consequences.

'Three days later more fighters arrived. They climbed up onto the highest roofs and called through megaphones for everyone to gather in the primary school. The roads were full of people for the first time since the village was surrounded but we were so scared no one spoke or greeted each other.

'The men were made to stay in the yard and we women and children were sent upstairs. They told us give us all you have then we will leave. They held out big bags and people dropped in money, phones and jewellery. My grandmother gave her wedding ring.

'Then they loaded men and teenage boys in trucks and drove them away. A few moments later we heard gunshots. People started screaming "They are killing the men!" then we saw ISIS fighters with shovels.'

As many as 600 men from that village were killed, including her father and five of her uncles – Nadia's brothers. Only those so young that they didn't yet have hair on their legs or under their arms were spared and taken away for training.

'The trucks then came back to the school to get us women and girls. We begged them what have you done to our men but they ordered us to get in. We were scared but we had no choice.

'They drove us to another school where virgins like me and Nadia were separated from the older women or those with children like my mum. Large buses with curtained windows came to collect us virgins.'

The buses took them to Mosul. The Iraqi city had been captured by ISIS in June and the group's leader Abu Bakr al-Baghdadi had appeared in its ancient Grand al-Nuri Mosque and proclaimed the Caliphate that he said would stretch from Iraq to Spain.

'They put us in a three-storey building packed with hundreds of women and children and lots of fighters. A man came through and began touching our hair, breasts, backs, feeling all our body parts. He told us we were infidels and *sabaya* – and said "If you scream I will kill you." I was with Nadia and when the man groped her she started screaming and all the other girls did too, so they dragged

Nadia out of the room and started beating her and burning her with cigarettes.

'We heard they were taking the most beautiful ones so we started rubbing dirt into our hair to try and look nasty but a girl told them what we were doing.

'Then in the night a very fat ISIS soldier came and we were very scared, he had a reddish beard and was in a white dishdash and so big he was like a monster. I was with Nadia, my cousin Katrine, and Nisreen, a friend from the village. The fat man shone torches in our faces and wanted to take Nadia but we held her and refused to let him. Then ISIS fighters came with electric cables and began whipping our arms and faces and backs and took all four of us. One of them, a thin man called Haji Salman, took Nadia and me outside then put her in his car. We screamed and held each other's hands but they pulled us apart. Then the bad fat guy who beat us at the beginning, came and said "Now you are mine."'

Until this point she had been speaking easily. Suddenly she put her head down.

'It was night,' she said. 'His name was Salwan and he was an Iraqi from Mosul. We got to his house and he kept trying to touch me and I didn't let him so he took my belt and beat me and slapped me so hard my eye was bleeding and there was a huge mark on my face. He told me "You Yazidis are infidels so we can do what we like to you." Then he sat on my back so I couldn't breathe and raped me from behind. After that he came every day to rape me three or four times.

'This went on for more than six weeks. My life was just rape.

'Then one day he told me he was going to buy another girl. I was relieved thinking it would make my life easier. The girl he brought home was just ten years old.

'That night they were in the room next door,' she said. 'I never heard anyone scream so much, crying for her mother. I cried more for that little girl than I ever did for myself.'

I hold her hand. It is cold. I asked her if she wanted to stop. She shook her head.

'One day the man brought us hijabs and took us downtown,' she continued. 'I could see the black and white flags [of ISIS] everywhere. I tried to flee but another woman caught me and brought me back.

'I'd heard the stories of how when girls were caught trying to flee they beat the shit out of them and killed the family so I told him I thought I saw my auntie in the car that's why I was running.

'I was almost giving up then one day I managed to steal his phone and get through to one of my uncles. He gave me the number of a contact person in Mosul who was helping Yazidi girls escape.

'Shortly after that the fat man took me to a meeting one morning in a kind of bomb factory. He left me in another building so I spilled tea on myself and told them I am just going to change my clothes. I called the contact, put on my hijab and jumped from the roof into the street.

'But the rescue car that was supposed to be outside was nowhere to be seen. I called again but the man told me you are being followed by three guys, it's too dangerous. I told him this was my second attempt at escape and I would be killed if I was caught. Eventually he gave me an address to go to.

'I got to the car and we were being followed by three guys on cars and motorbikes,' she said. 'But the driver called friends to come and block the way and he managed to take me to his family.'

However he had hurt his leg and ended up in hospital for six days, leaving her with his family. 'I was very afraid,' she said. 'I had heard they posted photos of escaped girls at their checkpoints. His family didn't know I was Yazidi, he told them I was his cousin and my father was in hospital.'

Finally the man got out of hospital and drove her through the checkpoints to Erbil and a rendezvous spot with her uncle. That wasn't the end. In a camp in northern Iraq, she was reunited with Nadia who had escaped from Mosul a few months earlier. 'I was happy to see her but where was everyone else? So many of the family were missing. My father had been killed as well as all five of his brothers and Nadia's mother, my aunt.'

That wasn't all. 'When the rapist found out I'd fled, he was so angry he took my mum from Tal Afar prison and kept her as his slave with my brother who was six and baby sister. He held them nine months.' When they finally got out the ten-year-old girl was still there being raped every day. Rojian had no idea what happened to her.

As for the other girls she was captured with, her cousin Katrine died when she eventually managed to run away with two other girls and were blown up by an IED. Nisreen, she thought, was still in captivity.

Eventually Rojian's mum also escaped with her baby girl and little boy, and when they heard about the air bridge to Germany they applied. On 1 December 2015, Rojian, her younger siblings and their mother boarded a plane for the first time in their lives and flew to Stuttgart.

In the shelter they were receiving 320 euros a month for food and clothes and Rojian had started school. Though she was happy to be safe in Germany, she said 'I don't like school because there are only two of us Yazidi girls. The others are Afghans and Syrians and are always saying ISIS things or playing ISIS prayers or poetry on their phones to scare us.

'I don't think I will ever get over this,' she added, 'it will never go away.'

German social workers visited each day but the women told me they were not receiving counselling.

'To start with we organised psychotherapy but it was not taken very well,' explained Dr Blume, when I asked him later. 'There was one session for example where a Yazidi woman came out and complained "She said she's a doctor but she only talked." In Iraq doctors give lots of pills and that's what they wanted.

'Also they don't really talk about personal suffering – when you ask the women, "How do you feel?" quite often they reply, "Thank you, my children are good."

'What's actually working is therapy like art, painting, yoga and being with animals such as horses to rebuild trust in their bodies and trust in other people. That's a big problem. Many feel betrayed by everyone.'

Turko told me she often felt desperate, particularly as the hostel was situated in the grounds of a mental institution.

'I feel like I am dying every day,' she said. 'I am crying every night. Those men took something from me I can't get back. Here I get worse and worse. I have nothing to do, just my own thoughts, and we are surrounded by people with mental problems. The town is thirty minutes' walk away and it's expensive. I feel like the place is crowding in on me.

'Often the kids sleep with me in the night and they were in ISIS slavery too and saw people being killed and us being raped so they wake up ten times in the night screaming "The men are coming, the men are coming!"'

I asked Dr Blume why the girls had been put in such remote locations and kept secret, almost as if they were outcasts.

'At the start they were very fearful and didn't want to be seen by others,' he said. 'Some were very ashamed.

'Also most had never left Iraq before and we didn't know how they would react to the cultural shock. At the start they were very afraid of men, especially of Arab or African origin, so to put them in big cities with lots of refugees would have really stressed them.

The psychologists told us it was important to bring them to a place where there were no triggers.'

As nothing like this had ever been done before, there was little for them to learn from. 'There was some experience of taking traumatised people in from Rwanda and Balkans but not in this huge number, and the culture and religion were different.'

He also pointed out that because Germany had taken in so many refugees in 2015 – over a million – there were limited locations available for the Yazidi girls. 'The places are not all ideal but the important thing was survival not beauty.'

'We couldn't put them with other refugees as most refugees coming to Europe were male – 70 per cent of those who came to Germany – and from families who could afford the trip so very different to these women who were really traumatised and the weakest in society.'

What they had been through was so terrible that it had taken some of the women a year to speak again. But not a single one had committed suicide since arriving in Germany. Dr Blume said he had watched them improve, starting with the children. 'For a whole year we didn't hear children sing or make a rhythm but now we see in the kindergarten they are laughing again and playing games and of course that helps their mothers.'

Some of the women, he said, had even started learning to drive. His plan was to gradually integrate them in society, putting them in apartments.

One major boost had been getting their spiritual leader Baba Sheikh to tell the community not to reject them but welcome them back. 'We asked Baba Sheikh to bless every group before they left and tell you did nothing wrong, the only people who lost their honour were the perpetrators not you, you are still our daughters and our sisters and can return any time. Now we see slowly, slowly, them being accepted in the community.'

I saw this for myself at another shelter on a wooded hillside where I was welcomed into a bedsit by a couple celebrating their first anniversary.

Vian, thirty-one, and Ali, thirty-three, both wearing gold peacock-angel pendants, sat on a green mattress on the floor next to a carrycot. Inside, was a perfect tiny baby boy wrapped in swaddling, just twenty days old. On the wall was a white and red pennant with a blazing golden sun – the Yazidi flag.

Ali smiled as he recounted how he had been pestering Vian for a year to give him her photograph. The day after she finally agreed ISIS arrived and Vian was captured and taken in a bus to Mosul.

'They had long beards and hair and no shoes and took us to Syria to a big school,' she said. 'I was very frightened. They told us if you don't convert we will kill you.'

Twisting the edge of the baby blanket round and round in her fingers, she continued: 'Every day fighters came with pieces of iron and wood and took some girls for a couple of days for pleasure. They divided us into three groups – the beautiful group, middle group and ugly group. I was in the middle group. I pretended I had mental problems, beating my head against the wall in the hope they wouldn't take me.'

Meanwhile Ali was desperate. When Vian managed to call from Mosul, he promised her he would do everything to get her back. 'I told her even if you marry an ISIS fighter and have kids by him, I will still marry you and you will be mine.'

She told him their location in this three-storey building and begged him, 'Tell the airstrike people to blow it up so we won't have to go through something worse than death.'

After that Ali heard screaming and the phone went dead. 'I was so worried I didn't eat for two days,' he said.

Instead he went to Mount Sinjar to join the fight against ISIS. 'Four of my friends were killed on the mountain and people were starving but I refused to leave because of my promise to Vian.'

Finally, when she was transferred to another village, she escaped with a small group and they managed to find their way up the mountain. Ali was overjoyed to see her but initially she didn't recognise him with his beard and uniform and weapons.

Vian had managed to get accepted onto the German programme and had moved there in June 2015. Ali borrowed $10,000 and made his own way on the refugee trail to meet her there. Three months after she arrived they married. The ceremony was attended by many in the community, as the first marriage to one of the abducted girls.

'These girls should be our heroes who we should be proud to marry,' said Shaker.

Such stories take a long time to tell. Darkness had fallen and everyone was drained. Later, I would learn that Shaker was so horrified by what these girls had gone through that every time we took a break, he had gone to the bathroom and vomited.

Turko and Rojian invited us to stay for dinner. I demurred, explaining we had a three-hour drive back to our hotel, and knowing they had little money for food.

But while we had been talking, some of the other women had been busy with pots and pans in the cramped kitchen. On the long table by the children's drawings, a feast was spread out on a plastic cover printed with pink roses.

Like many refugees cut adrift from home, recreating food is one way to connect and build a sense of community, and also remind the children of their origins. The women talked at once trying to explain each dish.

There were *kibbeh* parcels, fried pasties filled with bulgur, as well as onion, spices, parsley and minced lamb; *dolmas* – vine leaves stuffed with aubergine and rice; chicken in a tomato sauce, and *mier*, a sort of porridge of fried bulgur.

They asked me about English food. I explained that my country was not really famed for our cuisine and told them about 'toad in the hole' and fish and chips wrapped in newspaper, and that our national dish was chicken tikka masala brought by immigrants from India and Pakistan. They found this very funny and laughed for the first time, repeating the story to each other.

They told me they found German food pale and tasteless. I joked that maybe one day a Yazidi dish would be on German menus with bratwurst and sauerkraut but they looked at me uncertainly and I realised that such a suggestion of permanence was not tactful for those in such limbo between missing home and being scared to return.

A large plate of green melon was brought for dessert and the talk resumed as juice dripped down our chins. Afterwards, one after the other came and hugged me. 'That's the first time since all this happened that anyone has had a normal conversation with us,' said Turko.

I wished I lived nearby to visit. In the car winding through the dark forests, I thought of her and Rojian back in their small rooms with their bad dreams and the children screaming in the night.

3

The Power of a Hashtag

Northeast Nigeria

The name Chibok is said to come from the sound of feet being sucked into swampy land. It was a small sleepy town in northeast Nigeria on the edge of the Sambisa forest with a narrow dirt road cutting through and a marketplace in the centre with a large telecom mast towering above. There was a church, a mosque, a Union Bank with a fading blue sign and door that had long been shuttered, and women and children pushing carts of yellow jerry cans, for there was no running water, and despite its name, the land around was bone dry and cracked for lack of rain. If you kept on the road to the edge of town, you would come to a large red-roofed building with the sign Government Secondary School.

On 14 April 2014, the night Boko Haram snatched her eldest daughter from this school, Esther Yakubu was in bed with her four other children in their simple concrete home. 'Around 11 p.m. or midnight we woke to the sound of gunshots,' she recalled. 'My brother-in-law called and said Boko Haram is coming and we must flee. Boko Haram are butchers, everyone knows what happen when they come – they burn down homes, kill the men and take young women to be their bush wives.

'I said I am not leaving my house but then we heard more shots and my husband insisted we must go, so we ran with the kids still in nightgowns and boxer shorts. Chibok is a rocky place and we hid among the shrubs and the crevices.

'Boko Haram came and started setting fire to the marketplace and things till 4 a.m. We could hear them riding around on their motorbikes and see plumes of smoke but we didn't know they had gone to the school.

'Then my brother-in-law called again and asked "Where's your eldest?" I told him she was at school. My Dorcas was sixteen and she was in the middle of exams and boarding there. He said the school had been attacked. I didn't believe it but then parents started coming back and crying that the girls were gone. I still didn't believe it – how could they take all the girls?

'As daybreak came, around 5.30 a.m., we ran to the school. We saw the classrooms burnt, ashes everywhere and all the schoolbooks and backpacks and Bibles scattered about. I searched and searched for my Dorcas and screamed her name but she was nowhere.

Esther Yakubu, mother of one of the missing Chibok girls

'Someone counted the missing. They had taken 276 of our girls. That day the whole community was in mourning like a tide of tears.

'Then some of the girls started coming back. They told us that men had come into their dormitory at night and shouted to wake them up. The men were in army uniforms so they had not realised at first it was an attack. They had scrambled down from their bunk beds by flashlight. They saw the men were looting the foodstuff and were very young and scruffy and realised they were not army at all. Then they saw the buildings were on fire and screamed because they thought they were going to burn them alive. Then the men had ordered them onto open-top trucks and drove into the forest.

'A few got away at the start and some others had managed to escape inside the forest by holding onto branches. I recognised one of the girls and I asked her, "Was Dorcas with you?" and she said "Yes, but she was tired in the truck so didn't escape." She was not used to running, maybe she was afraid.

'My husband and other men went into the forest to try and search but it is huge and thick. Fifty-seven girls had managed to escape the first night but that left 219 somewhere in the forest with all the snakes and animals. Some people thought they had already taken the girls across the Gwoza Hills to Cameroon. Maybe they would sell them.

'I kept looking at her picture on my phone, trying to will her back to me. I was thinking, How could this happen? I only just moved her from Kano to this school in Chibok because I thought it was safer.

'Some people in the village said this was what happens when girls were educated too much. [Girls like Dorcas were an exception in northern Nigeria where only 4 per cent of girls finish secondary education and two thirds are married by sixteen.] But she was always a bright one and I really wanted her to be educated so she could have a better life.

'"Boko Haram" means "western education is forbidden". Not long before they attacked a boys' school at Buni Yadi and burnt fifty-nine boys alive. But we never heard anything like this.

'It seems like they weren't planning it as they didn't have enough vehicles for all the girls so broke into some houses and took some. Some of those girls who came back said the fighters actually came into the school looking for cement and a brick-making machine to build their base. They said they were arguing about what to do with the girls and even suggested burning them.

'You know some people say it's a conspiracy. We usually have a hundred soldiers on duty in Chibok because of all the attacks in the area but that night there were only fifteen as some had been sent elsewhere, and there were only twenty-seven police, most of them were drunk. The school had no light that night as the generator had run out of diesel. The headmistress was a Muslim and just two weeks earlier the school had a drill because of warnings of an attack and the principal told the girls to stay together in one place if anything happened. If they had run away they might have escaped.'

In his big white villa in the modern capital Abuja, the Nigerian president Goodluck Jonathan did nothing. Thousands of girls had been disappearing from villages across northeast Nigeria. The capture of the Chibok girls might have just been one more in a catalogue of Boko Haram atrocities, except for one thing. On 23 April 2014, nine days after the abduction, a commercial lawyer called Ibrahim Abdullahi was in his hotel room in Port Harcourt, packing to go home to Abuja, and switched on the TV. A live broadcast was underway from Port Harcourt Book Festival and Oby Ezekwesili, a former education minister, was speaking. She told the audience about the abduction of the girls, urging them to demand the government to 'bring back our daughters'.

Abdullahi was a regular user of Twitter so tweeted Oby's words and added two hashtags #BringBackOurDaughters and #BringBackOurGirls. He then rushed to catch his plane, thinking how devastated he would be as a father, were he to lose a child.

Across the world in Los Angeles, a film producer picked up the tweet. Within three weeks, the BBOG hashtag had been retweeted more than a million times worldwide. Supermodel Naomi Campbell, celebrity Kim Kardashian, US Secretary of State Hillary Clinton and First Lady Michelle Obama were among scores of high-profile people posting selfies of themselves holding placards bearing the words *Bring Back Our Girls*. With two teenage daughters of her own, Mrs Obama took over the president's weekly radio slot to express her outrage. 'In these girls, Barack and I see our own daughters,' she said, adding that her husband had directed his government to do everything possible to help find them. In London, prime minister David Cameron told the House of Commons 'this is an act of pure evil' and pledged Britain would 'do all it can'.

The US flew in CIA analysts and FBI hostage negotiators as well as Predator Drones they called 'eyes in the sky'. An Intelligence Fusion Cell was set up with Britain and France sending in military advisors and satellite specialists, though a promised RAF Sentinel spy plane was delayed after it broke down.

Like journalists all over the world, I was told by my editor to get a visa and jump on a plane. Suddenly the Nigerian Foreign Ministry was inundated with requests from media outlets apparently falling over each other to cover the World Economic Forum on Africa taking place that week in Abuja. I felt the familiar rush of breaking news as we piled off the plane into the sticky airless heat, then jumped into taxis into the strange modern capital to find a forest of satellite dishes marked CNN, ABC, CBS, BBC, ITN, Sky, Nippon TV … For the next ten days the abduction of the Chibok girls led news bulletins the world over.

At sundown every day, crowds of journalists would emerge from the Hilton and cross the road to Unity Fountain, a dusty traffic island with a non-running fountain inscribed with the names of Nigeria's thirty-six states. As flocks of birds silhouetted in black V-shapes against a reddening sky, campaigners dressed in red would gather to applaud the bustling Mrs Ezekwesili as she and others protested the lack of government action.

After each speaker a chorus would start up:

What are we chanting?
Bring back our Girls!
What are we asking?
Bring Back Our Girls! Now and Alive!

As people drifted off into the velvety darkness, I went for coffee in a nearby hotel with Mrs Ezekwesili who had gone from being a government minister to Vice President of the World Bank and was a co-founder of Transparency International. She was very angry, even more so when part of the hotel ceiling came down onto her dress. 'Without education I'd be just one more girl child forgotten and trapped in poverty,' she told me. 'How did we fail so badly as a society that we can have this wholesale abduction of our girls? This needs to be an awakening call.'

Oil-rich Nigeria had just overtaken South Africa as Africa's biggest economy, something its government had been planning to show off in the heavily guarded Economic Forum. Instead, all the world seemed interested in was the missing girls. This must have been extremely annoying for President Goodluck, a former zoologist with a penchant for fedora hats. He spent the next nineteen days holed up in his official residence in Aso Rock and said not a word about the kidnappings nor did he call a meeting to plan a rescue. His military denied it had even happened. His wife accused the protesters of 'playing games'. When the president was photographed dancing at a party rally, he was pilloried in an editorial in the *New York Times* as 'shockingly slow and inept at addressing this monstrous crime'.* The plight of the Chibok girls and his apparent indifference seemed to exemplify a government only interested in enriching itself.

Occasionally some of the parents of the missing schoolgirls would be at the Unity Fountain vigil. It was there I met Esther, a smartly dressed woman of forty-two, who worked as a finance officer for Chibok local government. She showed me a picture on her phone of her daughter Dorcas, radiant in a turquoise long-sleeved dress that shimmered like a mermaid tail. The photo had been taken the very week of her disappearance.

'You can see she loved fashion,' said Esther. 'We used to say she would tie her hair as nicely as the Yorubas – they are famous for it.

---

* 'Nigeria's Stolen Girls', *New York Times*, 6 May 2014.

'She's like a little bit of my heartbeat,' she added. 'She's a nice friendly girl, she is my main pillar. She always takes care of her younger siblings without being asked and cooks. She likes singing praises in the church choir and has a voice like honey.'

The family were all devout churchgoers. 'Most of the people in Chibok were Christians and we lived in peace with our Muslim brothers until Boko Haram came.'

Like most of the girls at the school, Dorcas had been doing her exams. 'She had done five papers. She always got good grades and studied hard. She wants to study business administration and be a lecturer.'

Four weeks after the abduction, a video was released by Boko Haram. It showed around 130 girls in black and grey hijabs under tamarind trees, holding their palms upward in prayer and reciting from the Koran. Although northern Nigeria is mostly Muslim, Chibok was a mixed community as Esther had told me, and many of the girls were Christian.

'I abducted your girls,' crowed Boko Haram leader Abubakar Shekau, cackling manically like an evil clown. 'I will sell them in the market, by Allah. I will sell them off and marry them off.'

Esther scanned the video in vain for her shimmering daughter. What were they doing to her?

Any mother would be terrified. Boko Haram was the world's deadliest terrorist group according to the Global Terrorism index, even if it did not receive the international attention of Al Qaeda and ISIS.

When I spoke to Nigerians there seemed considerable confusion about Boko Haram's objectives. In Abuja I met a former MP who headed an anti-corruption network, but turned up in an Audi R10 supercar and sported a gold and diamond Rolex. He described Boko Haram as 'a demonic sect capitalising on ignorance of religious beliefs to perpetrate Satanic activities' and 'mixed up with banditry and brigandry'.

Others claimed it was actually set up by the army or by northern politicians to create anarchy and derail Goodluck Jonathan, a southern Christian, and attain power for themselves. Or by southern Christian politicians to wrest power from the north.

Boko Haram was actually the movement's nickname – its real name was the rather less catchy *Jama'atu Ahlus wa-Sunna Lida'awati wal-Jihad* or the People Committed to the Propagation of the Prophet's Teaching and Jihad. But when the group started it had no name, leading some to call it the Nigerian Taliban.

Its founder was a baby-faced Salafist cleric called Mohammad Yusuf who in 2002 set up a madrassa in Maiduguri, the capital of Borno state, and named it after Ibn Taymiyyah, a Syrian who had advocated jihad against the Mongols in the thirteenth century. There, Yusuf taught that the earth was flat and denounced western education (boko) as haram.

Nigeria is Africa's most populous country with around 200 million people and hundreds of languages and tribes. Almost half are Muslim, mostly in the north, which is dirt poor compared to the booming south, following years of unequal distribution of the country's oil wealth compounded with economic mismanagement and looting by corrupt rulers.

It is also one of the world's youngest populations, more than half under thirty. Among thousands of young men without jobs or hope, Yusuf's preaching of radical Islam began to attract a following, particularly with fellow members of the Kanuri tribe. He and his acolytes toured the region in pick-ups stacked high with loudspeakers urging Muslims to ignore the Christian-dominated 'government of thieves' and follow Sharia law. The font of all this corruption, he raged, was the education system implanted by British colonialists.

Yet it was a law over motorbike helmets that really turned this into full-blown insurgency. Nigeria's roads were among the most dangerous in the world so, in January 2009, the government made helmets compulsory in a bid to reduce the death toll. But many people refused to wear them, claiming they caused head lice, could damage women's expensive hair weaves, or might even be used to cast magic spells on the wearer. Most thought it was yet another way for police to extort bribes.

The following month some of Yusuf's members were at a funeral procession in another northeastern town called Bauchi when they were stopped by police for not wearing helmets. The confrontation quickly escalated and security forces opened fire, injuring seventeen people.

Yusuf called on his members to respond with jihad and launched attacks across the five northern states. These were brutally crushed by government forces, leaving around a thousand dead and many more imprisoned, including many of the group's family members. In Maiduguri there were running battles in the streets. The military eventually caught Yusuf and handed him over to police custody where he was shot in the chest while 'trying to escape', they claimed. His bullet-ridden body was displayed to journalists.

The remaining leadership went underground and many thought the movement finished. But some ended up in jihadist training camps in Somalia, Mali and even Afghanistan, and around 2010 they re-emerged as a terrorist group under Yusuf's former deputy, Shekau.

Shekau looked terrifying to me in the video with the hijab-clad Chibok girls. People used words like 'psychopath' and 'delusional' but nobody seemed to know much about him other than that he had married Yusuf's widow. 'He is Stalin to Yusuf's Lenin,' one British diplomat in Abuja told me. 'He has walked the revolution and taken it in a particularly violent direction.'

Like Osama bin Laden, his preferred medium of communication to the world was through videos in which he usually cradled a Kalashnikov. Surrounded by masked lieutenants, he went off on hour-long tirades about anything from Abraham Lincoln to Queen Elizabeth II. 'I enjoy killing anyone that God commands me to kill the way I enjoy killing chickens and sheep,' he declared in one in 2012. 'We will kill whoever practises democracy … Kill, kill, kill!'

The first to be killed were moderate Muslim leaders shot dead by teams of gunmen on motorbikes. Most of the group's initial attacks focused on getting their members and families freed through jailbreaks, replenishing their ranks. They also began bombing churches, starting with two in Maiduguri on Christmas Eve 2010, then throughout the region, and they demanded all Christians leave the north. The following year they moved on the capital, bombing the police headquarters in Abuja then the United Nations building.

The 2011 collapse of the Gaddafi regime in Libya, memorably described in a British intelligence report as the 'Tesco of the illegal arms-trade', provided a ready source of weapons which poured into Niger and beyond.

By 2012, Boko Haram had become more indiscriminate, carrying out suicide bombings of mosques, bus stations, markets and hospitals across the region. True to their name they also burnt down schools and killed teachers, sometimes conscripting the boys to serve as lookouts and recruits. Other times they simply slaughtered them. Teenage boys were forced to dig trenches then line up to have their throats slit and fall in. One of their members was known as the Butcher, apparently because he could sever a spinal cord in one slice.

So ruthless were they that even Al Qaeda apparently saw them as too extreme. A letter from Shekau was among papers seized in the May 2011 raid by US Navy Seals on Abbottabad, in which Osama bin Laden was killed. In it he had requested a meeting with

Ayman al-Zawahiri, bin Laden's deputy, and to be 'under one banner'. There was no reply.

To raise funds, Boko Haram raided banks, stuffing the cash into big chequered nylon holdalls known as Ghana-Must-Go bags. To arm themselves, they seized army guns, trucks and even tanks – some said these were sold to them by corrupt military. Soon they were focusing on territorial control, annexing towns and villages across the north to control 70 per cent of Borno state and create a Caliphate, as ISIS would later, though even more brutal. They killed and captured thousands and sent hundreds of thousands fleeing.

Attacking schools, particularly girls' schools, was not unique to Boko Haram. Hundreds of schools had been bombed or attacked by the Taliban in Afghanistan and northern Pakistan, where, in October 2012, fifteen-year-old Malala Yousafzai had been shot on her school bus for campaigning for the right to study.

But one of Boko Haram's particular trademarks was seizing young girls and forcing them to marry fighters. This was partly to secure loyalty from followers by providing wives for unemployed youth who had no prospect of paying traditional bride price. It was also to provide future members of the Caliphate, the girls treated as incubators to produce Muslim offspring. Women who were already pregnant with Christian babies faced having their bellies slit with a machete and the foetus ripped out.

It may also have been revenge for the detention by Nigerian authorities of their own female relatives. There were some reports that Shekau's own wife and three daughters had been captured in September 2012 while attending a naming ceremony which was attacked by the military. Shortly after he issued another video warning: 'Since you are seizing our women, you wait and see what will happen to your women ...'

He added, 'I would like you to know there is slavery in Islam, even during the battle of Badr the Prophet Mohammad took slaves,' referring to the first military victory by Muslims in the seventh century over Meccans who outnumbered them.

Boko Haram was complicated and media attention-span short and the satellites were soon being packed up and journalists moving on to a new story, ISIS capturing great swathes of Iraq and Syria. The British Sentinel spy plane sent by Cameron was quietly moved on elsewhere. The FBI pulled out its hostage negotiators.

As for the girls, it was as if they had vanished off the face of the earth. The following year, in March 2015, President Goodluck Jonathan ran out of luck and became the first sitting president in Nigerian history to lose an election. His failure to find the Chibok girls and end the insurgency was one of the reasons.

The victor was Muhammadu Buhari who had ruled as a military dictator back in the 1980s. He had nine daughters of his own and told his troops that finding the Chibok girls was a priority of his first hundred days. But the deadline passed, Boko Haram attacks continued and attempts at negotiations with Shekau stalled. On 14 January 2016, President Buhari met with around 300 of the parents and told them his government had 'no credible intelligence' on the girls' whereabouts or indeed whether they were even alive.

Esther often sent me devotional messages and I couldn't get those girls out of my head. I knew that feeling of butterflies in my stomach when I woke in the early hours to find my teenage son's bed still empty. Imagine knowing your daughter was in the hands of brutal killers and rapists.

A spate of suicide bombings across northern Nigeria by young women had started in June 2014, two months after the abduction. Many believed these were Chibok girls who had been brainwashed and trained to be killers or forced to become suicide bombers, their vests triggered remotely, though others argued the girls were too valuable to Boko Haram given their international profile.

I met a man in London who flipped open his Macbook Air to show me stomach-churning videos of three of them being raped over and over until their screams became silent Os.

'Boko Haram make ISIS look like playtime,' I was told by Dr Stephen Davis, a former canon at Coventry Cathedral, who was living in Perth, Australia, and had spent several years negotiating with Boko Haram members. 'I met one girl who was gang-raped every day for a year.'

Between 2009 and 2016 they had killed more than 15,000 people, razed villages and forced more than two million to flee their homes. According to Unicef, they had also forced more than one million children from school, burning their buildings, killing hundreds of teachers and abducting thousands of boys and girls to work as cooks, lookouts and sex slaves. After being rebuffed by Al Qaeda, Boko Haram had affiliated with ISIS in 2015, becoming Islamic State West Africa.

And yet how could 219 girls be abducted and simply disappear? Dr Davis, who was himself a father of three daughters, was apoplectic. 'I couldn't believe you take so many girls and leave no trace,' he said. 'Think how many vehicles that means, yet they didn't even leave a single wheel track and not one villager saw them pass. It's totally beyond belief.'

Two years after the abduction of the girls, the dusk vigil still continued every evening in Unity Square. The swallows still came out in their V formations but the protesters had shrunk to a small huddle of perhaps a dozen, wearing red Bring Back Our Girls badges, and a stack of plastic chairs stood untouched. A few more drifted in from work and some passing motorists honked in solidarity.

'No one is giving up,' insisted Yusuf Abubakar, the sit-out coordinator. His megaphone wasn't working so he shouted the usual chant:

When shall we stop?
Not until our girls are back and alive!
When shall we stop?
Not without our daughters!

Various matters were discussed such as who could provide refreshments for a forthcoming candlelit vigil in memory of the slain Buni Yadi boys. As always the session ended with everyone singing John Lennon's 'Give Peace a Chance' reworded to say 'All we are saying – bring back our girls. Now and alive!'

Among those gathered was a teenage girl, Maryam, slim and still as a tulip, and her mother Fatima, their faces stricken. Maryam told me she had been at Buni Yadi school along with her beloved sixteen-year-old elder brother Shoaib on the night of 24 February 2014 when Boko Haram attacked. 'They herded all the girls into the mosque and told us that going to such school was wrong and if they caught us again they wouldn't spare us. Then they started shooting boys in the head in front of us.'

Others had their throats slit and they heard the screams. She never saw her brother again. 'He wanted to be an architect,' said her mother Fatima. 'I fainted when I heard the news.'

Fatima was paying for Maryam to go to school in Kaduna which she thought was safer. But Maryam cried as she told me, 'I can't concentrate because I keep thinking of my brother and what they did to those boys. I know my mum is sacrificing for me to go to school and I didn't want my education to stop but I don't know what to do. I have nightmares every night and they fill my mind.'

The next morning I met up with Esther Yakubu. She looked as if she had aged ten years in the past two and told me she felt as if she was living in a kind of limbo. 'I can't sleep, I can't breathe,' she said. 'My other daughter refuses to go back to school because she is scared.' Some of the Chibok parents had committed suicide, she said. No one had offered them counselling. 'The government just gave us dress material and rice,' she shrugged. 'What good is that?'

She still had faith her daughter would be returned. 'I believe she's alive,' she said. 'I used to dream that she was back. Once her sister woke in the night and screamed "Dorcas is here!" She dreamt she came back and was making herself up. She loved to do that.

'If she's dead I would know,' she added.

The international attention had surprised them and given them hope the girls would be quickly recovered, so they were mystified at the failure. 'We heard the Americans have satellites that could see even a man walking in a street in Baghdad or a goat on a hill in Afghanistan,' said Esther. 'How would they not see all those girls?

'What I think is the government was not serious. If they had been the children of the elite, they would have been found.'

The military checkpoint just outside Maiduguri airport had a large *Wanted* poster covered with menacing faces of dozens of armed Boko Haram fighters, in the centre of which was the leering face of Shekau. The soldiers standing behind piles of sandbags looked surly, not surprisingly perhaps as they were poorly paid and equipped – partly it was said because their commanders were pocketing the funds or selling off their equipment to the terrorist group.

I had flown to the birthplace of Boko Haram to meet some of their former hostages to learn what it was like to be a girl like Dorcas in their captivity. On the flight I sat next to Professor Abba Gambo who was head of the crop-production department at the university. He told me all eleven of his brothers had been killed, including one who was shot in front of him. He blamed Boko Haram on high levels of poverty, illiteracy and climate change, which meant the area was getting just three months of rain, with

Lake Chad shrinking and crops declining. He pointed outside the window at the parched brown land.

I was not the only foreigner on board. Denise Ritchie was a feisty blonde barrister and anti-sexual-violence campaigner from New Zealand who told me she was carrying suitcases of bras and knickers she had collected to give to the abducted women. First, I thought she was mad then I felt humbled that someone would save their money to fly halfway round the world to try to bring a little dignity to women she had never met.

We both checked into Satus guesthouse which had been recommended as safe because an army unit was stationed there, though this may have been a questionable advantage given they were the main target. The website showed Scandinavian-style rooms of stripped wood and white Egyptian cotton duvets – but the rooms were brown and dank with stained candlewick bedspreads. I accosted the manager and he laughed and told me those were pictures of another hotel which he had liked so had cut and pasted.

Maiduguri was much livelier than on my previous visit two years earlier in 2014. Then it was under curfew having recently been attacked. Now everyone seemed to be selling something. On the street young men were playing table football and people grilling skewers of river fish and tiny sparrow-like birds with red beaks called quelea, which were sold in paper and crunched whole.

Hundreds of thousands of people from surrounding villages and towns that had been taken over by Boko Haram had fled into the city. Twenty-five camps had sprung up to house them all. Among them were thousands of girls who had escaped or been rescued from Boko Haram. While all the international focus was on the Chibok girls, it soon became clear that their abduction was just the tip of the iceberg.

* * *

'They put their dirty hands over our mouths and made us show them our breasts,' said Ba Amsa, who, like Esther's daughter Dorcas, had been sixteen when she was taken prisoner by Boko Haram. 'You couldn't resist because they had guns and if you did, they took you to the bush and killed you.'

She was from a small town called Bama which had been attacked several times by Boko Haram then captured in September 2014, five months after the Chibok abductions.

Even by their murderous standards it was bloody. Afterwards Boko Haram put out a video showing their gunmen mowing down civilians lying face down in a local school dormitory lined with bunk beds. Most appeared to be adult men. There were so many corpses that the gunmen had difficulty stepping between them to finish off those still twitching.

'We have turned the floor of this hall red with blood, and this is how it is going to be in all future attacks and arrests of infidels,' said the group leader in a message. 'From now killing, slaughtering, destructions and bombing will be our religious duty anywhere we invade.'

As Boko Haram moved in, people tried to flee. Ba Amsa had a limp because of childhood polio so could not run fast. 'They caught me and my sister and took us to a kind of prison of women where they kept us three months, making us do lessons on Islam.

'It was a place for Boko Haram fighters to choose wives. They would tell us men are coming to look at you and made us stand up and show our breasts then they would pick five or ten of us. More than twenty girls had been taken away before they came for me.

'The man who picked me was someone I knew from Bama and we stayed in a house of people they had killed. He was young and didn't seem to know anything about religion. He told me anyone who joined Boko Haram would go to Paradise.'

When I asked how he treated her, she looked down at the ground. 'I couldn't resist him,' she replied. 'He was armed. One day the army came and bombed the village and I managed to run away even though I was pregnant.'

I met Ba Amsa at Dalori camp which was based in a former technical college on the edge of town on dusty ground dotted with bare baobab trees. Dalori was the largest camp with around 22,000 people and also the oldest. It was said to be the best equipped and had rows of white tents, but it seemed a miserable place, with just one tap where barefoot people were queuing to get water. The tents were no escape from the 40-degree heat. Rations were just rice and a monthly bar of soap – I later spotted the flour, cooking oil and beans they were supposed to get on sale in the market just down the road.

Camps were organised by place to try and keep communities together and most people in Dalori were from Bama. Ba Amsa was attending a workshop organised by a local group for women and girls who had escaped Boko Haram and wanted to speak out. It was in a small trailer set up with rows of desks at which sat forty women and girls, several holding babies even though they looked like children themselves. It was sweltering.

Ba Amsa, who was by then eighteen, was nursing a baby boy – her four-month-old son Abuya who had been born in the camp. She had been reunited with her parents who were also in the camp. Her other siblings – two elder brothers, one younger and a younger sister – were all still missing.

Ba Amsa said she was lucky because her family still supported her. But she worried about the future of her son. One day the elder sister of her Boko Haram husband came to find her, wanting to give the boy a name.

'In our tradition the husband names the baby but I told her he had no right after what he did. This baby is a reminder of all the pain but this child doesn't even know of its own existence so it has no blame,' she said. 'All the bad things that happened to me are because of the father not him. This child is innocent.'

It didn't seem so to me at first but as I met more girls I realised she was right about being lucky. Most of the girls in the workshop were ostracised by their community and made to stay in a separate tent for what they called Sambisa wives.

Among them was Raqaya al Haji, who at thirteen was already four months pregnant by a Boko Haram terrorist she had been forced to marry.

When Boko Haram came for her, she was just eleven and about to start high school. 'I was asleep in my parents' house in Bama when two men with guns forced their way in and took me,' she said. 'I knew who they were as they were from the neighbourhood and everyone knew they were members of Boko Haram.'

They took her to a village called Bu Nafe and made her one of three wives of a young fighter called Khumoro even though she was so young she had not yet started her periods.

'If I refused they would make me a concubine,' she said. 'I knew if I ran away there were people on the roads who would take us back and kill us.

'He was a troublesome man,' she added. 'If I resisted him he forced me to drink blood. Often they made us gather and to watch women be lashed or have their heads broken with rocks for adultery.

'Sometimes Khumoro went off to fight and I thought about running away but I knew Boko Haram had people on the roads and would kill me if they found me.'

Eventually she became so desperate that in December, after more than a year and a half of captivity, she pleaded with him to let her go to visit her sick grandmother.

'I fled. I walked at night so they wouldn't see me then hid in the day. I was dizzy from no food or drink. It took me three nights to get back to Bama. It was under the control of the Nigerian army and they kept me for a while … Then in January they brought me here to the camp. I was so happy at first then I realised no one would talk to me. They call us *annova* which means epidemic or bad blood.'

'People believe the women who were abducted have become sympathisers and had a spell cast over them,' explained Dr Yagana Bugar, a lecturer at Maiduguri University who also came from Bama and had researched a report on the stigmatisation of these women. 'Because camps are organised by village, everyone knows your story and no one wants to associate with those taken by Boko Haram. So after everything else they have been through they end up ostracised in camps and can't go back to their original places.'

In other words they were victims twice over. Or maybe three times if you included what happened in military custody.

Some had been so brutally raped they had fistula, a tear in the walls between the vagina and the bladder or rectum which meant they leaked urine or faeces and could barely leave their tent because they reeked. Others had been infected with HIV by their captors and some had tried to abort their own babies or been forced to by their families. What they were going through mentally, I couldn't begin to imagine.

Then another girl came forward. Zara Shetima, at eighteen, had a fine-boned beauty, carefully plaited hair, and an adorable twenty-month-old baby girl she had named Kellu Kariye.

'The insurgents came to my village in Bama and told my father they wanted to marry me,' she said. 'I refused so they came back with guns and said they would kill me and my father unless I agreed. They brought 2000 naira [£7] as dowry.'

When the village was captured and others ran away, the man kept her there in her family house. 'He was short and dark in complexion,' she said.

Asked how he treated her, first she said fine. But there was a hollowness in her eyes. 'He forced himself on me, they all did,' she added, looking down. 'It was very hard.'

Tears started streaming down her face. Little Kellu took the end of her mum's red scarf and dabbed at the tears. 'If I resisted they made me watch him slaughter other people.'

That was not the end of the story. 'Some others came and said we should move and he refused so they shot him,' she said. 'Then they told me to marry another one. When I refused they took my sister.'

Later, when a military jet bombed the villages, she took the opportunity to flee, scrambling through thorny scrubland. She had no idea what had happened to her sister and the rest of her family.

'Nobody is taking care of me,' she said. 'I am alone here. Often I think it would be better to die but who would look after Kellu?'

Apart from the twice-daily ration of rice, and monthly bar of soap, she got no other food or help. To supplement it, she weaved traditional prayer caps which took a month to complete and sold for just 2–3000 naira (£7–10) each.

There was only one other way girls like Zara could afford any more food. All the aid workers told me sexual abuse in the camps was rife. The superintendent of one camp was on trial for raping children.

Some women found the conditions in the camps so unbearable they preferred to live outside, begging on the streets.

Back in Abuja, I went to see Brigadier General Rabe Abubakar, spokesman for the Nigerian military. 'Please Keep Moving. No Loitering. Maintain Silence' read a sign at the entrance. There was a power-cut and his office was sweltering. He told me that Boko Haram was now 'extremely weak because our military activities are really punching on them' and that the army had rescued 'thousands of girls' – more than a thousand that January alone. It seemed surprising that none of them were Chibok girls, particularly given all the international resources deployed to find them.

He suggested that the international attention had made things worse for the girls. 'You have turned those girls into their crown jewels,' he shrugged.

Dr Andrew Pocock, who had been British High Commissioner in Nigeria at the time of their abduction, later admitted to me that one large group of girls had been located early on in the search. 'A couple of months after the kidnapping, fly-bys and American eye-in-the-sky spotted a group of up to eighty girls in a particular spot on the Sambisa forest around a very large tree they were calling the Tree of Life, along with evidence of vehicular movement and a large encampment.

'They were there for a while – six weeks – and the question to Whitehall and Washington was what to do about them and answer came there none.'

Despite all the fervour western leaders had shown round the BBOG hashtag, there was no appetite to send in their own boots on the ground. 'A land-based attack would have been seen coming miles away and had the girls killed,' explained Pocock. 'An air-based rescue such as flying in helicopters or Hercules would have required large numbers and meant a significant risk to the rescuers and even more so to the girls. You might have rescued a few but many would have been killed.

'My personal fear always was what about the girls not in that encampment?' he added. 'Eighty were there but more than two hundred were taken. What would have happened to them?

'It's perfectly conceivable that Shekau would have appeared on one of his videos a week later, saying "Who told you you could try and free these girls? Let me show you what I've done to them …"

'So you were damned if you did, damned if you didn't,' he said. 'They were beyond rescue in practical terms.'

* * *

Far away in Australia, Dr Stephen Davis could not believe it was so hard to find more than 200 girls. He had been involved in hostage negotiations in the oil-rich Delta area as well as previous peace negotiations with Boko Haram so made some calls to commanders he had got to know.

'Three calls, three commanders,' he said. 'They said, "Of course we know who has the girls." So they spoke to some of those who had them and they said they might be prepared to release them.'

On the strength of that Davis went to Nigeria in April 2015 and spent three months in Boko Haram territory in the north, his white skin making him 'stand out like a lighthouse'.

He asked for proof of life. They gave him videos of girls being raped – the ones I had seen. They also told him that eighteen of the girls were ill so he suggested taking them off their hands. Three times a deal was almost concluded. 'Once it got as far as them taking some of the girls to a village for a handover but then another group took them, sensing a money-making opportunity.'

Frustrated and facing threats, eventually Davis had to leave for medical reasons – he had terminal cancer.

He insisted that the Boko Haram camps were easy to spot. 'It's not hard to see where the five or six main camps are,' he said. 'I can see them on Google Earth. You tell me the Americans, British and French can't see them from satellite tracking or drones?

'Meanwhile every week Boko Haram set off from those camps to slaughter and kidnap hundreds more girls and young boys,' he added in frustration. 'How many girls have to be raped and abducted before the West will do anything?'

In June 2016, shortly after my second trip, another video of the girls was released. In front of several rows of girls in floor-length robes, some seated and others standing, stood a masked militant in camouflage holding a Kalashnikov. 'We still have your girls,' he declared. 'The Nigerian government knows what we want – the release of our jailed brethren.'

He pulled out a girl in faded black abaya and tattered yellow headscarf and held the small microphone to her lips. Speaking nervously and looking down, clutching her robe to her neck, she explained who she was and read a scripted plea for the Nigerian government to free them by releasing Boko Haram prisoners in exchange. The girl was Dorcas.

Esther was relieved to see her daughter still alive but horrified at what she was enduring. 'Seeing my baby next to a terrorist with ammunition round his neck is not easy,' she said.

One of the girls standing behind Dorcas was clearly pregnant and another was carrying a baby. 'I have nightmares about her being raped,' she added. 'But in those nightmares I embrace her. For me it's not a problem if she's been raped, pregnant or converted to Islam. We just want our daughters back, no matter what the condition.'

The video ended disturbingly. The camera panned over a number of dead girls lying in pools of blood. Some of the bodies

were yanked over by soldiers so their faces were visible. The militant said they had been killed in a government airstrike and warned, 'We cannot keep protecting these girls.'

One Saturday in October 2016, a few months later, came unexpected news. Twenty-one of the Chibok girls had been released. Then in May 2017, three years after their capture, eighty-two more were handed over near the Cameroon border. A photograph shows them standing in a line in floor-length hijabs, guarded by seven militants, one of whom asked if anyone had been raped or touched in captivity. 'No,' came the answer.

Excited by the news, Esther scanned the pictures in vain, looking for her daughter. 'I really hoped Dorcas would be among them because someone called me and said she had been let out. But eventually, we saw the picture of the freed girls meeting President Buhari and she wasn't among them.

'Later I heard she had been in the group – she was supposed to be the eighty-third girl – but they decided not to free her and took her back to the forest.'

The releases were the result of negotiations involving the Swiss government and the Red Cross and facilitated by Zannah Mustapha, a barrister in Maiduguri who had represented Boko Haram families in court and set up an orphanage and widows' school sheltering victims from both sides. 'Even dogs don't eat their own children,' he said, explaining the trust he had built up.

The first handover of girls, he said, had been 'a confidence building measure', the second the main deal.

In return, five Boko Haram prisoners were released and the group was said to have received a black duffel bag containing three million euros. Mustapha said he knew nothing about that. 'I am a son of the soil, brought up in Maiduguri who just wants to bring peace to my area,' he insisted. 'I don't know if any money was paid.'

He claimed that more girls could have been freed but they didn't want to come, which he attributed to Stockholm syndrome. 'I met one of the girls who told me she and others didn't want to because they had converted and married Boko Haram men. The parents don't want to hear this but I heard it for myself.'

A week after the second handover, another video was released of girls in black hijab sitting on the floor saying they were not coming back because they had got married and converted. Once again Dorcas was speaking, her face covered. Once again an AK47 was in shot.

'She looked taller and slimmer than when she lived with me,' said Esther.

She insisted Mustapha was wrong about the Stockholm syndrome. 'Everything the girls say on these videos is being fed to them by Boko Haram. I know my daughter. She would not say the things she said unless she'd been forced to. If presented with the opportunity to come home, she would take it. Her mind cannot be at rest there, in the forest, miles away from her mum.'

The returned Chibok girls were kept in a secret location in Abuja for a deradicalisation programme and counselling, and only allowed back to their families in Chibok at Christmas. Some were then enrolled at the American University in Adamawa, housed away from the other students in a dormitory named after Malala, and highly protected.

Esther desperately tried to meet them but the authorities refused. Finally, in October 2018, she managed to speak on the phone to one of the girls. 'She used to plait Dorcas's hair. She told me that Dorcas is alive, that she is fine, that the terrorists used to teach them Arabic and that some of the girls are married, though not Dorcas.

'I used to dream she was back and I'd wake with a start, but now sometimes I have nightmares in which Dorcas says she will never come back.'

She had given up her job and left Chibok. 'Chibok is a sad place,' she said. 'I used to keep all my daughter's belongings in her room in Chibok but I cast her things out as I don't want to see them anymore.

'If she could, I know my Dorcas would have contacted me. She has my phone number in her head. I've been calling and calling her old mobile for five years now, but she never answers. I don't care if she's converted to Islam or not, if she's had a baby or not, I just want her to come back.

'They say some of the girls have died, but I'm sure Dorcas is alive. I go to church every day and pray for her to come back. I hope one day God will answer.'

4

Queue Here for the Rape Victim

Cox's Bazar, Bangladesh

How do you decide which child to save when Burmese soldiers are pointing guns at you? That was the impossible dilemma of Shahida, a Rohingya mother I met in December 2017 shortly after arriving in Kutupalong camp to which she and hundreds of thousands of others had fled. And how do you live with the decision?

Afterwards, when I think about that camp, I think about noise. And children everywhere. With uncertain faces and inappropriate clothes from well-meaning donations, a boy in a belted woman's cardigan of cream wool with a fur collar, a girl in a fairy dress with pink tutu and high heels like boats for her tiny feet. Someone had been teaching them a few words of English. 'Bye-bye!' they shouted as they passed by.

It was all a bit overwhelming after the long series of flights from London to Doha then Dhaka then Cox's Bazar in northeast Bangladesh, where the airport terminal carried the unlikely message 'Welcome to the Honeymoon Resort', and the Mermaid Beach hotel greeted me with a green coconut adorned with a cocktail umbrella and an invitation to sign up for a romantic candlelit dinner on what was apparently the world's longest beach.

I dumped my stuff in one of the small thatched cottages with psychedelic names amid a grove of palm and papaya trees, watched by an audience of chattering monkeys, and set off along the coast road.

Dotted along the way were piles of concrete pyramids stamped disconcertingly with the words Tsunami Protection. 'Like the Venus of Willendorf,' said my interpreter Reza, who turned out to be an artist.

Banners hung across the road emblazoned with large photographs of Prime Minister Sheikh Hasina under the words 'Mother of Humanity'. The title might surprise minorities or opponents abducted, tortured or locked up by her regime. Human rights organisations had recorded at least 1300 extrajudicial killings by state forces since she came to power in 2009 as well as an election in 2014 in which almost half of MPs won seats without anyone voting for them.

The banners referred to her opening of the border to fellow Muslims from neighbouring Burma. The refugees were Rohingya, a name few outside had heard of until the last few days of August 2017. People started pouring into Bangladesh from Rakhine state in western Burma, crossing the Naf river by boats or makeshift rafts or even swimming. Soon as many as 10,000 a day were coming.

It was monsoon season so they were arriving bedraggled and muddy, some bloodied from knife or gunshot wounds, and many starving after days or weeks in the jungle with nothing to eat but leaves. Most were mothers and children and they came with unimaginable stories of Burmese soldiers and Buddhist mobs moving into their villages, slaughtering the men, setting fire to their huts, then raping the women and girls often in front of their family.

Within three months more than 650,000 had been driven out – two thirds of the Rohingya population. The UN called it a 'textbook example' of ethnic cleansing.

As we turned off through emerald paddy fields where women in colourful wraps were standing among the rice shoots, and into what aid workers called a 'mega camp', I feared that I might have become a bit jaded after all the refugees I had spoken to over the previous few years,

Then I met Shahida, wrapped in a raven-grey scarf, and batting away flies, inside a flimsy shelter of black plastic over bamboo poles on a muddy path. Across the path was a leaking latrine and the stench was overpowering, as was the screeching from two cocks scrapping outside. A boy who looked about five passed by carrying a bundle of firewood almost the size of himself, occasionally stopping to put it down and look at it, as if astonished by the absurdity.

She was one of three young widows staying together from the same village in Rakhine state. Each wore a different-coloured scarf and each had lost a husband and a child.

Raped, beaten and widowed – Madina, Munira and Shahida

Munira, the eldest at thirty and brightest in canary yellow, was the most anxious to speak. 'First they came for the men,' she said, recalling the night a few months earlier in late September when Burmese soldiers burst into their homes in Borochora in Maungdaw. 'Then two days later they came for us.

'It was around 2 a.m. and I was breastfeeding my baby when I heard the first shot. Then there were so many it was as if it was raining fire. I could see flames in the distance from all villages around burning and rockets flying overhead.

'That's when the soldiers took the men, tying their hands with bind. Then two days later they came back, again after midnight, shouting, "Come out and see what happened to your husbands!" They entered our homes, pointed guns at our hearts and dragged us out.

'They took all the girls and women of the village to a rice field and lined us all up – maybe forty or so – and forced themselves on us. To start with we were all screaming but in the end it was quiet, we could cry no more.

'I was raped by five men, first one then the next. They beat me and slapped me and kicked me and bit me. I was too terrified to move. I saw two girls dead near me. By the time the sun came up I was barely conscious.

'When I came to, I couldn't walk but only crawl. There were bodies all around. I tried to find my children. Then I saw a small boy lying face down, shot in the back. It was Subat Alam, my eldest. He had been running towards me. He was eight.'

Also in the paddy field that night was Shahida, twenty-five, the lady in grey. She had grabbed her six-month-old baby son and two-year-old daughter when the soldiers burst into her hut. Tears spilled from her eyes as she told me how desperately she tried to shield them.

'They were in my arms and soldiers came to snatch them away,' she said. 'I tried to hold them but I could only protect one. They grabbed my baby boy and threw him to the ground then I heard a shot as I was running. I didn't look back as I worried I would lose my daughter too.'

Pushed into the line of women at gunpoint, her heart was pounding so much she could barely stand. 'I'd heard about women being raped in other villages,' she said. 'Then they bound my wrists against a banana tree and raped me.

'I was raped by one solder and was crying and shouting as he assaulted me. Afterwards he wanted to shoot or knife me but it was too dark.'

Somehow she escaped to the jungle where she found her three remaining children huddled together in terror.

'As the sun rose, we saw everything,' she said. 'All the cattle, chicken and goats killed and our houses burnt down. People beheaded, their limbs cut off, or shot.'

The call for prayers from the mosque on the hill started up, making it hard to hear, as the third widow Madina, in a dusky pink scarf, recounted her tale, particularly as the little boy she was nursing had joined in with his own wailing. His left hand was swollen and badly infected.

'I was sleeping when the soldiers burst in,' she said. 'I managed to flee with my three children to the hill behind. I was very scared because I was five months pregnant. If a woman is pregnant they cut out the foetus from her belly. They think Rohingya are not humans. They want to wipe us out.

'Then one soldier saw me and grabbed me. I was terrified he would feel my swollen belly. They had big knives and machetes.'

As he raped her in the forest, she repeatedly prayed for the baby she was carrying. 'I was shouting so my children cried,' she said. 'They were scared. That's when they took my eldest.

'I never saw him again. We know if the children are taken they are killed.

'I think the Burmese army are the worst people in the world,' she added, using her scarf to wipe away her tears.

'If we had knives we would kill them,' said Shahida.

The three women eventually managed to escape, passing a graveyard east of the village then hiding for a month in the jungle with other rape survivors as well as elderly and children from the village.

'We were hiding under bushes, moving from one place to another,' said Munira. 'It was raining day and night and we had no hope. We women had lost our appetite because of all the horror but our children were crying for food. All we could give them was fruits and leaves. Some days all we had was water from streams. We had to keep moving as the military were searching everywhere. Some people had managed to bury their crops before fleeing so after a week they went back to the village to dig up some millet but the soldiers saw them and shot them in the head. We kept seeing dead bodies. Some had died a few days before. Others were fresh.'

'It was hard to sleep,' said Shahida. 'I would see those soldiers on me and pray for help.'

Eventually they crossed the river to Bangladesh and safety. But their torment was not over and perhaps never would be.

Apart from the ghosts in their heads, the slaughter of their husbands had left the women as sole providers and protectors of their children, not easy anywhere but particularly in this conservative Muslim society, and they were struggling. 'The children have no sweaters or warm clothes and the babies have diarrhoea,' said Madina.

'We just get basic needs, rice, lentils and oil but we have no mat to sit on or pillow or utensils or jerry can to collect water,' said Shahida. 'And no one will marry us after what happened and with all these children.'

*　*　*

Even the most conflict-weary of aid workers and journalists seemed shocked by the Rohingya. It was not that their individual stories were worse than anything we had heard before, though many were, but it was more the sheer scale of what had happened. Every single shack had terrible stories and I had never come across such widespread violation of women and girls.

It was also the conditions. The camp was filthy with pools of green fetid water dotted along the path. There were lots of latrines – 30,000, the relief commissioner informed me later. But these had been erected so hastily that many were already blocked and none seemed to have locks. Many were next to wells where children were collecting water from a tap. These had been dug so shallow that aid workers told me that more than three quarters of the wells were contaminated by faeces. Not surprisingly most people were suffering from diarrhoea. A quarter of the children were suffering malnutrition. Many of the women with babies were so stressed that their breast milk had dried up.

Nor was there any privacy. Bangladesh was already the world's most overcrowded country, and its 165 million people among the poorest, so finding space for hundreds of thousands more was not easy. It was, said one aid worker, as if the whole population of Manchester had suddenly turned up on your doorstep.

Around half a million had been put into Kutupalong. If you climbed a hill the area looked like one of those relief maps in museums, dotted with makeshift dwellings up and down the hills as far as the eye could see. It was hard to believe that a few months earlier this area had been mostly forest. Some of it used to be an elephant reserve, which meant in the early days some refugees were trampled to death, though soon there were so many refugees even the elephants had been driven back.

The camp covered ten square miles and was divided into sections from AA to OO. There were signs for every aid organisation under the sun, some of which were marked 'Child friendly spaces' as if

Tents stretching in every direction – Kutupalong houses
more than 600,000 Rohingya refugees

other places were not. The mosques seemed to command the best spots on the hills.

Through it all was an endless stream of people. A bearded man passed with a plastic bag of fish and an air of purpose. Pathways were lined with stalls of people selling things. A young man stood at a table with digital scales on which he was trying to weigh live chickens. A makeshift barber's had a mirror and a painted board of hair styles, including the footballers Neymar and Cristiano Ronaldo. I marvelled at the resilience of people who lost everything. What would we in the West do if we lost our homes and were dumped in a place with no electricity?

The refugees were living so on top of each other that they had less than half the internationally recommended minimum space. In other words all the conditions in which disease can thrive. There had already been an outbreak of measles and while I was there diphtheria broke out. António Guterres, the UN Secretary General, called it a 'human rights nightmare'.

Every evening as dusk fell, the air darkened with smoke from thousands of campfires and made my eyes sting. There was so much coughing going on it was almost like a soundtrack to the camp, that and the cries of 'Bye-bye'.

Foreigners were not allowed to stay after 5 p.m. I would often hear rumours of what happened then, how men on motorbikes would appear to snatch girls for prostitution. Refugees told me that at night they heard screams of children being taken. I never managed to find anyone who had lost a daughter this way but I did see scantily clad young Rohingya girls on the long beach in Cox's Bazar touting their trade. Some said they were sold by their own families, desperate to supplement the rations of rice and lentils.

Yet talking to Rohingya it soon became clear that what was happening to them was nothing new. On a muddy island in the river where 6000 Rohingya had been stranded, I was greeted by Din Mohammad, a community leader in pebble-lensed glasses held together with tape, who presented me with a green bottle of fizzy drink. 'We may be refugees but can still offer something to guests,' he said and smiled.

I commented on his fluent English and he told me he had a psychology degree from Rangoon University. 'I graduated in 1994, just before they barred Rohingya from higher education,' he said. 'Now I am fifty-one and I have never been allowed to practise. I scraped a living growing subsistence crops.

'To the Burmese regime we are non-people. For decades they harassed us every day, sent our people to jail, didn't give us citizen rights but alien cards as if we were foreigners. We had no rights, no education – there were primary schools in our villages but no teachers. We weren't allowed to travel to another village without permission, which they refused, or even to get married, and they demanded more and more money for a licence.'

Nor were these the first to flee. Kutupalong was first established in 1992 when 300,000 Rohingya fled an earlier wave of repression. On the main road into the camp were shelters that looked more permanent made from corrugated iron.

Inside one I met Shahida Begum, a mother of five, who had arrived in that earlier wave twenty-five years earlier, when her village was burnt down. 'In Burma the Buddhists are the majority and so have all the power and they don't like the Muslim people,' she explained. 'I think they will not stop till they make all the Rohingya leave.'

She had taken in a Rohingya girl of fourteen called Yasmin who was sitting on a bed, wrapped in a marigold orange shawl patterned with red flowers. Above her was knotted a green mosquito net.

Yasmin never smiled and her small hands kneaded over and over as she explained how she ended up there. Her voice was so quiet I had to lean in to hear, straining to understand the unfamiliar place names which over the coming days I would hear over and over again. The noise of the children outside was soon lost.

'I grew up in Chali Para village in Maungdaw district,' she began. 'We lived on rice and fish from the river. I was the bread-winner as my parents became too old and sick to farm, and we had to beg for food, which made me cry. I was the eldest – I had two little brothers aged three and four. I told my parents if I was a boy I would work then a neighbour taught me to sew teak leaves into garlands on bamboo rods for the thatched roofs of our huts. It took long but if I sewed a hundred garlands I would get 1000 myanmar kyat [about 47p] which was enough for a kilo of rice.

'I would like to have learnt to read and write but we had no school: the Burmese authorities didn't allow us. There was just a madrassa to study Koran.

'The morning the Tatmadaw [the Burmese military] came, it was about 10 a.m. and I was taking a break from stitching leaves and playing outside our house with some friends. We didn't hear the trucks as there is no road to our village so the soldiers had stopped on the main road and walked.

'Five or six of them came to our house. They were in uniform with black masks and rucksacks. One soldier took a grenade from his rucksack and threw it inside where my mum and dad and two little brothers were. Immediately there were flames and I could hear them screaming.

'I tried to run in but my friends pulled me back. Before our eyes the house burnt to ashes. We tried to run away as we knew the soldiers often took girls to rape. But they caught us. They took us to the jungle. I was scared and crying and screaming but one of the men put his hand over my mouth to stop me. They ripped my clothes, tied my hands behind me then two soldiers raped me, one after another.

'The second one was saying "kill her" but I pleaded with them not to. I told them I already lost all my family, why kill me? Two of my friends bled so much they died, I don't know what happened to the other. I can't say what they did to me because when I think about those incidents I cry.'

She fell silent. Eventually she resumed the thread. 'They left me naked. I just had a yellow scarf which I wrapped around me then I made my way very slowly to the river bank as I couldn't walk well.

'In the jungle I met a lady with her sons and she saw I was bleeding down my leg and asked me what happened. She gave me cloth to wrap round it and helped me to the river bank. It was full of people trying to cross. Boatmen wanted money and I had nothing. I told them all I have is this nose ring so they took that. It was the only thing I had from my parents.

'We were about thirty people crowded into the boat. It had an engine but no roof against the rain and it took long, from dawn to early afternoon, maybe eight hours. Still, it was our good luck to find one as lots of people were on makeshift rafts which were very risky.

'The boat took us to the island on the Bangladesh side. When we got there I left the lady because I was afraid. She had two sons about my age and I was scared they could also harm me so I said to her, "I will find my own way, Allah will be with me."

'Then I sat down and I was crying so hard that people of the island asked me what happened. They gave me rice cake and water and also some money to cross to Teknaf [on the Bangladesh mainland].

'After that I walked ten minutes along the broken road and saw some Bangladesh army. They could see I was Rohingya and gave me biscuits and water then put me in a bus to the transit centre. I stayed there two days and was so tired I couldn't talk. I was lying on the ground, my foot and stomach all swollen. Someone said she has no one and took me to Balukali camp.'

It was there that Shahida Begum found her. 'I had gone to the camp with some food to meet relatives who had just arrived but when I got out of the tuk-tuk I saw a crowd of people round a girl so I went to see what had happened,' Shahida explained. 'She was so sick and weak and dressed only in a shirt on so I put her in the tuk-tuk and took her to the UNHCR clinic. They treated her for an infected thorn and also gave her a pregnancy test.

'I thought I have four girls already, why can't I look after her too? It's difficult but by the grace of Allah we can manage. She has no one.'

She showed me around the small dwelling of four rooms with a cooking area in an outside lean-to. They had electricity in the form of a bulb but water had to be fetched from a pump. Yasmin shared a room with Shahida and one of her daughters. It was extremely cramped as another of her daughters was married with a son and husband who also lived there, making ten altogether. And things had become more difficult as Shahida's husband had just lost his job as a schoolteacher. I wondered how many of us in the West would just take a girl in like that.

'For the first few weeks I had nightmares every day about my family burning but I sleep with my auntie and sister and now they are fewer,' said Yasmin. 'They don't make me do anything – I don't go outside yet and stay inside helping with the cooking. Only occasionally I go to collect water from the tube well.

'I'd like to go to school and learn to read and write. I know I am lucky that some girls who were raped died but I survived. I think those soldiers are the worst people in the world. Don't they have daughters or sisters?'

Before I left she fixed her eyes on mine. 'What happened to me was really bad and I don't think any boy will marry me,' she said. 'Who can marry me now?'

The question was heartbreaking. Of course, life was never easy for Rohingya girls in their villages where they were often married off by her age. At least Yasmin was not pregnant and had found a caring family. But how do you get over something like this? There was little to distract them in the camps for once girls hit puberty most were rarely allowed out of the huts.

I have to admit I find all these stories not only shocking but disorienting. I had grown up associating Buddhists with peace, lotus flowers and meditation, and admiring Aung San Suu Kyi as a beacon of courage against tyranny. Awarded the Nobel Peace Prize for her years of struggle, she had spent fifteen years under house arrest, separated from her British husband Michael Aris and their two sons. Even when he was dying of cancer back in Oxford, all she could do was send him a farewell video, dressed in his favourite colour with a rose in her hair. It arrived two days after his death.

Yet Aung San Suu Kyi was now Burma's de facto head of state

and had stayed silent as all these Rohingya were made stateless by her government and the appalling atrocities wreaked on them by the military.

The Burmese authorities did not even use the word Rohingya, instead calling them Bengalis as if they were migrants from Bangladesh, or demonising them as 'maggots', invaders or 'a black tsunami'.

In fact, the Rohingyas had lived in Burma for centuries. Rakhine state, the rice-growing area where they live, used to be the Kingdom of Arakan and some reports had Muslims living there since the eighth century.

Persecution and rape were nothing new. Arakan was plundered by the Burmese monarchy after they conquered it in 1784. Francis Buchanan, a Scottish surgeon with the East India Company, who travelled there afterwards, wrote 'The Burmans put 40,000 to death; whenever they found a pretty woman they took her after killing the husband and the young girls they took without any consideration.'*

It was plundered again by the British when it came under their rule in 1826 as part of the Indian Empire, later to be joined by the whole of Burma. Colonial authorities encouraged many more Muslims to come from Bengal as cheap labour in the paddy fields which caused resentment among the Buddhists.

During the Second World War, when Burma's nationalists supported the Japanese occupiers, the Rohingya sided with the British who had promised them a separate land. Afterwards, the British rewarded the Rohingya with prestigious government posts. But when partition of British Indian territories in 1947 etched a line between what is now Rakhine state and what was

---

* Willem van Schendel (ed.), *Francis Buchanan in Southeast Bengal (1798): His Journey to Chittagong, the Chittagong Hill Tracts, Noakhali and Comilla* (Dhaka: Dhaka University Press, 1992).

then East Pakistan, now Bangladesh, the promised autonomous state never materialised.

After Burmese independence in 1948, some Rohingya mounted a rebellion but this was crushed. When the military seized power in 1962, their situation deteriorated. The junta in Rangoon saw minority groups as a threat to Buddhist nationalist identity. They were disenfranchised, denied citizenship, corralled into slave labour, banned even from travelling outside their villages or marrying without permission.

The first exodus was in 1978 and there were waves again after further attacks, such as the one which had sent Shahida fleeing in 1992, and others in 2012 and 2016. Inside Burma, more than 100,000 Rohingya had been picked up and put into what were basically internment camps near Sittwe, the capital of Rakhine. A conference at Harvard in 2014 described their situation as a 'slow-burning genocide'.*

One might have thought things would change with the 2015 elections which swept Suu Kyi and her National League for Democracy to an overwhelming majority in Parliament. Burma was welcomed back into the international community and sanctions lifted.

She had after all told the Nobel Women's Initiative in 2011: 'Rape is used in my country as a weapon against those who only want to live in peace, who only want to assert their basic human rights. Especially in the areas of ethnic nationalities, rape is rife. It is used as a weapon by armed forces to intimidate the ethnic nationalities and to divide our country.'

A year after that, however, she took a very different line when Samantha Power, then US ambassador to the UN, used a visit to bring up the issue of state violence against the Rohingya, and

---

* Dr Maung Zarni and Alice Cowley in *Pacific Rim Law & Policy Journal*, University of Washington, June 2014.

appealed to her to raise her voice. 'Do not forget there is violence on both sides,' Suu Kyi replied, adding, 'you should not rely on propaganda for your information. Muslim countries are hyping events.'*

In October 2016, a year after her election, security forces conducted what they termed 'a clearance operation' in northern Rakhine state. Villages were burnt down, hundreds killed, including children, and women gang-raped. Around 90,000 were forced to flee.

A UN report said 52 per cent of women had been raped and told of children as young as eight months having their throats slit. 'The devastating cruelty to which these Rohingya children have been subjected is unbearable,' commented Zeid Ra'ad al Hussein, the Jordanian diplomat who was then UN High Commissioner for Human Rights, which put out the report. 'What kind of hatred could make a man stab a baby crying out for his mother's milk? And for the mother to witness this murder while she is being gang-raped by the very security forces who should be protecting her.'†

Once again they got away with it. Indeed the campaign saw the regime increase its popularity at home as defender of Buddhist values in the face of 'invading Muslim hordes'. They used Facebook, which is very popular in Burma, to incite hatred against the Rohingya, posing as fans of pop stars and creating celebrity pages full of incendiary comments that portray Islam as a global threat to Buddhism and the Rohingya as a threat to national identity, even though they made up only 5 per cent of its population of 54 million.

Meanwhile they prepared for what some called 'the Final Solution'. The 2017 onslaught was the worst of all. It was appar-

---

* Samantha Power, *The Education of an Idealist* (London: William Collins, 2019), pp. 315–16.

† Flash Report of OCHCR mission to Bangladesh, 3 February 2017.

ently triggered by an attack by the Arakan Rohingya Salvation Army (ARSA), a small militant group, on a series of border posts on 25 August. But the retaliation was unforgiving and clearly pre-planned.

Within three months more than 350 villages were wiped off the map and 700,000 people driven out – the largest forced human migration in recent history. A report by a UN fact-finding mission published in September 2019 stated that at least 10,000 Rohingya had been killed. Based on interviews with nearly 1300 victims, it included graphic accounts of women tied by their hair or hands to trees then raped, and villages scattered with bodies of women with blood between their legs, in a regime campaign to 'erase their identity and remove them from the country', and warned that the 600,000 still in Burma 'remain the target'. The investigators said they had a confidential list of 100 names involved in war crimes and called for the international community to act and for the prosecution of senior generals.*

Pramila Patten, the UN's Special Representative on Sexual Violence, accused the Burmese military of using rape as a 'calculated tool of terror to force targeted populations to flee'.

The Burmese government dismissed the reports as 'Fake Rape'. Colonel Phone Tint, Rakhine's minister for border affairs, even told journalists: 'These women were claiming they were raped, but look at their appearances – do you think they are attractive enough to be raped?'

We could not independently check these stories as Burmese authorities would not let journalists into Rakhine state. But satellite images taken by Human Rights Watch clearly showed 345 villages destroyed. And in the accounts of rape of the women I was interviewing there was a sickening similarity. Some of the women showed

---

* Report of Independent International Fact-Finding Mission on Myanmar, 16 September 2019.

me bite marks on their hands or cheeks and shyly lifted trousers to reveal scars from shot wounds or bruises. Their eyes spoke pain.

Why had the international community turned a blind eye? Were they so dazzled by the lady with the flowers in her hair and story of courage that they ignored the attacks? Did they care more about not wanting to rock the transition than the fate of the poor Rohingyas?

Azeem Ibrahim, a Scottish academic who had written a book on the Rohingya as well as endless newspaper columns warning of impending genocide, had another view. 'The problem is the Rohingya are right at the bottom of the global ladder,' he said. 'No one can name a single Rohingya, they have no leadership, no office on K Street. They are mostly rickshaw pullers, fishermen and subsistence farmers.'

Were anyone to take action, they would need evidence and I kept asking if anyone was gathering it. The difficulties of such an enterprise became clear one morning when I was taken to OO section of the camp by a Save the Children press officer to meet a woman who had been raped and shot and apparently was very keen to tell her story.

Sanoara Begum, thirty-five, was about to have lunch when we arrived at her shelter so we left her and went for a walk. Along the way was a washing area where men and boys in lungis were shampooing and soaping themselves from buckets filled from a tap.

What did women do? I wondered. Some told me they were hardly eating so they could avoid using the latrine.

When we got back to Sanoara's shelter there was a queue. The *New York Times* and a local journalist were waiting outside. An NBC crew was hovering nearby.

'Can we do it as quickly as possible?' Sanoara asked me. 'You can see there are others.'

I wondered about leaving. But having hung around that long, it seemed churlish not to at least hear her story, so I squatted inside on the jute matting marked UNHCR. Her husband and son sat behind me by the entrance, which was not ideal given the nature of the discussion.

She told me she was from Boli Bazaar, in Maungdaw, a village which had already been targeted in 2016. 'First the military came to our village and burnt all the houses so we fled to another village called Leda. But then the next night they came there about 9 p.m. and shouted all you people must leave Myanmar, why are you still here? Then they started killing the men. They took my older son Mohammad Shaufiq and shot him in the chest and slit his throat. He was fifteen.

'After that around midnight they seized younger girls and married women and took us to a school. There were six of us, four young girls and two married women and me. Two of us were pregnant. I was eight months pregnant.

'They bound my hands and legs and threw me on the ground. I was raped by twelve soldiers, three at a time. I kept thinking about the baby and what would happen. They bit me. When I tried to resist they beat me with the gun, look I lost two teeth.'

She pulled back her top lip to show me a gap.

'After a while I was senseless then three more men came. One of them told me if you tell anyone we will kill you. Then another came in and shot me – they shot me twice, in my right knee and by my vagina.' She lifted up her trousers to show me. 'Once with a pistol and once a big gun.

'I lay so still I didn't even dare move my eyeballs. Then I can't remember anything. My husband and brother came to me and carried me. They thought I was dead but my fingers were moving a little so they realised I was alive.

'They sold my daughter's gold nose ring and took me to a

doctor who gave me some medicine. I gave birth to the baby on the banks of the river but it was dead so we buried it there. I was a mother of four but now there are only two.'

She started crying then gestured around the small black plastic shelter, barely larger than a disabled toilet cubicle, with its mud floor and a fire at one side for cooking, which was surely a fire hazard.

'Look how we live,' she said. 'In Boli Bazaar we had lots of property. Our bathroom was bigger than this shelter. My husband had a tuk-tuk and my elder children had bicycles to go to school. My husband had magical healing powers. We had fourteen cattle and sixteen goats. I had a good bed, good food. Now we are in this nasty place. We have no money, we can't even buy a fish.'

At that point I sensed a movement near my rucksack just behind me. My interpreter Sonali had also noticed and suggested I moved it in front of us. I vaguely noticed the husband and son had gone. We continued.

'My husband and brother carried me the whole journey on a blanket because I couldn't walk. It was six days walking to the river and we had to stop three days on a hill so they could rest.

'We crossed by boat then we got to the border at Utipara. I was bleeding from the shot wounds so they took me in a tuk-tuk to Kutupalong camp and I was treated. I feel very much pain.

'Now I don't want to have sex. But my husband beats me. He says if I don't cooperate he will take another wife.'

She began weeping. Then she said it was time for the next interview.

It wasn't something I normally did but I asked if I could take her photograph, not for publication but to remember. I slid my hand into the rucksack pocket for my iPhone. I noticed a fleeting moment of panic cross her face. The phone wasn't there. I was baffled – I'd been using it just before we went in the tent and tucked it in the pocket when we got in so I knew I had it.

'You shouldn't have left it by the entrance!' she scolded. 'A beggar took it.'

'But your husband and son were sitting there,' I replied. 'Where have they gone?'

She started yelling. Soon a beggar was produced. She was an old woman with a string bag that Sanoara demanded she empty out. There was no iPhone, just a woollen hat.

'This poor woman is nothing to do with this,' I told Sanoara. 'Where is your husband?'

The Save the Children representative told her that we would have to call the camp police and suggested she might like to find her husband. I waited outside the tent and the husband was fetched.

'He knows black magic so maybe he can find it,' said Sanoara.

After a heated discussion between her and her husband, the phone was miraculously produced and thrust at me by the husband. 'He found it from a boy using his black magic and beat him,' said Sanoara.

'Black magic,' I nodded.

I stepped over a cesspit outside and walked away. That evening at Mermaid Beach, a raucous group of fellow journalists and aid workers had gathered on a table on the grey sand, ordering spicy lime prawns and drinking beer. Holding court was an enthusiastic American from something called the Institute of the Future in Palo Alto, explaining his plan to erect towers throughout the camp from which to beam Bollywood movies to bored refugees. I asked if he realised the Rohingya were Muslims and there was no way the imams would agree. Then I felt mean – he just wanted to give them something to do in a place where there was nothing to do and nowhere to go, just wait and remember.

I was sitting next to Hannah Beech, a *New York Times* journalist whose work I greatly admired. She asked about my day so I recounted the story of the rape victim and the phone. She told me that she had spent the day with three unaccompanied children she had met and their uncle in order to write a profile. She had gradually become suspicious that something didn't stack up. It turned out they were not unaccompanied at all but the children of the man who had presented himself as the kindly uncle.

We were both annoyed. But we also wondered how desperate must people be to do such things or make up such stories. Or were they so traumatised they didn't know what was real anymore? The refugee commissioner had told me some Rohingyas were so disoriented that they were confusing antiseptic liquids for milk and drinking them. And what of us, the beast we were encouraging them to feed, endlessly looking to devour ever more horrific accounts. Were we really any different to that perhaps apocryphal TV reporter who shouted 'Anyone here been raped and speaks English?' to a planeload of Belgian nuns who had just been rescued from a siege in eastern Congo?

5

Women Who Stare into Space

Sirajganj, Bangladesh

> *A little boy was crossing the street in Jamalpur carrying a can of*
> *milk when he was beckoned by a security guard to come into the*
> *Pakistani army camp. He took the milk and they paid him with a*
> *two anna coin. Inside the room the boy saw three naked women*
> *with torture marks all over their bodies. He could never forget*
> *what he saw and never spent the coin.*

Wartime memory displayed in Liberation War Museum, Dhaka

In the centre of the gallery stood a sculpture fashioned from twisted bark of a woman in long wavy robes who looked distressed in a way that reminded me of the Yazidi women I had met in the ruins of the mental asylum. The sculptor was Ferdousi Priyabhashini, a well-known Bangladeshi artist who became the first middle-class woman to break the silence in the 1990s over the sexual violence she had suffered during the country's war for independence. Her artworks were created from branches of trees and twigs combined with discarded scrap iron because, she said, 'We are like that thrown-away bark no one wants.'

On a nearby wall was a triptych of black-and-white photographs of three women who conveyed unimaginable distress despite their faces not showing. Instead, the photographer Naib Uddin Ahmed had shot each woman with a river of dark dishevelled hair covering her face, her fists tightly clenched in front, wrists adorned with bangles almost like handcuffs.

I was in Gallery Four of the Liberation War Museum in Dhaka, looking at its small display on sexual violence. An astonishing 200,000 to 400,000 women are thought to have been raped by Pakistani soldiers in the 1971 war for independence, yet a plaque on the wall stated 'there are not many records of this hidden suffering'.

They call them *birangonas* from the Bengali word *bir* which means brave or war heroine. It was a title given by Bangladesh's founding president Sheikh Mujibur Rahman in 1972, and meant to recognise them as war heroines and bestow respect. I would soon learn it had brought unfortunate consequences.

I had gone to the museum after meeting Honorary Captain Abdul Suhan, a retired Bangladeshi army officer with orange hennaed hair, milky eyes and a pronounced limp, who lived near the Rohingya camps. We sat on his terrace on a sofa with no springs, batting away mosquitoes, as over tea and biscuits he told me that the terrible stories I was hearing in those camps were not new to locals.

'The problem of course started with you Britishers,' he began. He was referring to the independence of India in 1947 and its partition to create the Muslim homeland of Pakistan as two separate wings, with 1000 miles of hostile India in between. What later became Bangladesh was then East Pakistan, in a country it was hard to imagine anyone could have expected to work. When the Awami League led by Sheikh Mujibur Rahman of the more populous east won the majority in the 1970 elections, West Pakistan refused to accept.

Sheikh Mujib, as he was known, laid out six demands for regional autonomy in a historic speech in Dhaka on 7 March 1971 and when these were refused, called a general strike. Pakistan's military leader General Yahya Khan responded with Operation Searchlight, a massive military crackdown.

On 25 March 1971 three battalions secretly took up position in Dhaka. Just before midnight, as everyone was sleeping, they pounced. University hostels were set on fire, students and academics gunned down. Intellectuals, poets and Bengali nationalists were assassinated, newspaper offices blown up and Hindu districts set ablaze. Sheikh Mujib was arrested. Death squads roamed the streets of the capital, killing 7000 people in a single night.

That was only the beginning. Within a week, half the population of Dhaka had fled, and at least 30,000 people had been killed.

Similar purges were soon underway around the country. Suhan was at that time a major havildar in the Bengali regiment of the

Pakistan army, and he and other Bengalis fled their barracks in Chittagong and joined the rebels in the hills. He soon realised that the Pakistani soldiers were doing more than fighting and killing.

'They raped a lot of women, it was a terrible atrocity,' he said. 'Sometimes they hung them from the banana trees, sometimes they bound and raped them. Countless women were taken to Cox's Bazar by the al Shams and al Badr [collaborators] for the Pakistan army to rape over and over and in the camp at Comilla. They kept them like chattels. Young and old, it didn't seem to matter.

'Because ours was a conservative society and the women shy, they didn't dare disclose what had happened to them, but we fighters knew what was happening and those victims greatly helped inspire and motivate us.

'Yet after the war men like me got garlands and help while these women got nothing and had to hide away. Those women who were well-off ended up in silence while those who were poor ended up begging. Some hung themselves with their saris. It was worse than what you are hearing happened to the Rohingya but they won't speak. They just stare into space.'

Tears began falling from the old man's eyes. 'I founded a girls' high school in memory of those female martyrs,' he said. 'I didn't know what else to do.

'When I die, like all the freedom fighters, government people will come, they will place a flag on my coffin and a bugler will play. When a *birangona* dies, there will be nothing.'

Below the gallery, in the museum lecture theatre, a conference was underway comparing the attacks on the Rohingya women across the border in Burma to what had happened in Bangladesh forty-six years earlier. There I met Mofidul Hoque, a writer and one of the museum's founders, who had fought a long and often lonely battle to try and win respect for the *birangonas*.

'Women are always soft targets in conflict,' he said. 'The Pakistanis thought with massive killing they could subjugate the population for once and for all – a kind of Final Solution for Bengali nationalists. So they entered the countryside, set up camps and the very next thing they were looking for the women. Girls and women of all ages were abducted from their homes and picked up in the streets, fields, bus stations, schools or collecting water at the well.'

Some were raped there and then – so-called spot rape – often on their own beds and in front of their own family. Others were strapped to banana trees and gang-raped. Women were taken to army camps as sex slaves and kept naked so they could not run away. People talked of seeing trucks of semi-conscious women being unloaded. Porn movies were shown at the camp to work the men up before letting them loose. Many women died in the camps, some bayoneted through the vagina and left to bleed to death.

Australian journalist Tony Clifton wrote in *Newsweek* that he had doubted the stories until he visited the refugee camps and hospitals on the Indian border. There he met victims such as orphaned Ismatar, 'a shy little girl in a torn pink dress … her hand covering the livid scar on her neck where a Pakistani soldier had cut her throat with a bayonet'. He came away 'believing the Punjabi Army capable of any atrocity'.* Clifton had covered Vietnam, Cambodia and the Biafran War so was no stranger to horror. Yet, describing the babies shot, the daughters dragged into sexual slavery, the men whose backs had been whipped raw, he wrote, 'I find myself standing still again and again, wondering how any man can work himself into such a murderous frenzy.'

He could have been describing the Rohingya camps more than four decades later.

---

* 'The Terrible Bloodbath of Tikka Khan', *Newsweek*, 28 June 1971.

Among those he interviewed was John Hastings, a Methodist minister from Britain who had lived in Bengal for twenty years. 'I am certain that troops have thrown babies into the air and caught them on their bayonets,' he said. 'I am certain that troops have raped girls repeatedly then killed them by pushing their bayonets up between their legs.'

Many survivors had mutilated breasts. Doctors from the International Planned Parenthood Federation, brought in to set up clinics after the war, found almost every woman had some form of venereal disease. One said she had been raped by fifty soldiers.

It was one of those doctors who alerted the world to what had been going on. Dr Geoffrey Davis, an Australian known for his work on late-term abortions, was brought in to supervise abortion of unwanted babies, as well as facilitate international adoption of those who had been born. He was, he said, carrying out abortions 'on an industrial scale', a hundred a day just in Dhaka.

Years later, he was asked if the numbers of women raped were exaggerated as Pakistan has always claimed. 'No,' he replied. 'Probably the numbers are very conservative compared with what they did. Some of the stories they told were appalling. Being raped again and again and again. By large Pathan soldiers. All the rich and pretty ones were kept for the officers and the rest were distributed among the other ranks. And the women had it really rough. They didn't get enough to eat. When they got sick, they received no treatment. Lot of them died in those camps. There was an air of disbelief about the whole thing. Nobody could credit that it really happened. But the evidence clearly showed that it did.'*

The numbers went far beyond what might be seen as a 'common by-product of war' and the objective far more than humiliating the enemy and damaging their morale. Just as I had seen with the

---

* Interview with Dr Bina D'Costa from the Australia National University in Sydney, 2002.

Yazidis, the girls in Nigeria taken by Boko Haram, and the Rohingya, this was rape as a systematic weapon of war.

'It was not individual cases, it was a deliberate policy and that policy was ideological,' said Mofidul. 'What happened here was one of the largest killing of Muslims by Muslims, branding us as inferior, not proper Muslims. Rape was their "duty" to purify the heathens.'

Just as ISIS fighters years later would be given religious 'justification' for taking Yazidis as slaves, imams in Pakistan issued a fatwa declaring that the Bengali freedom fighters were 'Hindus' and that their women could be taken as *gonimoter maal* or war booty.

In his memoir, *A Stranger in My Own Country*, published after his death, Pakistani Major General Khadim Hussain Raja wrote that their commander General A. A. K. Niazi had told officers to 'let loose their soldiers on the women of East Pakistan till the ethnicity of the Bengalis has changed'.

Dr Geoffrey Davis heard similar explanations from Pakistani soldiers he met who were being held as prisoners of war in Bangladesh. 'They had orders of a kind or instruction from Tikka Khan [Pakistan's military governor in the East] to the effect that a good Muslim will fight anybody except his father. So what they had to do was to impregnate as many Bengali women as they could ... so there would be a whole generation of children in East Pakistan that would be born with the blood from the West. That's what they said.'

The war was brought to an end by the entrance of Indian forces. At one minute past five in the afternoon of 16 December 1971, Pakistan's commander General Niazi signed a surrender at a trestle-table set up on Dhaka racecourse. Slowly, he unstrapped his pistol and handed it to the Indian commander who compounded the humiliation by stripping Niazi's insignia of rank off his shoulders.

Cheering Bengalis who had gathered around the racecourse threw flowers. Sheikh Mujib was released by the Pakistanis and returned to lead his newly independent country.

One of his first acts was to embrace its violated women as war heroes. He declared them *birangonas* to give them honorary status, like male freedom fighters, eligible for preferential educational and employment opportunities, and encouraged men to marry them.

He also established rehabilitation centres for the women and clinics to treat medical damage and temporarily legalised abortion.

In a landmark act of 1973, the International Crimes Tribunal Act, he also declared rape a crime against humanity.

It was a bold and unprecedented initiative.

But his good intention backfired for the title branded them. To society these were shamed women who had had sex with someone not their husband. Many were driven from their own families and villages, even killed by their own husbands or made to kill their children.

Like the girls taken by Boko Haram in Nigeria, they became double victims, first suffering the rape, then ostracised when they tried to return home.

'We have one case,' Mofidul told me, 'where a girl was raped and got pregnant and her mother took out her gold earrings and said, "Take these, go away and never come back." She was given shelter by a porter at a port on the river and gave birth to a baby boy. Then the porter's family told her you should kill this baby and go and start a new life in Dhaka. So she put salt in her baby's mouth and put him in the river to drown. After that she was very disturbed.'

Some women were accused of prostituting themselves by telling their story and there were rumours of them receiving bags of money. Others were accused of fabricating stories to cash in.

If the survivors' situation was hard before, it became far worse after 1975 when Sheikh Mujib was assassinated and an Islamist government took over. This included some of the very people who had been collaborators in the war, sourcing women for the Pakistani soldiers or even raping them themselves. The rehabilitation centres closed and the women were thrown out onto the street.

'They spat at me crossing the road and called me "wife of Pakistani soldier".'

'"How could you let them touch you?" That's what my own family told me!'

The women telling the stories were gathered in a corrugated-iron shack down a muddy pathway, near the river's edge, in Sirajganj, a small town on the floodplains northwest of Dhaka.

The shack was one of a line leaning against each other facing an enclosure of muddy ducks and they looked more like animal sheds than human dwellings. Inside, large cobwebs, lit up by a bare light-bulb, hung like drapery from the ceiling. The only furniture was a bed, a wooden dresser stacked with chipped cups and plates, and a small black-and-white TV. On the wall was a picture of Mecca and a 2014 calendar.

Six women in colourful saris sat on plastic seats or huddled on the bed. Their clothes were vibrant orange, pink, yellow and green even in the dusty half-light, but their faces were anguished and their bodies seemed to fold in on themselves.

The women clasped my hands as I walked in and one in pink kept stroking my hair as if I were a child.

This was the Mothers' Club. They were all mothers – and grandmothers – but they had something else in common. They referred to it as the 'ghotona' which my interpreter translated as 'the event', adding 'everyone knows what that is'.

Before we started talking they shooed away a gaggle of curious grandchildren who had gathered in the doorway. The children immediately began grizzling noisily outside. Soon the ducks joined in squawking, and occasionally there was a loud spitting sound from someone passing by.

I was relieved to find the women. It had been a long journey from Dhaka through a grey sheet of never-ending rain. About two hours in, the road had collapsed, forcing traffic to the side, and we were stuck in an endless line of cars, trucks and buses trying to overtake each other on the single lane. It took more than six hours to finally get to the Bangabandu bridge over the wide Jamuna river, one of the largest tributaries of the Ganges, and through the green paddy fields into Sirajganj.

I had been put in touch with the women by a local activist called Safina Lohani who had set up a woman's centre after the war where they all met. But communication had not been easy and I wasn't sure if at the end the women would be waiting, or if they would talk to me. Instead, they could not have been more welcoming.

For more than four decades they had been meeting every couple of weeks, usually at Safina's house, and for many of those years secretly. Then in 2015, Safina had suffered a stroke, so since then they met in each other's homes, though not in villages where people would talk.

'When we get together we talk about our past and how the Pakistani army destroyed our lives,' explained Hanzera Khatam, her face lined and leathery under her scarlet scarf. 'Because of them we had a life that was completely wretched. Because of Safina we have survived.'

Hasna, who at seventy was the eldest and wearing an orange shawl over her yellow dress, spoke first. She told her story almost without taking a breath.

'It was a Thursday when the soldiers came to our village Khaji Para. I was cooking with my daughter on my lap; she was five. The soldiers arrived by train and summoned the entire village. Almost all the women fled but the station was right next to my house so they were there before I could do anything and I didn't have time to get away. They grabbed me and threw my daughter to the ground so hard her skull split and her mouth was frothing. Fifteen days later she died. Two of the soldiers raped me there and then. I was screaming so the soldiers beat me with the barrel of their rifles. May Allah give them the punishment they deserve.

'After the war everything was a struggle. My husband died immediately after. All the villagers knew what had happened to me and I was castigated and shunned. They called me *birangona* and the word has a bad connotation. The neighbours called me names. I had a son and I worked as a housemaid then in the women's rehabilitation centre then that closed. I got work separating rice from chaff and as an agricultural labourer even though I was often in pain in my belly.

'My son became a rickshaw puller but now he is sick and can't work so I have to look after his four children.'

A hen wandered in and started pecking on the floor, only to be chased away by a scrawny stray cat which hissed and slunk back out.

In just three minutes Hasna had depicted a life of complete misery.

Koriman, the woman in the light pink shawl over a faded black-and-lilac dress who kept stroking my hair, picked up the thread.

'I am also seventy,' she said. 'When the war started I was 23 and living with my husband in the village of Tetulia. He worked in a tobacco factory making cigarettes so we had a good life. We had two sons and I was pregnant with a third child. Then the military came to our village and burnt down the whole place. We fled and took refuge on an island in the river. A few days later we went back to our village to try and get some things and found everything destroyed and saw lots of our neighbours dead and decomposing.'

She started to cry. 'The soldiers had gathered all the men and put them in a line and opened fire. So we left again without taking our cattle or valuables.'

By now she was sobbing. She dabbed her eyes with the end of the pink cloth. It was my turn to pat her. Her voice grew softer.

'We saw the Pakistan army setting fire to everywhere including Sirajganj town. The whole sky was lit up with smoke and flames. We were so frightened we would just go back to the village for a short time, not stay.

'One day I had gone back to my home with my children and was making bread in the yard when I suddenly noticed Pakistani soldiers. I tried to take my son in my lap but the soldiers were already in the yard and knocked him to the ground with their rifles and raped me. I was so frightened I closed my eyes till they had gone and don't know how many took me and for how long but they left my breasts and my body swollen. My husband came and saw everything and was so affected that he was struck dumb from that day till his death thirteen years later.

'Because of that I had to suffer a lot. I felt it would have been better if they had killed me. Villagers insulted me so much. No man would marry me. For a long while I could not bear the smell of making bread.

'But then I met Safina who ran the women's centre and I worked there. In 1975 Sheikh Mujib came to Sirajganj and addressed all war heroines as his own daughters and said we should be looked after. Eight of us even visited his home.

'Then he was killed and everything got worse. The centres closed and we had to do everything on our own.'

The other women nodded in agreement. The hubbub outside seemed to have stopped and I noticed the drip drip of water coming from the edge of the roof and splashing onto the dresser.

Seated in front were two sisters. The shack where we were meeting belonged to the elder of them, Raheela, in a black, red and yellow printed scarf. She was chewing betel leaf and shaking her head as she listened to stories which she had heard over and over.

'I am sixty-five. I was married three years before the war and my husband and I had been living in Shinapurna, about eight or nine kilometres from here,' she started.

'First the war was in Dhaka then Pakistan military arrived in large numbers at a station called Jamtoli Bazaar and people were frightened. I was at my father's house and my father-in-law came and said the situation in Sirajganj is deteriorating so we should move. We went to his house but then the army came to a neighbouring village and took two brothers and shot them dead and raped two women, one the mother of a newborn and one a virgin, and took them with them to their camp.

'The news spread quickly and my mother-in-law took us to a cornfield to hide. But my father-in-law said it was not safe, so late at night we left with my father.'

She stopped for a moment to pat away her small granddaughter who had wandered in clutching a filthy ragdoll to her chest and who kept trying to clamber onto her grandmother's lap.

'Then we saw that the house we were going to had been set on fire by the Pakistani army so we kept going and came to my aunt's house. By then it was 10 a.m. – we had walked all night. Suddenly we heard the sound of army jeeps. My father told me to hide in a nearby house which was the home of some Hindus. Those vehicles stopped in front and then I heard boots and the men came in and found two Hindu women trying to hide under the divan. They dragged them out by their hair, beating them, then saw me hiding behind the door.'

At that point she sent the children out of the hut and shook her head.

'First, three of them were trying to rape me. Then some other soldiers entered dragging in another Hindu woman and raped us both over and over. The men were big, not small like us and our Bengali men. Then they left us and took the other two Hindus away.

'By the time they finished I was unconscious. When I came round, it was evening, about 7 p.m. I found my father and some other people on the bank of the river, some of them injured. It was hard for me to walk but he helped me to another aunt's house. After a couple of weeks my husband came to visit and discovered what had happened and never came back.

'Three months later, when Bangladesh was liberated, everyone was celebrating and went home but me. Instead of going to my husband's house, I went to my parents.

'After a while I heard about the rehabilitation centre which was full of women like me tortured by the Pakistan army. I told my father I would like to go and first he refused because he said everyone knew what kind of women went there. But then I did and worked there three years, learning to weave cloth, with maybe forty other women.

'One day we got the news that Sheikh Mujib had been killed and we were frightened. The guard at the centre made us go home because he feared there would be retribution.

'I went back to my father's and eventually he persuaded the villagers to get my husband and convince him to take me back for I had done nothing wrong.

'He did and I lived with him till his death and we had five daughters and two sons. But it wasn't easy. My husband could not forget what had happened. He did not speak nicely to me. Some of the villagers said I was an impure woman so should not live in the village. They told me you should have killed yourself rather than enduring this dishonour, and often I thought they were right, what the Pakistanis had done had killed me anyway. When our daughters married we had to pay higher dowries because people did not want to be associated with us.

'A few years ago I went on TV to talk about being a *birangona* and my son-in-law was very angry. He divorced my daughter and she was very upset with me. "You ruined my life too," she told me.'

Raheela wasn't the only one in her family to have been raped. Her younger sister Maheela, sixty-three, in a yellow, black and gold shawl, began speaking next.

'When our father took Raheela to our aunt's house and she was raped by Pakistanis, he left me and the younger ones with my uncle, his brother. I was just sixteen and my husband had gone off to join the freedom fighters.

'One day a Pakistani plane came and bombed the jute mill and the embarkation point on the river so everyone was frightened. A few days later the soldiers came to our village and my uncle took me to a different village where his in-laws lived. But then soldiers came there and we had to hide in the jute field in a bunker in the dry earth. The following day the villagers thought the soldiers had gone and we came out, but some collaborators told the Pakistanis and they came to the house. I hid behind a fence and my cousin's wife under the mattress. They found us easily and raped us in the house then they took my cousin's wife with them. Later, when they brought her back, they had sliced off her breasts and she died.

'After a few months Bangladesh was liberated but our house had been burnt to ashes by Pakistani military so we had nowhere to go and had to stay in my grandparents' house and get treatment. When my husband came to know I had been dishonoured by the Pakistanis he left me and married another woman.

'Then Raheela joined the rehabilitation centre so I also started as a tailor and we supported each other. But then it closed which seemed the end of hope.

'I heard that my husband had fallen ill and was sick for a long time and that woman left him. After that he returned to me so I cared for him and from then till his death we were together and we had five children, three boys and two girls.'

Like Maheela, Hanzera Khatam was the widow of a freedom fighter.

'I was twenty-three when the war started and lived with my husband Hatam Ali in the village of Chuna Hati. When the war started our home became a den of freedom fighters and I would be cooking all night to feed about forty a day. Often there would be firing or shelling from the Pakistan air-force and lots of people in our neighbourhood were killed. Then one day there was a heavy reinforcement of the Pakistan army in the camp near our village and they started firing mortars and guns from different directions, so the freedom fighters were surrounded and many were killed so we had to flee.

'I ran into the bush with my seven children. But it was hard to hide because the ants and insects were biting relentlessly. The soldiers set fire to our village. They started at one end and burnt down one house after the other. My husband was watching from the bush and thought if he couldn't take the cattle it would also be burnt and it was all we had, so he went to get it. I heard a shot, they had got him, and I raised my head to see and three soldiers spotted me and ran towards me. I was carrying my three-year-old daughter so they grabbed her and stamped on her to death then they raped me so much I lost consciousness.

'My children were running in different directions. Afterwards the villagers helped bring me round and find my children. By the time I found my little daughter ants had already eaten her eye and part of her nose.

'My husband never really recovered. All we had left was a small piece of land just three decimals (three hundredths of an acre) and we sold it to buy him medicine but he died three years after the war.

'The villagers wouldn't let me back in the village so I had to build a hut by the railway where I still live. My children would collect firewood to sell in the bazaar and made cow pats for fuel but it wasn't enough. Safina helped us a lot, she gave us clothes and food, but we still had to beg.

'You can see we are very poor. But it's not just money we ask for but recognition that we are the people wronged.'

She picked up a plastic bag from the floor and out spilled files of letters and forms, many of them with official stamps – fruitless attempts at validation in a nation of bureaucracy.

The other women shook their heads knowingly and proffered their own paperwork.

Last to speak was Aisha Khode Bhanu. 'When the war started for three months there was no railway but then all of a sudden one night the trains started and we realised the Pakistani military was coming to Sirajganj,' she said. 'Before they came, they bombed the area indiscriminately. The planes were buzzing overhead like flies.

'My husband like most people in our area worked in the cotton mills but they had stopped. When we heard the trains, me, my husband and in-laws walked twelve hours through the night. When we looked back, the Pakistan army was setting fire to everything, the flames rising so high we could see from far off.

'When we returned to our house a few days later we found everything burnt to ashes – utensils, cushions, even rice. We had nothing. We were all staying at relatives' except for my father-in-law who went back and made a home from that burnt corrugated iron.

'One day he was visited by a razakar [collaborator] who insisted he should bring back all the family members as the army wouldn't come back there again so they didn't need to be worried. So three months later we all moved back. But I felt uncomfortable. I used to keep a lamp burning at night and was frightened to leave the hut.

'One morning we heard the razakars were coming so we ran to the pond to hide and covered our heads with water plants. They found us and assured us the army wouldn't come back but, around noon while we were waiting inside the house, we saw soldiers – eighteen of them. My mother-in-law told me to stay silent but within a few moments the soldiers started banging on the door so vehemently we were scared.

'My husband went out to face them and they beat him with the barrel of a rifle and forced him to the fields and also my father-in-law and I knew they were coming, then two of them entered and raped me.

'Then all the soldiers came alternately and raped all of us on the string bed, me, my mother-in-law, my husband's other wife. The rape was so violent that the other two died within a month.

'My husband also died a year later because of the torture he suffered. I was left alone with three daughters and one son.

'I survived because of Safina. We were all making handicrafts in the women's rehabilitation centre and got some rations but when Sheikh Mujib was killed and it became defunct we had to go through a life of misery and distress. After that I worked as a housemaid.

'My son now works in the jute mill and my daughters are chronically poor, finding it very hard to subsist.

'I don't like the term *birangona* – to me it meant distress and disrespect,' she said. 'Things improved a bit when Mujib's daughter Sheikh Hasina came into power in 1996 and she tried to rehabilitate *birangonas*. Recently we started getting an allowance of 10,000 taka [£90] and neighbours and villagers started to respect us finally. But even today I jump when I hear banging on the door.'

As she spoke, the thin wail of the muezzin called for prayers from a mosque in the distance. Outside darkness had fallen. The women were restless, needing to get back to their villages.

Aisha had one more thing to say. 'We have given our most precious thing but you won't find our names engraved anywhere.

I would like my rapists to be killed for what they did. Let them be hanged.'

That night in a small shabby guesthouse in Sirajganj, I was reading in bed with a torch when someone started banging on the door. I froze. The banging became more insistent and there was shouting. I could not smell smoke so I stayed in my bed, hoping the lock would hold. When I opened the door the next morning there was a bottle of water outside. I smiled sheepishly at the manager as he handed me my breakfast of fried egg swimming in oil.

I set off early to go and visit Safina who lived above the bazaar. On the street outside a man had built a fire and was boiling water and Nescafé in a pot to sell to passers-by. 'Bangladesh Starbucks!' joked my interpreter.

Safina's husband Amin-ul-Islam Chaudhry was sitting at a table in the apartment scanning the morning papers. Photographs of Sheikh Mujib were dotted round the room. Amin told me he had been a freedom fighter along with his father and brothers and was shot when they attacked a Pakistani army camp.

'I went to India to get military training. The Pakistan army was searching for me and my father so Safina and our little boy stayed in her parents' house and moved from village to village. What the Pakistan army did here was genocide, taking away women and girls and torturing them.'

Safina came in pushing a walker, wrapped in a colourful embroidered shawl. Her eyes were deep and kind. Since her stroke she struggled to speak, so Amin helped.

I asked about the rehabilitation centre she had started that the women had talked about so fondly. 'At the beginning it was very difficult,' she said. 'Even though Sheikh Mujib had said all the rape victims should be recognised as freedom fighters and provided help, none were willing to come forward. Bangladesh is a very conservative Muslim society. No one spoke about sexual harassment and those violated by the Pakistan army were hated by their own family and persecuted. Many of the women were hiding in the jungle so I went to find them and arranged them refuge in the centre.

'We had maybe sixty women. Their stories were so terrible I spent most evenings in tears. Often when they were raped the soldiers had grabbed their babies and stomped on them to death or thrown them so hard their brains came out. You see now Rohingya going through the same. The sad thing is when war breaks out, women are the easiest victims.

'I got the women some training to weave cloth, tailor or make bangles so they could be self-reliant as I thought that would help their self-esteem.

'But when Mujib was assassinated, the military regime ordered the centres to close within twenty-four hours and police came and told the women to leave then put the centre under lock and key.

'Some of the women went to relatives but their families didn't want them. Some lived in the jungle and sometimes family members gave them food secretly but most had to beg.

'I was told to cut off all communication with them. But I couldn't leave them like that. So I tried to find them. I found about thirty and formed an organisation which I called the Mothers' Club. They were all mothers, after all.

'It was hard to raise funds so I created an NGO called Sirajganj Women's Development Organisation. We had to do most things clandestinely. The problem was those collaborators were still alive and threatening us.

'From 1975 to 1995 I worked in the community, arranging small meetings where I sat with local people to try and change their opinions of *birangonas*. I tried to make them understand how it was because of those women and how they suffered that Bangladesh was liberated. But it was very hard. We were castigated for working with the *birangonas*.

'Finally, in the late 1990s, things started to improve. Under Sheikh Mujib's daughter, Hasina, the government once again declared the women freedom fighters.'

That was when Ferdousi, the sculptress, came forward and told her story. But most had spent too many years in denial.

According to Safina, the Sirajganj women had been getting a monthly allowance and medical support since 2013 after a local female social worker Mitalee Hussein, whose own mother was a *birangona*, filed a case in the High Court for their recognition.

'But it was too late for most of them. Many had died. And to qualify they had to tell their story so not many came forward. Some had been accepted by their families so did not want to risk that. Sometimes the families did not even know, particularly the children. But there were some rape victims where their own families raped them, saying they were already defiled.'

In 2010 the International Crimes Tribunal was finally set up by Sheikh Hasina's government based on her father's act of 1973. Operating out of the old High Court building in Dhaka, by March 2019 the court had tried 88 collaborators and party leaders for torture, murder and rape. Twenty-six had been sentenced to life, and 62 given death penalties, of whom six had been executed.

Pakistan had never apologised. A commission of inquiry into the war and how it lost half its territory reportedly accused senior military of 'shameful atrocities' but was never made public and no one ever brought to book. The military museum in Lahore carries no mention and history taught in schools gave the impression that Pakistan actually won the war.

Back at the Liberation Museum in Dhaka, Mofidul told me that a Pakistani artist Nilofar Butt had recently visited and made a minute-long video called *Amnesia* with just three sentences:

> *You have hidden the fact*
> *The nation has hidden the fact*
> *I have hidden the fact*

As I had seen, even today these women live in the shadows. 'It's still a hidden suffering,' said Mofidul. 'I met a girl recently whose mother had scars on her body and only after many years had told her daughter why. That girl wrote a song, "I'm the daughter of a *birangona*". It was so beautiful but she cannot go public as society is not ready even now.

'We need a movement to say these women should be saluted by the state,' he added. 'We have a lot of rape in this country and even today when a girl is raped she is considered an outcast and often blamed. We should unearth our own history so we can learn from it. When our young researchers meet a *birangona*, they always say how inspired they are by their resilience and they get strength from them.'

6

The Women Who Changed History

Taba, Rwanda

The small town of Taba seemed an unlikely place to have made international legal history. About an hour south of Kigali, passing through brilliant green paddies and skirting the brown ribbon of the Nyabugogo river which was gushing onto the road, the tarmac abruptly ran out at the foot of a small hill. At the top was a red mud road, the main street of Taba, busy with women in colourfully printed *kitenges* – waxed cotton wraps – selling tomatoes, cucumbers and airtime, as well a few meandering goats, and men on brightly painted bicycles, the local form of taxis. Pink and white hibiscus flowers grew along the sidewalk and a yellow-billed hornbill was trumpeting from a banana tree.

Waiting for me there was a tall fifty-something woman with high cheekbones and a gap between her front teeth, Victoire Mukambanda. She got into my taxi and we bumped along a clay track to her home along one of the green terraced slopes. Rwanda is known as the Land of a Thousand Hills and the scenery was easy on the eye, all around us deep valleys and undulating hills laced with mist. Then Victoire started pointing at the box-shaped houses. 'Here were the teachers dead, there that family were all shot … From the top to the bottom were Tutsis and they were all killed.'

Over on the hills were the groves of banana trees where she hid in the teeming rain. 'I died many times in those banana trees. I prayed to God to die. I knew my parents had been killed because they shouted the names from the tops of the hills. I heard the names of my four brothers and my sister. Sometimes I heard them shout my name as one still to be hunted down.

'They were people I knew, neighbours actually, acting like animals. They killed thousands of Tutsis. The machetes they used to cut people were the same as they used to cut crops and cows, they didn't care.'

Eventually our driver was defeated by the muddy track and we walked the final part. Thunderous clouds were massing overhead. The sound of birds was all around, the *kar-kar-kar* of a white-breasted crow heralding our arrival.

We came to a squat house with adobe walls, a corrugated-iron roof and no windows. Behind was a small lean-to where a young

Victoire, remembering the past

boy tended a black-and-white Jersey cow tied up and mooing, part of a government scheme to give a cow to each genocide survivor.

The house had two rooms, a bedroom with a dirty mattress on the floor and a living room where the only furniture was a brown sofa and coffee table, and the only decoration a picture of President Kagame and a calendar two years out of date.

Outside it began to rain, giant raindrops pounding onto the corrugated iron like fistfuls of stones.

It was raining like this in April 1994 when the season of killing started that saw a tenth of Victoire's countrymen slaughtered in a hundred days, including most of her family, as everyone became either hunted or a hunter.

We sank into the brown sofa and Victoire began to tell me what she remembered. 'I grew up here in Taba and before it was an easy life,' she said. Like everyone I met in Rwanda, she referred to the time pre-genocide simply as 'Before'.

'My parents were farmers and had plenty of land where they kept cows and grew beans, potatoes, cassava and groundnuts as well as trees with passion fruit, oranges, mango and papaya. I went to school and loved it but I could only continue up to the end of primary as the government did not favour us because we were Tutsis and it said so on our ID cards. We were very much a minority and would be bullied. Even if you passed the exams to high school, they would replace you with a Hutu student who had not done as well.

'We were taught that Hutus and Tutsis were a separate race. They said Hutus were the real people of Rwanda and we Tutsis had come as invaders from Ethiopia. It was very shameful to be a Tutsi. If a Tutsi did well they would come and loot and burn their house down and kill their animals so they had to start anew. My father had to do a "Huturisation" and forge a Hutu ID which made him feel dehumanised. But the government knew people were doing that and cross-checked, then arrested my dad and beat him.

'All this problem started long before 1994. There were killings of Tutsis in Taba right from independence in 1959, before I was born. And in 1973, when I was in Year 4, they expelled Tutsis from schools and burnt and looted many homes so I saw people fleeing to the Catholic church. We always went to the churches when there was a problem.'

Hutus made up about 84 per cent of the population, Tutsis about 15 per cent and the Twa, a local pigmy group, the remainder. People often talk of physical differences – Hutus are generally described as darker skinned and rounder faced with flatter noses, while Tutsis are taller and slimmer with long faces and finer features, yet I met tall thin Hutus and short round Tutsis. Generally the divide is traced back to the late nineteenth century when 'race science' was popular among European colonialists who classified Africans by skin shade and cranial size. The Germans who colonised Rwanda in 1897 saw the paler Tutsis as warrior kings ruling over peasants, while the Belgians, who took over after the First World War, entrenched these distinctions by printing ethnicities on official identity cards.

Nowadays all this is discredited and the two groups regarded not as separate tribes but more like social classes or castes, Tutsis having been traditionally cattle herders and Hutus agricultural farmers. Cattle is more valuable so over time the Tutsis had gained higher status and became rulers, prompting resentment among Hutus. Eventually in 1959 the Hutu Revolution deposed the Tutsi king and forced tens of thousands to flee into exile. From then on there had been periodic purges.

'The harassment we felt as Tutsis had always been by officials not person to person,' said Victoire. 'That changed in 1994 when they launched the "final solution" of doing away with our *ethnie* [ethnicity]. The first step was so-called "security meetings" where Tutsis were always excluded, which was when they were training militias they called Interahamwe which means those who work together – because they called this thing work. They told them Tutsis are the enemy. On the radio, they started all this hate-speak calling us *inyenzi* or cockroaches.

'I was married by then and my husband owned a bar, and we had seven children. On the night of 6 April we heard President Habyarimana's plane had come down in Kigali and he had been killed. The Hutu Power roadblocks appeared on the streets of Kigali the next day and the killings started there. About eleven days later, our Bourgmestre [mayor], Jean-Paul Akayesu was invited to a meeting in Muchakaberi in the south of Rwanda where he was given the command to kill every single Tutsi.

'Next morning, 19 April, we were woken up by someone screaming for help. People went up the hill to see and found the school had been burnt down and Akayesu holding a meeting. He declared the killings are starting and not a single Tutsi should be left alive.

'That's when they came down the valley where we lived. We were very scared. They started by killing educated Tutsis. They took the teacher Alex Gatrinzi and his older brother Gosarasi who were our neighbours and killed them, and another teacher was beaten and buried alive, accused of favouring Tutsi children. Seventy-six children were killed in the school.

'After that someone went to the top of the hill and announced, "Today is the final day for Tutsis." That night every cow belonging to a Tutsi was killed. People were looting our crops from the fields.

'It was like these people had lost humanity. They were people we knew and exchanged goods with. People we shared moments with and beer. They used to come to the bar and we invited each other to ceremonies.

'They destroyed our house and took everything, furniture, even the iron sheets of roofing, nothing was left. What could we do? We all ran away and scattered.

'I had no idea where my husband or my children were, only my baby girl who was on my back. As I ran, someone struck me from behind with a club. They were trying to hit my head but they hit my baby and smashed her skull. I felt the whack then I heard no cry and I knew. I took her dead body off my back, put her down and continued running. I could not even bury her.

'Some hid behind trees for many days. It was April, the time of rains, so it was very wet and muddy. We were hiding but we had already accepted death would be our final destination.

'One day I came across the body of one of my sisters, hacked to death with a machete. I don't know how I survived. I was raped many, many times. Any time someone caught me they would rape me. "We want to taste you Tutsi women," they said. One by one, one coming after another. I was raped so many times I lost count.

'You can't imagine being raped, not showering, you can't change clothes, then in the morning heavy rain pours on you and it rains until it's done, then at night it rains again.

'One day I was raped by four men so violently I couldn't walk. Afterwards a woman found me on her way to the fields and she gave me a cassava, telling me to eat it piece by piece. By then, after so many days of not eating, my jaw hardly worked.

'For a while we sought refuge in front of the bureau communal [the mayor's office]. There were dozens of women and children there. We knew that the mayor had ordered the killings but we had nowhere else to go. Over the next weeks the militia and locals raped and beat us repeatedly. When people died, dogs were eating the bodies but if we tried to bury them they beat us. We begged Akayesu to kill us because we could not live like this anymore. He said he would not "waste bullets on us".

'I went back to the hills but they caught me and beat my eye so it was red and swollen for months and threw me in a latrine pit. Every day I was praying to God to die because I was so tired.'

The rain outside on the metal was becoming deafening. The equatorial darkness had fallen quickly, like a curtain, as always in Africa. The boy who was tending the cow brought in an oil lamp. A sharp crack of thunder was followed by lightning flashes in the hills that illuminated the recesses of Victoire's face in the dim light.

'Eventually someone told me to go south to Musambira because they were not killing women there anymore. I pretended to be a Hutu and an old woman took me in. I stayed a week then I saw a big number of Hutus moving toward Congo. The old woman told me the RPF was coming and she was fleeing. I said I would stay.'

The RPF was the Rwandan Patriotic Front, a guerrilla force of Tutsis exiled in neighbouring Uganda and Burundi led by Paul Kagame.

'When the RPF came, we ran toward them and they were so happy to see us. They told us you are in safe hands now and gave us water and food.

'It took me a month to find my children. They had been sheltered by my younger sister Serafina who was also raped and had been forced to marry an Interahamwe. We were all that remained of our family.'

She stopped for a moment and looked at me. 'I wish those people who did these things to us were also killed,' she said.

'Afterwards I couldn't speak or eat – I would forget to cook. I barely uttered a word for months. How could anyone begin to put what happened into words?'

But Victoire did something else. She not only got her voice back but became Witness JJ behind a thin curtain in a courtroom in the Tanzanian city of Arusha, in a trial which led to the world's first ever conviction for war rape.

* * *

God passes the day elsewhere but sleeps in Rwanda, locals like to say. Where was this God as neighbour turned on neighbour with club and machete in a nationwide effort to exterminate Tutsis, all while the world turned a blind eye?

Everyone seemed so friendly and everything so beautiful, yet, just like Victoire, everyone and everywhere carried tales of such evil. 'I hid in a septic tank for two and a half months,' my driver Jean Paul told me. 'When I came out my entire family had been killed – my father, who was a doctor, my mother, a primary-school teacher; and all my seven siblings.'

He showed me the bridge where hundreds of people were pushed off; the Hotel des Mille Collines where more than 1200 people hid in terror as its heroic manager bribed the Rwandan army with money and Johnnie Walker; the church where those who had sought refuge were clubbed to death, rows of cracked skulls now arranged along the pews.

Josh and Alissa Ruxin, the American couple who ran my guest-house Heaven, with its popular weekend brunches, told me that when they started building in 2003 they would find bones washed up every time it rained.

Eight hundred thousand people killed in 100 days from a population of 8 million. It was a rate of murder unequalled even by the Nazis and it forced the UN to use the word genocide for the first time in its history – even as it did nothing to stop it.

The UN Special Rapporteur on Rwanda estimated that in this tiny country from 6 April to 12 July 1994 there were between 250,000 and 500,000 rapes. That's between 250 and 500 a day. Victims as young as two or as old as seventy-five. Rape was the rule and its absence the exception, found the UN report in January 1996. In some areas, almost all women who survived had been raped.

It was clear the rape was not circumstantial but an integral part of the campaign, used as much as a weapon as the machete and club. Hutu propaganda included a tract called *The Ten Commandments of the Hutu* which warned that the Tutsi 'will not hesitate to transform their sisters, wives and mothers into pistols' to conquer Rwanda. One commandment stated: 'A Tutsi woman works for the interests of her Tutsi ethnic group. As a result we shall consider a traitor any Hutu who marries a Tutsi woman, befriends a Tutsi woman or employs a Tutsi woman.'

How does a country and a people recover from something like that? The post-genocide government had tried to legislate away animosity between the Tutsi minority and the Hutus who wanted to exterminate them, by launching an 'I am Rwandese' campaign and scrapping ethnicity from the identity cards. Most people looked away when I asked if they were Tutsi or Hutu. The official language alongside Kinyarwanda was switched to English from French, which was associated with the past Belgian colonial masters as well as what was seen as the support of the government of President François Mitterrand for the genocidal regime. Place names had been changed so I found it hard to track down towns and villages on my map.

On the surface it seemed to have worked. Rwanda was regarded as a model in Africa. The centre of Kigali, where the gutters had literally run red with blood, now had roads lined with streetlights, manicured hedges and swept pavements, for every citizen had to give one day a month to cleaning. It was the neatest most crime-free capital on the continent, as if by cleaning one could scrub away the past. The government had even criminalised plastic bags, divesting tourists of them at the airport and making them buy hessian replacements.

As for women, it was the only government on earth where the majority of Parliamentarians were female – an astonishing 64 per cent. Rwanda was also promoting itself as a tourist destination, spending £30 million to advertise on the shirts of Arsenal players, and recommended by the *New York Times*. At Kigali airport the blonde American woman and her daughter in front of me told the passport officer they were there for 'reconciliation tourism'.

All this seemed remarkable and pleased western donors who had turned Rwanda from the land of a thousand hills to what locals jokingly called the land of a thousand aid workers. The World Bank had poured in $4 billion since the genocide. The UK in particular had got behind the new government, the then Tory leader David Cameron even leading a group of his MPs there in 2007 to help rebuild schools and do other good works for a few days.

But could one really legislate and scrub away such a bloody past? Indeed, many people told me what they had instead was dictatorial government. Paul Kagame, tall and beanpole thin so that his jackets seem to flap around him, had been President for eighteen years after leading his Tutsi forces to end the genocide. He had been re-elected for a third time in 2017 with 99 per cent of the vote, after changing the constitution so he could run again. Meanwhile his would-be challenger, US-educated accountant Diane Rwigara, was barred from standing and locked up in a maximum-security prison with her mother for over a year. Other opposition figures disappeared or met violent ends. A friend of mine who had taught a journalism course there had told me how local journalists who dared criticise Kagame were beaten or killed mysteriously.

'I do what I have to, to make sure my country never goes through such a terrible thing again,' Kagame told a British general who questioned his authoritarian ways.

The International Criminal Tribunal for Rwanda (ICTR) opened in November 1994, shortly after the trial for the former Yugoslavia. They were the first international criminal courts since those in Nuremberg and Tokyo following the Second World War. The chief prosecutor of both courts was South African judge Richard Goldstone, highly respected for his work dismantling apartheid laws.

There was little confidence it would achieve much. The new Rwandan government had drawn up a list of around 400 top génocidaires and appealed to the UN for help in apprehending them so they could be tried in Rwanda before their people. Instead the UN created the Rwanda tribunal as a subset of that for former Yugoslavia, and very much its poor relation. It wouldn't even be in Rwanda but in neighbouring Tanzania.

The aim was to try high-level perpetrators such as government officials and military officers for the genocide. But, under-staffed and under-resourced, it seemed a gesture by the international community to look as if it were doing something after its failure to act at the time.

Many of the prosecutors were young and inexperienced. One of them was Sara Darehshori, whom I met in New York where she was working for Human Rights Watch as senior counsel, looking at sexual assault in the United States.

Over hot chocolate on a crisp autumn afternoon in Manhattan, she told me that, while studying at Columbia Law School, she had volunteered in rape crisis centres then worked in Bosnia for a year resettling refugees and rape victims from the war. She had just graduated and was in her first job at a law firm when she heard about the new tribunal for Rwanda, and applied for a post as an investigator.

'I was just twenty-seven and when I got the job thought I would be carrying the bags of some senior counsel,' she said. 'But when I got there, there were no other lawyers, no one in the office at all, just two forensic guys and a secretary. We had one car and had to bring our own computers and to walk two blocks to the UN office to make photocopies. On the first day we caught our security guards trying to steal our generator.

'It was hard to believe this was the UN and a serious endeavour. Everything was thrown together.'

No one met her at the airport on her arrival. 'It was completely dark as all the streetlights had been shot out and I was all alone. Eventually, I managed to get a lift from a passing car from an aid agency. The first night I stayed in a hotel room with a door that didn't close properly and a bloody handprint on the wall.

'We had just started investigating in the field when we got a call from the Zambian government to say that they had arrested a group of Rwandans from our Most Wanted List. We didn't yet have a list! But at the time Judge Goldstone was prosecutor for both Rwanda and Bosnia and he was sitting in The Hague with all these staff and a great office and no one in custody, so was under a lot of pressure, with people asking why don't you have any trials for all this money. When he heard we could start trials, he was very keen.'

She ended up as one of two co-prosecutors with another young American, Pierre Prosper, who had come from working on gang cases in Los Angeles. The pair found themselves putting a war criminal on trial for genocide in front of a panel of three international judges – the first such trial ever.

'When I went to present the first indictment there was no courtroom, literally just me and a judge who lived in Tanzania in this makeshift office,' Darehshori laughed.

That first indictment was Jean-Paul Akayesu, the mayor of Taba, not because he was a key figure, but was among the group picked up in Zambia.

'It was ironic because he wouldn't have necessarily fallen in the basket of people we were looking at,' she added.

When he was brought in, she went to interview him. 'He was the first suspect I had ever interviewed,' she said. 'He was tall and polite and told me he had not seen a thing as he had stayed in his home during the genocide.'

The next challenge was getting people to testify. Most Tutsis in Taba had been killed. Although there was clearly no shortage of witnesses, many Rwandans were afraid of what punishments might come down on them or their families. It quickly became dangerous for people to collaborate with court investigators. By September 1996, at least ten witnesses had been killed before they could testify in Arusha.

Victoire was one of five brave women from Taba who testified. 'I was hesitant at first,' she said. 'Friends and relatives tried to put us off. They said people will know and it will be dreadful. But in the end I decided that for justice to take place someone had to say what happened and tell the world, and I was prepared to do it so these people would be punished and this wouldn't ever happen again.'

'I didn't want to die a hater,' explained Godeliève Mukasarasi, a Hutu woman married to a Tutsi, as she recounted how she persuaded five village women to board a plane for the first time in their lives and describe in a foreign court the terrible ordeal they had gone through.

'Our Mission is Extraordinary, Our Mission is Healing Hearts', read the sign outside the small brick building on the main road of Taba which housed Sevota, the organisation she set up for widows and orphans of the genocide. Inside, a group of children in blue uniforms were sitting in front of a blackboard on which someone had written 'a lion is chasing us' and learning English. They sang and danced in welcome as we entered.

'After the massacre I hated everyone,' said Godeliève. 'Then I got sick and almost died. After I was cured I said I must do something to forgive and love. I had survived twice. In the genocide I was being chased and taken to the river like the other women to be raped and killed but I wasn't killed.'

Godelième

Her house was a few doors along the main road, solidly built of brick with a green door and a papaya tree in the front yard. She was much darker skinned than Victoire and fabulously dressed in a red, yellow and white printed jacket and skirt that reminded me of a morning sunrise. She looked younger than her fifty-nine years and her smile was warm, making her the kind of person you immediately trust. The house was immaculately kept and on the table a pile of woven baskets made by women in her organisation.

'When the genocide started I was thirty-three and had five children,' she said. 'My husband Emmanuel was a businessman and owned a grocery which sold food, cosmetics, beer, sodas, everything. I was working as a social worker. We were happy. Emmanuel was head of local businessmen, we had a car, a house and plantations. We were among the richest people here.

'When the killings started my husband had to escape first as he was a Tutsi and a rich person and then my children also left. I remained to look after our property because I thought I wasn't a target as a Hutu.

'The killings started on 19 April. They were going to family after family, over hills and mountains killing, using different weapons – spears, clubs and machetes or throwing people into the river.

'On the 20th they attacked my father-in-law's family and on the 23rd they came to our place in the night and threw a grenade. I was scared. I knew families in the same situation when they killed everyone, including those who were not targets.

'They were dressed in banana leaves and smoking weed and they chanted and whistled. Maybe they had been drinking banana beer. They had smeared white stuff on their faces and shouted, "Look for them! No one should survive!"

'I knew them, they were neighbours. Some were workers at our store, some teachers at our primary schools.

'I tried to negotiate with them. We had two houses in the compound so I said "Destroy one house and leave one because one is mine and I am a Hutu," and I gave them some money. But they came back at night and destroyed both and looted everything in our store and took all our cows and pigs. We had three cows.

'Also in our compound was my younger sister and around fifty children from Kigali who had fled here. The kids were hiding in the backyard of the bar.

'Luckily, five minutes before the Interahamwe came back, I was warned by a friend. "Be ready, they're coming to kill you," he told me. He took me and my younger sister to another place where an old man was living. That same man went to look for my children who'd been hiding in a prayer room, and brought them to where I was. One of the boys had climbed an avocado tree when the killers came and another was hiding in a basket of beans.

'I knew everyone involved, both the killed and the killers. I couldn't imagine they could do such things. How could a young boy command people to cut neighbours down with machetes and rape their daughters? It was as if we had all lost our minds. I thought I can no longer be living in the real world, that's the only explanation.

'Girls were first raped before being thrown into the river. They took me to the river but then they left me because they were more interested in looting.

'We stayed only one night with that old man. The next morning he'd left a cigarette packet on which he had written, "Leave Run Fast They Are Coming."

'When we were running there was a roadblock and I fainted because by then I'd spent days without eating so my sister gave me water from the puddles to revive me even though it was very bad water. When I came round, we went to my office in the district administration block. I had nothing in my office just a Bible and a framed picture of Jesus so I slept on the ground. After two days an old man brought us a mat to sleep on and some food.

'I could see people digging deep pits and throwing in dead bodies. They were torturing women and some would even rape dead bodies. I saw that with my own eyes.

'Some days later my husband was brought to the office and beaten very badly. We were there about two weeks. While I was hiding him, a big group of Interahamwe came in a truck and took him away, back to our former residence, to show them what they could loot. They grabbed from the smaller militia what they had taken from us. Afterwards they told him, "We won't kill you. You will go and die anyway."

'We knew we didn't have much time so Emmanuel found a car of a Tutsi who had been killed and took it to drive us at night to my parents' area. My sister, who had also married a Tutsi, was there too so they said we must punish them because they have snakes in their homes. Sometimes they called Tutsis snakes instead of cockroaches. "We must finish those snakes," they said.

'They came back with guns so we fled to the safe zone of the UN mission of French troops in Kibuye in a convoy of eight vehicles.

But on the way we kept coming to roadblocks. I was in the first car and would just keep saying there are no Tutsis here and give them money but after a while I ran out. My mum had some 50,000 francs, so I told her to give me the money to save my husband and children. That's how we survived.

'We only returned to Taba when the new government took over. It was really hard to come back because we had no money and I was ill and also of course because of what had happened here. My husband got a contract from the RPF who were then in government to supply wood for rebuilding in Kigali.'

After Godelieve recovered she set up Sevota to support widows and children. As Taba is not far from the capital, soon it started getting visitors from NGOs as well as government officials. When they asked how they could help, she suggested bringing chickens or goats for the women, most of whom were widowed, to help them make a living.

Gradually more women started coming. Victoire attended one of the meetings and was given a goat which she said helped her find her voice. 'If you have a goat, you have something,' she laughed. 'You can take it outside to eat. You can talk to it. You can yell at it. Even if you're shouting and chasing it, at least you're opening your mouth.'

Meeting the other women at Sevota also helped. 'That's when I realised this didn't just happen to me and us here,' she said.

When UN investigators came to the centre, the women agreed to talk to them, hoping to bring their tormentors to justice, though unsure if they were being taken seriously.

Then came the news that Akayesu had been indicted. Godelieve was approached if any of her members might be prepared to testify in Arusha.

'I wanted to make sure the truth was known,' she said. 'I helped the court to find witnesses and prepare them psychologically before they went to Arusha.'

She was reluctant to go herself. 'They asked me and I refused. Because a woman who came from Norway had told me people who give evidence are always killed. And there were two of us who had seen the same thing at the Mayor's office so there was no need for us both to be witnesses.'

Her husband Emmanuel, however, said he would go and testify. 'We discussed it, particularly after I got a threatening letter saying they will kill you – but he wanted to. Then on the evening of 23 December 1996, we got word there had been shootings and eleven people had been killed. Some of the defeated militias who had fled to Congo had come back to attack the country. It was in the area where Emmanuel was doing building work. Then I heard that he was among the dead as well as my daughter, she was twelve. The next day we went to bring their bodies from the hospital and on Christmas Day we buried them.'

She got up and searched around the room. 'I have a picture of them but the frame is broken.'

Emmanuel's murder left her a widow like the women she had been helping. The tragedy only made her more determined to help others and bring the perpetrators to justice.

I asked if any of the killers and rapists of Taba had returned. 'People came back,' she nodded. 'Some were first jailed then returned. Others fled to Congo then came back. Some live in my street. I had a watchman who was a killer. Also the person living opposite was a killer. We greet each other every morning but we both know.'

I stared at her. I hadn't expected perpetrators would return to the same places. I couldn't imagine what it must be like to see them every day.

'When we see killers we can never say publicly, but we know inside and of course we discuss at home,' she replied.

It turned out some of Akayesu's family were back in Taba though his wife and children were thought to be living in Mozambique.

'But of course the current political agenda is to unite people and foster reconciliation and ethnicity has been removed from identity cards so nowhere is it indicated. So being Hutu or Tutsi means less or nothing.'

Can you really legislate that? I asked.

'Well people cannot forget of course, but it's a mechanism to help them move on. And of course perpetrators always say they were misled.'

Do you believe them? I asked.

'I don't know,' she replied. 'For example if someone is your neighbour and knows everything about your family, for them to kill your kids is beyond imagination. They must have been brainwashed.'

'They were telling people that we Tutsi women were more beautiful and sexy and looked down on Hutus,' said Serafina Mukakinani, Victoire's younger sister, who also agreed to testify, becoming Witness NN.

We were sitting in a restaurant of thatched cabanas on a hillside in Kigali as she did not want people where she lived to see her talking to a *mzungu* or white person. 'They will talk or think I have money and want some,' she shrugged. 'That's how it is.'

It was raining again and George Michael's 'Careless Whisper' was being muzak-ed over the speaker in our cabana as we ordered rice and goat stew.

Serafina moved to Kigali after the genocide and worked in a market in Nyamirambo, a poor suburb in the southwest, selling charcoal that she bought from a truck coming from the north. On a good day she made 1000 Rwandan francs – less than 90 pence.

When the genocide happened she was twenty-five, and like her sister, had been at home in a village near Taba when militias came.

'They destroyed the roof, took our chairs and bed and everything,' she said. 'We ran with nothing but what we were wearing to a neighbouring area. After that Akayesu started a meeting in which he said we have been telling you about your enemies, now your enemy is your neighbour and I hope you know what to do.

'Then they started killing anyone they could find. Everyone ran in different directions, into the fields and hills. I didn't see my family again. They killed our parents, our brothers and sisters. My parents were mining tiny gemstones for an investor so the Interahamwe threw them in the mines and stoned them to death.

'Whenever someone was killed we would know because they would shout "We killed so and so!"

'I went under a tree and stayed there many days and it was raining on me, I couldn't move. They were cutting down banana plantations and trees so everything was open and it got harder to hide. They found me and took me to one of their killing sites. I don't know how I survived. There were latrines around so they put you in these filthy pits to bury you alive.

'These were our neighbours. As it was officially organised they were also doing it in the day so it was easy to recognise them.

'Of course they raped me. Women are weak physically and the government had abandoned its protection for women and even told the men to go after us. Wherever you were hiding under a tree a man would find and rape you and sometimes kill you. There were lots of different men doing this and they used sticks and bottles into the private parts of many women right up to their stomach but they didn't do that to me. I was not conscious a lot of the time.'

She fell silent. I stared at my goat stew then stupidly asked, 'How did you feel?' wishing I could take the words back as I spoke them.

'Can I ask you a question?' she replied quietly. 'If someone finds you under a tree after three days, you've had nothing to eat or drink, he has killed your parents and family, then takes you – do you think you would feel anything? You are just numb. Just be in my shoes and imagine.

'After some time Mayor Akayesu told people to bring those you are hiding but it was a trap to take us to his district headquarters. People kept coming and Akayesu said we should all be killed.

'Then one of the killers said he would marry me if he took me from there, and save me. What would you do? That's how I survived. And saved Victoire's children.

'I had protection because he was a militia but it was not a good situation as he was going off killing my people. Also his comrades were not happy. They said why have you married this cockroach, not one of our sisters?

'So he took me to another place. Eventually the RPF came and he and his friends ran away to Congo and the soldiers found me hungry and alone and just waiting to die. I was in a bad state because of the severe beatings, hunger, rain and fear but they counselled us and said they would protect us.

'I went back to Taba after 4 July when it was over. Most of the homes of Tutsis had been destroyed but there were several houses empty of Hutus who had fled so they gave them to us. I thought I was the only survivor in my family but then Victoire came back in August. I was so relieved to find her. It was just us. Our younger sister was raped and killed, she was cut all over. Our brothers were killed.'

Rwanda is a very overcrowded country where arable land is at a premium so many women had little choice but to go back to their family land where they suffered such terrible ordeals.

'I was scared to stay in the same place after what happened,' said Serafina. 'Once Victoire had come back to get her children, I moved to Kigali. First I stayed with an uncle who had lost his wife and eleven children in the genocide so wanted someone to look after him. He had a job but after some time he remarried and his wife didn't like me so I had to leave. Then I rented a place and survived by doing odd jobs like cleaning and gardening.

'I went to Arusha to testify because I was determined to see this crime punished and wanted to play my role in ending this bad thing. I had no fear because I knew it was the truth.'

Yet initially, Akayesu wasn't even charged with rape. Not because there was no evidence of mass rape: it was well documented. But it wasn't seen as an issue important enough to win the attention or other resources of a financially strapped, overworked team of investigators, prosecutors, and other court officials.

Then in September 1996, a Human Rights Watch report called *Shattered Lives* was published, documenting horrific stories of rape, forced marriage, gang rape and women speared to death through their vaginas – the first comprehensive account of sexual violence during the genocide. Some of the survivors interviewed were from Taba. Questions began to be asked from women's organisations and in the *New York Times* why the international tribunal was not prosecuting anyone for this.

The tribunal sent Lisa Pruitt, a thirty-two-year-old American, to Rwanda as a gender consultant to investigate whether witness statements could support charges of sexual violence against Akayesu. Pruitt later became a law professor at the University of California Davis in San Francisco where we spoke. 'I think they sent me because the tribunal was drawing a lot of internal criticism and they needed to be seen to be doing something,' she told me. 'I'd worked as a rape counsellor and just written a dissertation on feminist legal theory so was in the right place at the right time and had the right credentials. I was very excited.'

She came away disheartened, convinced that court investigators had largely dismissed the issue, discrediting rape survivors such as Victoire for spurious reasons such as 'losing their train of thought' or appearing 'less than coherent'.

'What would you expect from someone describing the kind of trauma she was?' asked Pruitt. 'It wasn't helped by the fact that the investigators were mostly white men.'

She also found them completely focused on the genocide, which they thought was the more important crime. 'Many of the investigators said, "Well, we can't be concerned about some women who got raped. We can't divert resources to investigate those crimes. We had a genocide down here."'

When she wrote a memo advising on how to interview deeply traumatised women, suggesting making them comfortable and offering them water, she was laughed at.

She flew to the tribunal's headquarters in The Hague to present her findings to Louise Arbour, the Canadian jurist who had taken over from Judge Goldstone as Chief Prosecutor, but was told there was no interest in pursuing rape charges after all.

'After I left Rwanda and met Louise Arbour, it was very clear nothing was going to be done with my memos. I thought oh, I get it, this really was a ruse, they are not committed to pursuing these issues, they just needed to be able to say we had a gender consultant and looked into it.'

Her October 1996 report *Taba Commune Sexual Assault Evidence Summary* was filed away.

'It was really devastating. I had been raped myself in 1984 when I was at college so there was the pain wrapped up in my being a survivor and also in working so hard, investing so much of myself in something I felt so strongly about, only to be told, Thank you, but no, we are not going to amend the indictment.'

* * *

For the young prosecutors in Arusha, amending the indictment seemed too risky. They had their hands full proving genocide based on killings, which had never been done before, and didn't want to complicate things and risk losing the whole case.

'As far as we knew, there was nothing linking Akayesu specifically to the widespread rape in Taba,' said Dareshshori.

On 9 January 1997 Akayesu went on trial for genocide – the world's first such trial. There were three judges, Laïty Kama from Senegal who was the presiding judge, Lennart Aspegren from Sweden, and Navanethem Pillay from South Africa, the only woman.

'I was reluctant,' Pillay admitted. 'Mandela had just taken over as President [of the first majority government] in my own country and I wanted to be part of that change. But I agreed to try it for a year.'

The daughter of a bus driver in Durban, she had grown up during apartheid and says it was because of what she experienced that she became a human rights lawyer. Having managed to not only get through high school but also gain a place at Natal University, she said: 'I could not enter parks or beaches as they were reserved for whites. I did not have money to get the bus home between classes so I sat in the library and read Nuremberg cases.' When no white law firm would hire her, she ended up starting her own, mostly focusing on domestic violence cases.

Like the prosecutors, she was shocked at the lack of support. Yet she ended up there for eight and a half years. 'Why? It was because of the women witnesses who told us we waited for this day to see justice being done.'

It was her question to one of those witnesses in the Akayesu trial which changed everything. In the third week of the trial, Witness J took to the stand and described how she was six months pregnant when militia came and killed most of her family, and she and her six-year-old daughter managed to escape by hiding in a banana tree. Then, almost in passing, she mentioned something else.

'The woman had climbed a tree to hide and she said she was with her six-year-old daughter who had been raped by three men and she knew the names. But the prosecutor interrupted her and said, "Yes, well I didn't ask you about all that." Investigators had never asked her! I suppose it wasn't in her witness statement so he was concerned it could be grounds to discredit her if she was saying new stuff in the witness box.

'But I thought this person has had the courage to come here to testify, she's getting nothing out of reliving this horror, so who are we to say we will only hear you on this and not that. She had the right to give a full account of what happened. She told us she had heard of other rapes at the bureau communal – the mayor's office.'

Pillay had recently given a talk at the UN on Human Rights Day where a female aid worker had asked why there wasn't a single charge of rape among the thirty-seven indictments at the ICTR. 'I gave her the appropriate response: that you need to speak to the prosecutors, judges just look at the indictments,' said Pillay. 'But that really made me think – out of thirty-seven indictments not a single count of sexual violence! Yet the report on Rwanda that the UN Security Council had commissioned to set up the court, and given to us judges, had factual information of large-scale incidents of rape and sexual violence.'

When the next woman, Witness H, came to the stand in March, Pillay again insisted she be allowed to tell her full story. She told of her house being attacked and hiding, then being found and raped in the sorghum fields. Eventually she had fled to the mayor's office where they had heard people were taking refuge. There were around 150 people there she said, mostly women and children, and she mentioned a new detail.

'Then I saw the women being dragged to the back of the bureau communal, and I saw them being raped,' she said, adding that the men were 'signing out women to rape'.

Judge Pillay picked up on it. 'Would you say that Akayesu was aware these rapes were going on?' she asked.

'It happened at the bureau communal and he knew we were there,' replied the witness.

'That was always the missing link,' said Sara Dareshori. 'Rapes *at* the bureau communal would have been something that Akayesu couldn't have missed.'

The prosecutors asked for remand to investigate the rape allegations and the trial adjourned for two months. 'This was unusual as it was late in the case,' said Pillay. 'But we thought this is the first trial of a huge crime, the first genocide trial, so we shouldn't be restrictive on time.'

The prosecutors found Lisa Pruitt's buried memo, which helped lead them to Victoire, Serafina and three others that their investigators had previously interviewed.

'The information was there all along,' said Pillay. 'You have to wonder ...'

In June 1997, prosecutors added rape and sexual violence charges to Akayesu's indictment and prepared to prove that even though Akayesu may not have raped anyone himself, he had known that the militias were dragging Tutsi women away to do so and did not use his power to stop them.

The women were asked to go to Arusha to testify.

'We were strong because we were together,' said Cecile Mukarugwiza, who was the youngest, only fourteen at the time of the genocide, and thirty-eight when I met her all those years later. 'We could not have done it alone.'

Like Serafina, she had moved to Kigali and was living in a rural district called Kabuka, east of the city, in a mud hut on a hillside reached by a dirt track. There was birdsong and the occasional moo of a cow. Clothes were drying on a bush outside. Inside, on the wall, was a picture torn from a magazine of Jody Phibi, a Rwandan pop star, next to the obligatory Kagame poster.

I raised my eyebrows at my interpreter who on the way had shown me a message sent to his phone of Kagame holding a large black umbrella above him, like Mary Poppins, with the words Happy Birthday. 'It's not his birthday,' he had laughed. 'We get things like this every day.'

Cecile was both striking and stylish – later, I discovered she was a dressmaker. Waiting in the hut was a tall young man in dark jeans and a stripy shirt and an air so serious that it stilled the noisy day. 'This is Clemente,' she said. 'He is one of *les enfants mauvais souvenirs* [the children born out of rape].'

'I found out I am born of bad blood when I was twelve,' he said, 'and my mum was cutting my nails. I always knew the man I called Dad didn't treat me like a real son.

Clemente found out when he was twelve that he was born of rape

'For a long while I couldn't study. I wanted my mum to take me to my real father's family but she said she didn't know who he was. She didn't want me to get help because then people around would know there was something wrong.

'In the end she took me to Sevota [Godeliève's organisation] and I met other children like me and also Cecile.'

'You see, for so many of us in so many ways, how what happened in the genocide did not end with the killing,' said Cecile.

Clemente had to go to his job painting cars and he left as quietly as he sat.

Cecile then told her story. 'I grew up in Muhanga, a village next to Taba, at my grandmother's as I'd been sent to look after her. Then she died in October 1993 and I moved to my parents' place.

Cecile

There was discrimination at school and the workplace against us Tutsis but we were all living together. My brother was married to a Hutu. Then suddenly things changed.

'One morning when I was walking to my aunt's, some people told me, "It's not safe, go back." I didn't understand. When I got home I could hear people screaming and saw that our neighbours, who had many cows on the hill, were being raided.

'My parents said we must go so we all ran into the banana trees. I was not familiar with the area because I had only lived there a few months and didn't know where to hide. Anyone who was found was killed. We saw people we knew being killed day after day by people we knew. Even children were taking part. We were being hunted down like criminals or animals.

'When they got a woman or girl, they would undress her, force her to the ground then one after another come and take her. It was so bad because it was public. They would shout, "Hurry up! I also want her!"

'I was raped countless times. The last group that raped me were so many people and one man shouted, "I can't use my penis in that dirty place so I'll use a stick!" I know many women who died like that. They sharpened the sticks and forced them right through their vaginas.

'I'd lost my parents – my last sight of them was when we were fleeing the house. My father was thrown into the latrine pit with clubs then they smashed the house on top of him. I saw my little brother of seven being killed. He'd tried to climb a tree and they grabbed him and clubbed him till he died. My nine-year-old brother, they gave him a tool and told him to dig a pit, then buried him alive in it.

'Whenever they caught someone they would shout in celebration in the hills: "We have so and so, it's his final day!"

'My father had two wives – he had five children with my mother and two from the other, and all were killed.

'What I was waiting for was death. If you're raped and lying there and they use these sticks and things, you can't think of anything else, there is so much physical pain. I thought, I might die now, or in a few hours, or maybe tomorrow. That was my life every day.

'One of the militias took me as his slave, he kept me in his home, continuously raping me, then would go off killing.'

A small scrawny tabby cat ran in then out and someone started playing jazz synthesiser nearby. 'It's one of the new evangelical churches,' explained the interpreter. The genocide had left traditional Catholic churches tainted for their failure to protect their flocks.

Cecile resumed her story. 'Eventually the RPF came so the militia fled to Congo and took me with them. There was a man who had lost his wife but had a baby so he forced me to carry it. There they set up a tent and put me outside; a woman gave me a mat to sleep on. We would cross to Rwanda to get food and eventually I managed to run away. One day I saw some RPF and they asked what are you doing there and took me back.

'When I returned to Taba the only person I found from my family was my aunt as she was married to a Hutu. No one else had survived. I went to live with her but her husband didn't like me so my life was a struggle.

'At the start I couldn't imagine ever talking about what had happened. But I joined Sevota and met Godelième and one day came the news that Akayesu had been arrested and they needed witnesses. As an association we had agreed wherever it was needed we would testify so I felt an obligation to speak to the investigators.

'Akayesu was the leader – I was actually being kept in the commune so saw him giving orders. I saw teachers put in a room and him order people to kill them. I personally didn't see him ordering rape but I know others who did.

'Later when they asked us to go to Arusha to testify, of course we were scared. We knew people were attacked and got threatening letters to stop them, but given how grave the killings and rape were, how could we not?

'I was seventeen and had just got married – my aunt and uncle had forced me to marry a Tutsi man of thirty-seven so they could inherit my parents' property and build a house on that land. That man beat me every night and didn't care; he thought I would get money going to Arusha.'

Cecile became Witness OO.

For the five women of Taba, it was their first time on a plane and they were terrified. As the eldest, Victoire calmed the others even though she had only given birth ten days before and was feverish with malaria. 'I was afraid to fly and it hurt my ears,' she said.

In Arusha they were put up in a safe house. The night before the trial they all prayed together that they would speak the truth, say what happened and seek justice, not revenge.

When they arrived at the court the next morning they were horrified to see Akayesu sitting there, though he could not see them as they were behind a curtain. Victoire – Witness JJ – was first to testify and began nervously, her voice thin and reedy, as the prosecutor described the act of penetration then asked: 'Did your attacker penetrate you with his penis?'

Then she grew strong. 'That was not the only thing they did to me,' she replied. 'They were young boys and I am a mother and yet they did this to me.'

She said she had lost count of the number of times she was raped. 'Each time you encountered attackers they would rape you.'

Asked about Akayesu, she recounted him coming to the town's cultural centre while she was being taken there by force from the bureau communal in a group of about fifteen girls and women and then raped repeatedly by Interahamwe. On the second occasion she heard him say loudly, "Never ask me again what a Tutsi woman tastes like.""*

The women electrified the court. 'Though I had to speak in a foreign court, with foreign judges in robes speaking a foreign language, I was not afraid because when you speak the truth, you have nothing to fear,' said Victoire.

Twenty years on, Judge Pillay, herself a mother of two daughters, said she would never forget the women's testimony. 'As a woman listening to that, women talking of being gang-raped, of men jumping on the belly of a pregnant woman and forcing her to abort, you can never forget because you feel in your mind and body it's happening to you.'

Her male colleagues were horrified. 'They wanted to put their hands over their ears and not hear any more,' she said. 'They told me we don't know what can be done with this evidence so we leave it to you.

'There was no internationally accepted definition of rape and sexual violence so I decided to create one.'

Akayesu finally took to the stand in March 1998. He pleaded not guilty, claiming that he was simply a figurehead and had done all he could to reduce violence in his commune. His main argument was that if Major General Roméo Dallaire, commander of the UN peacekeeping force, could not stop the abuses, how could he? He denied he had witnessed rape and argued that the rape allegations were a result of public pressure from the women's movement, not based on reality. He also questioned the credibility of the witnesses, asking for example how Witness JJ could have climbed a tree when

---

* ICTR 96–4 transcript of Witness JJ, 23 October 1997.

six months pregnant. After fourteen months the chamber retired for their deliberations.

Back home in Taba the women were struggling. Witness H had disappeared. Another one of the five had been infected with HIV by her rapist, and later died. Cecile also fell ill.

'The constant beatings from my husband gave me mental problems and the court in Arusha arranged a counsellor who suggested I leave him. But I had nowhere to go and by then we had a daughter. To start with I stayed with a friend but she was a prostitute living in just one room. So it was very hard to be there with my child and I ended up going back.

'I got very sick because of the beatings and malaria and people would come and mock and say you are dying of HIV because you were raped. I ended up in hospital and once I heard the doctor say to someone, tend to that old woman. I was nineteen!

'When I recovered we had a second daughter and eventually, when I was twenty-three, I left. I had a little money so I rented a room for 3000 francs per month. It was just like a toilet. I bought one spoon, a plastic plate and a mattress, as well as a basket to trade bananas, and that was my life.

'One day a young man came and proposed. I told him I'm used to suffering on my own, don't come and share my pain. But later I thought it would be nice to feel safe, so he came to live in my room. Within a few days I realised he was a drunk, a thief and a womaniser.

'He stole a motorbike and went to jail. When he was released, he stole a bicycle and was arrested again. By then I was pregnant with his son. I told him you are adding to my pains.

'He was taking people on his motorbike for money but one day Kigali city decided to ban bikes as they made the city dirty. Even my business of selling bananas had to stop.

When bad days come they come in a bad way and I fell pregnant again.

'Then my aunt died and I inherited her land so I sold part for transport to my husband's hometown on the border with Congo. I went and lived with his parents for a year but they were Hutus and didn't like me.

'I couldn't live in my own parents' plot in Taba because I feared that place after what had happened, and my neighbours the killers. To this day I can't spend a night there.

'So I came back. My husband had got a job as a nightwatchman in a bank and they gave him a loan of 50,000 francs which he gave me to start a business.

'Here in Kabuka you can get cheap cassavas so I started coming here to buy them to sell in the city centre. I saw that homes here are very cheap so moved here. Then the bank closed down so my husband started working on construction sites. We had another son but he was killed in 2013 in a road accident when he was five.'

She took out a picture of a gorgeous little boy, eyes like saucers with curiosity.

'My husband became a foreman but as his income went up he forgot where he came from and started going after other women. After our son died he asked for a divorce.

'My first husband had remarried and wasn't good to our two daughters. He sent them out on the streets, so I brought them to live with me.

'There was a scheme for survivors so I did tailoring and learnt to make clothes. But Kabuka has many tailors so there is too much competition. All people who have failed in life, especially women, become tailors.

'Recently I took a decision and went to the president's office where they help survivors and asked for a house. The man said we can give you a house in the south in Taba in your father's area. I explained that because of what happened to me I could never live there.

'He said, "Well, then we can't help you." He told me, "You look young and fit. You have time to make life happen. This is not a good place to bring your problems."

'That's my life. It's not a good life but we're surviving. My mind is so numb nothing pains me anymore. I might look nice but no one knows what's on the inside.'

On 2 October 1998, the court found Jean-Paul Akayesu guilty of nine of fifteen counts of crimes against humanity, including extermination, torture and murder, and count thirteen which was rape. He was sentenced to life and imprisoned in Mali.

Apart from the killing of at least 2000 Tutsis in Taba, the court concluded: 'The rape of Tutsi women was systematic and was perpetrated against all Tutsi women and solely against them.'

The 169-page judgment had been signed at 2 a.m. by the three judges. They, along with their legal officers, had worked round the clock to finish writing it and producing it on their one printer.

After a few hours of sleep, they met in the small antechamber to announce the verdict to the international press waiting to report on the first ever genocide verdict.

But Judge Pillay had a problem. 'The summary that Judge Kama [the presiding judge] was going to read was in French so I said I am not going into the courtroom until I see an English version,' she said. 'They went and got one and told me, Please hurry. I look at it and guess what, there were pages missing and what did they include – the last four counts about sexual violence.

'When I complained, the Swedish judge said, "What do you mean? It's all there." We were all getting irate. Eventually they saw so they yelled at one of the legal officers who went and rescued the missing bit from the terrible printer.'

In those pages the tribunal ruled that rape and sexual violence 'constitute genocide in the same way as any other act as long as they were committed with the specific intent to destroy, in whole or in part, a particular group, targeted as such'.

It was the first time ever that rape had been recognised as an instrument of genocide and prosecuted as a war crime in an international court.

'From time immemorial, rape has been regarded as spoils of war,' stated Judge Pillay at the time. 'Now it will be considered a war crime. We want to send out a strong message that rape is no longer a trophy of war.'

The ruling included the definition she had formulated of rape and sexual violence – the first ever definition in international law and one that was deliberately gender neutral:

> *The Tribunal considers that rape is a form of aggression and the central elements of the crime cannot be captured in a mechanical description of objects and body parts ... The Tribunal defines rape as a physical invasion of a sexual nature, committed on a person under circumstances which are coercive. Sexual violence is not limited to physical invasion of the human body and may include acts which do not involve penetration or even physical contact.*

'Until then rape had been regarded as collateral damage and also something mechanical with no understanding of the effect on the women,' she explained. 'We picked up what the women like JJ said that it destroys life itself for them.'

For the women of Taba who had risked so much to speak out, the verdict came as a huge relief. 'For months I listened to the radio waiting for a decision, worrying that our decision to speak out would be in vain,' said Victoire. 'When I heard the news that Akayesu had been found guilty I danced!'

'Their actions changed the law and criminal justice for every woman,' Erica Barks-Ruggles, the US ambassador in Kigali, told me. 'These women showed you can take the worst trauma and turn it into a story of strength and victory.'

Patricia Sellers was legal advisor for gender to the court at the time and went on to become special advisor to the prosecutor's office in The Hague, as well as teaching law at Oxford. To her the Akayesu case was 'as significant in international criminal terms as Brown v. Board of Education', the landmark case in 1954 when the US Supreme Court ruled unanimously against racial segregation of children in state schools.

But while the women of Taba may have changed international justice, their own lives had never recovered.

'I was very pleased with the convictions because it was always haunting me whenever they categorised a rapist with someone who stole potatoes or a goat: it was really, really unfair,' said Serafina. 'We opened the eyes of the world. Many women told me they felt empowered to speak out after. But it hasn't helped my own life. It's been almost twenty-five years since the genocide but I still can't trust anyone and can't go back to my house or hometown and have never had a relationship since.'

Cecile agreed. 'At the beginning when we went to testify it was really frightening but when we took the first step others followed. If we hadn't had the prosecutions we would still be looking at each other with evil eye and wouldn't be neighbours.

'I was very happy to see Akayesu convicted but it's been hard personally. I felt broken inside. One never heals but healing is a journey: you don't stay where you are. I no longer think about the past so much because every day when I wake I think about what shall we eat, how to pay school fees.'

They had received no compensation, they told me, and as I had seen were all struggling to survive.

In 2005, nearly ten years after the Akayesu verdict, Judge Pillay wrote in the foreword to *Listening to the Silences*, about women's experiences in war: 'I have now learned that Witness JJ [is] living in ... a ramshackle hut on bare ground amidst sparse provisions, rejected by and rejecting the society of others ... The international community has responded to only one aspect of the aftermath of the genocide: that of bringing perpetrators to justice – but not the needs of women to help feed, clothe, house, educate, heal and rebuild.'

When I visited them in 2018, JJ – Victoire – still didn't have electricity. Yet their main frustration seemed to be that their courage in speaking out had not stopped such atrocities against women elsewhere. Some of them had been taken to the UN in New York to meet Yazidi survivors.

'We condemn the international community and the UN because they just stood by and watched us be raped and the same things are happening over and over again round the world,' said Victoire. 'We are just simple women but it's hard for us to understand.'

She seemed loneliest of all in her hut in the hills of Taba, looking out at the banana groves where she was repeatedly raped. 'You may think we are the lucky ones because we survived the genocide and were not diseased,' she said. 'But we are like dead women walking.

'I think rape is even worse than killing someone because I have to live it every day. It was something I experienced as a grown-up so I remember everything. People from the same country, the same town, speaking the same language, with the same skin colour, born the same way, did this to us. I still live with them – the boy you met who helps me is a Hutu and people ask, "Why do you have that guy?"'

All the women complained they still suffered physical effects. 'Even today when I go and hoe the fields or fetch water, I feel so bad, and I have backache which never goes,' said Victoire.

Before I left her in her dark hut with the thunder and lightning in the hills, she told me she rarely slept. 'I live alone and feel lonely but what can I do?' she asked. 'I lock the doors and windows and then the memories come ...'

The international tribunal in Arusha continued for twenty-one years, hearing more than 3000 witnesses and indicting ninety-three people of whom sixty-two were convicted.

No one was actually prosecuted for carrying out rape but, as with Akayesu, for supervising and encouraging it.

Shockingly, one of them was a woman, Pauline Nyiramasuhuko, convicted along with her son after a ten-year trial. The court heard how the former Women's Development Minister had summoned Interahamwe from Kigali to her home region of Butare to kill and rape women with other militias led by her son. She personally forced women to undress before loading them onto the trucks.

The total number of convictions was small, given the cost of more than $2 billion, and punished only a fraction of the number of perpetrators. Some of the masterminds were still on the run, including in the UK and other European countries, much to the irritation of Rwanda's Justice Minister Johnston Busingye.

Like many in Kagame's government, Busingye was not in the country during the genocide but grew up in Uganda where his family fled after earlier pogroms against Tutsis in 1959 and 1963. He had been involved in the justice system since the post-genocide government took over, so he seemed a good person to ask if there ever really can be appropriate justice. A tall man in a violet shirt and dark suit with metal-rimmed glasses, Busingye sat at a long table surrounded by cabinets lined with box-files marked *European Arrest Warrants*. The ministry's fugitive tracking unit had found more than 500 *génocidaires* still in hiding overseas.

'Some of the people responsible for all these rapes and mass murder are on your soil but your government refuses to hand them over,' he said. 'The UK is rapidly joining France as a safe haven. They [the suspects] say if you take me to Rwanda they will torture me, kill me, there will be no fair trial … But imagine you are a family who believe those people in the UK are the ones who wiped out their loved ones and raped their women. What signal does it send to leave them free?'

I asked if he thought Rwandan society could ever recover from what it went through. 'Our healing process has built on the passage of time,' he replied. 'Nineteen ninety-four was raw, very brutal. Every April we hold memorial events. In the first years people would shriek in their hundreds. Now they are quiet and sombre and walk home silently after.'

An important part of the healing, he said, had been a community-justice programme started in 2002 called *gacaca*, pronounced ga-cha-cha, referring to the grass on which people sat as they came forward to confess or recount atrocities they had suffered. Almost two million cases were heard over ten years.

For many this was a remarkable feat of truth and reconciliation. I met one woman called Alice with a stump where her right arm should be, who had become friends with her old classmate Emmanuel who had hacked it off. But to others it was perpetuating the myth that only Tutsis were killed. The gacaca courts were silent on the revenge crimes carried out by Tutsis after the genocide, when Kagame sent his RPF army into Congo to force back home Hutus in UN refugee camps or pursue them into the jungles, killing thousands.

Apart from the Akayesu verdict on the international stage, the Taba women had helped secure a significant victory back home, getting rape changed from a category-4 crime like pickpocketing, to category 1 along with murder.

Rape cases in the gacaca courts were held behind closed doors to protect identities. But many women did not come forward as they feared their communities would see them going into the buildings to testify.

'A good number were convicted in the gacaca and are serving time for rape,' said the minister. 'But the number in my view is not equal to the crimes committed as we didn't have the evidence.'

He turned pensive. 'You asked about how society can overcome this but society doesn't overcome. In 1994 we thought we Rwandans have weathered so many storms, even this we will manage. We have removed this government which was killing us, let's restore sanity.

'But Rwanda has been a school. I've worked in the justice system since 1995, I've been a prosecutor, judge, permanent secretary in this ministry and now minister. I have spoken to thousands of people, I've been a student of trauma. And some of my initial hopes have met a U-turn. The idea that because the threat has been removed you can lead a full life – you can't, particularly for these women.

'That's why rape really was a calculated weapon. The fellows who raped them and planned to rape them: they knew you either die now or die later but you'll never be human again after this ordeal.

'You meet these women, here in the city, or go out to villages, to Taba, and meet them and they seem normal. But I think when they go home and close their doors at night, there is a space inside them which no one can break into, no matter what you do.'

7

The Roses of Sarajevo

Sarajevo

It was snowing as my plane touched down in Sarajevo in March 2018 and the mountains all around were white and majestic – this after all was where the Winter Olympics took place in 1984 and Torvill and Dean scored perfect sixes for their *Bolero* routine which made teenage girls like me all over Britain long to be ice dancers.

It's also known as the place that triggered the First World War. A simple grey plaque on the corner of Franz Joseph street at the northern end of Latin Bridge, marks the spot where on 28 June 1914, a sunny Sunday, nineteen-year-old Serb nationalist Gavrilo Princip shot dead Archduke Franz Ferdinand, the heir to the Hapsburg throne, and his pregnant wife Duchess Sophie as they drove past in their open limousine.

My guide Resad, who learnt his English from listening to Annie Lennox lyrics after becoming obsessed by 'Sweet Dreams (Are Made of This)', tells me it almost didn't happen. Princip was part of a team of six and the plan had been for one of his colleagues to throw a grenade into the couple's car as they drove in to visit this outpost of the Austro-Hungarian empire. But the grenade bounced off the car's back canopy and hit the driver behind and the Archduke and his wife continued on to the Town Hall for tea.

Afterwards, however, they decided to visit the wounded man in hospital. Their driver took a wrong turn up Franz Joseph Street then stalled right in front of the delicatessen where Princip was standing with his Browning pistol. On such accidents of fate, wars start. Austria-Hungary blamed Serbia for the assassination of its crown prince and a month later declared war, backed by Germany, setting off a domino effect which drew in all the major powers and left 17 million people dead.

In the 1990s Sarajevo became known for something else – the longest siege of a city in modern history. It's hard to imagine now with its cheerful yellow trams, bustling cafés and Zara store, but for almost four years, from 5 April 1992 to 29 February 1996, Sarajevo was under siege as the former Yugoslavia tore itself apart and Bosnian Serbs tried to wipe out the Muslims with whom they had lived for centuries. It was a war that introduced the term ethnic cleansing to the world.

Day after day, Serb forces on the hills shelled the city below, demolishing many buildings including the Town Hall which had become the national library. Snipers in high-rise buildings picked off people queuing for water, a small girl skipping, lovers on the bridge, mourners at funerals.

'My hair was blown off by a sniper,' said my interpreter Aida, a middle-aged woman with spiky black hair and a passion for all things purple.

'I was twenty-four, it was New Year 1994 and we had a get-together at friends'. By that stage in the war we all had become expert at making do. My biggest problem was my long mass of hair because it needed so much water to wash and power to warm the water and we had neither – the Serbs had cut them off and all the trees had been chopped down for wood the first winter.

'We all gave each other gifts that we had made or that would be useful. My friends had got together to give me seven litres of warm water – exactly enough for my hair – which was the best possible present. I was so happy when I washed my hair that new year's morning. I left all my hair loose like a cloud around my face and started walking home. In my hands was a miniature Christmas tree I'd taken to be festive.

'Suddenly I heard a crack and felt something fly past. It was my hair! A woman was shouting at me to get down. The thing was, you knew in your own area the bad spots for snipers but not when you went somewhere else. I couldn't have looked less like a soldier with all my hair and my mini Christmas tree.'

Those snipers, and artillery, under the orders of the Bosnian Serb military commander General Ratko Mladić, left some 11,000 of the city's residents dead, more than half of them civilians. Among them was his own daughter Ana who shot herself in 1994 with her father's favourite pistol, so horrified was she at what he was doing.

The war ended a year later after NATO finally intervened with airstrikes. Richard Holbrooke, the US diplomat who brokered the 1995 Dayton Peace Accord, called the Bosnian War 'the greatest collective security failure of the West since the 1930s'.

The Bosnian Book of the Dead, the casualty report published in 1997 by the Research and Documentation Centre in Sarajevo, records 97,207 deaths of which 40 per cent were civilians. Two thirds of the dead were Muslims.

And then there was the rape. No one really knew how many but estimates were between 20,000 and 60,000 mostly Bosniaks (Muslims) but also Croats and Serbs – and some men.

The victims ranged from between six to seventy years old and were raped repeatedly and often kept captive for several years. Many women were forcibly impregnated and held until termination of the pregnancy was impossible. The women were treated as property and rape was used with the intent to intimidate, humiliate and degrade.

What was new was the attention it got. The proliferation of rape as a tool of war in the former Yugoslavia and women held in rape camps shocked the world. No one could say they didn't know at the time. For the first time in modern history, journalists and historians documented the deliberate and methodical use of rape and sexual violence as a weapon of ethnic cleansing and genocide.

'The enormity of the suffering being inflicted on the civilian population in this conflict defies expression,' stated the Warburton report issued in February 1993 by investigators sent from the European Council.

Rapes, it said, were being committed in 'particularly sadistic ways to inflict maximum humiliation on victims, their families, and on the whole community'.

This 'could not be seen as incidental to the aggression' but part of 'a deliberate pattern' and 'serving a strategic purpose in itself … usually perpetrated with the conscious intention of demoralising and terrorising communities, driving them from their home regions and demonstrating the power of the invading forces.

'In many cases there seems little doubt that the intention is deliberately to make women pregnant and then to detain them until pregnancy is far enough advanced to make termination impossible, as an additional form of humiliation and constant reminder of the abuse done to them.'

Bosnia is a mix of Muslims (who since 1993 have called themselves Bosniaks), Serbs and Croats, but they all look the same and speak the same language – what used to be known as Serbo-Croat, though Serbs use the Cyrillic alphabet. Only the names and religions are different, Serbs being Orthodox, Croats Catholic and Bosniaks Muslim. For centuries they had intermarried.

The old town of Sarajevo seems like a melting pot of religions. Down ancient cobbled alleyways where coppersmiths hammer away as they have for centuries, there is a cathedral, an Orthodox church, a synagogue and a mosque with a lunar clock, maintained by the same family for generations.

How did such long-time neighbours turn on each other so savagely?

'Where logic ends Bosnia begins,' shrugged Resad, my Annie Lennox-loving guide. He was nineteen when war broke out in 1992 and overnight found himself thrust from being a student who had never used a gun to a soldier with an AK47 and three bullets. 'My uniform was the boiler suit my dad used for gardening. The frontline was only just over a mile from home and my family were so short of food that when I came back from fighting, I would go to the hospital and give blood to get a can of meat for my mum. Then I would go back and give blood from my other arm to get another one. The only certainty when you woke up each day was this could be your last.'

The Town Hall where Archduke Franz Ferdinand and his wife drank their last tea had recently been rebuilt in all its Moorish splendour. On the wall was a plaque in awkward English: ON THIS PLACE SERBIAN CRIMINALS IN THE NIGHT OF 25–26 AUGUST 1992 SET ON FIRE NATIONAL AND UNIVERSITY'S LIBRARY. OVER 2 MILLION BOOKS, PERIODICALS AND DOCUMENTS VANISHED IN THE FLAME. DO NOT FORGET, REMEMBER AND WARN!

'Not forgetting' was the aim of the International Criminal Tribunal for the former Yugoslavia (ICTY), or the Hague Tribunal as it became known. Voted into existence by the United Nations Security Council before the war ended, it was a special court to track down and punish those responsible. What it really represented was an embarrassed recognition by the international community of its own failure to prevent Europe's worst atrocities since the Second World War.

The Tribunal started inauspiciously. For the first eighteen months the UN provided so little funding that it could not afford to lease a court building. It was given weight when Nelson

Mandela persuaded South African judge Richard Goldstone, who had dismantled apartheid laws, to become chief prosecutor. Even so, the first defendant, in November 1994, was not a mastermind but a lowly prison guard, if a particularly nasty one. He had fled to Munich, where he was recognised by a Bosnian refugee who informed a German TV reporter.

It took the worst massacre since the Second World War to shock the international community into real action. In July 1995, more than 8000 Bosnian men and boys were slaughtered by Serb forces in what was supposed to be the UN protected enclave of Srebrenica. A handful survived by hiding under bodies and crawled out of the mass graves with accounts so bloodcurdling the world could no longer turn a blind eye.

A list was drawn up of 161 indicted war criminals from all sides. Eventually, the biggest ever international manhunt, prior to 9/11, was launched involving intelligence services and special forces from a dozen countries including the SAS and US Delta Force.

Yet the bloodshed in the former Yugoslavia continued. Heading the list of the indicted was Serbian President Slobodan Milošević, the so-called Butcher of Bosnia, who in 1998 had gone on to start another Balkan war – this time in Kosovo where thousands of ethnic Albanians were slaughtered and forcibly deported and many women raped.

Finally, in October 2000, he was toppled from power and the following March, men in ski masks and fatigues arrested him from his luxury villa in Belgrade. It was the eve of a US deadline for Serbia to cooperate with the War Crimes Tribunal or lose aid and face crippling economic sanctions.

Then, late one night in June of the following year, a helicopter landed in the courtyard of the UN jail in The Hague. Inside was Milošević to become the first former head of state to be tried by an international court.

His trial took years for he was accused of instigating three wars in Croatia, Bosnia and Kosovo and he mounted his own defence, cross-examining witnesses. In the end he died of a heart attack in jail in 2006 before the verdict. But the sight of his large head and mobster-sized body in the dock was still a powerful symbol.

Radovan Karadžić, the Bosnian Serb leader behind the pogrom, was caught in 2008, hiding in plain sight in a Belgrade apartment, almost comically disguised with long snowy white hair and beard, working as a spiritual healer under a new name.

General Mladić, the military commander, managed to remain sixteen years on the run before becoming the last to be captured. He had fled to a nuclear bunker built for Tito, the long-time ruler of Yugoslavia, deep inside a mountain in eastern Bosnia, then he had moved to Serbia where he was finally tracked down in May 2011 in an upstairs room of his cousin's rundown farmhouse in Lazarevo, a small village in the north. The wizened old man in a black baseball cap huddled in front of a single-bar heater was almost unrecognisable from the barrel-chested general strutting about barking murderous commands.

At his trial in 2016, radio intercepts were played of him instructing his forces to rain artillery fire on the people of Sarajevo. 'Let's drive them out of their minds so they cannot sleep!' he ordered.

The arrest of Mladić meant all 161 people on the Tribunal list had been caught.

Day after day in that sterile Dutch courtroom a thousand miles from Bosnia, with its judges in crimson robes presiding over benches of lawyers in black, and rows of court clerks sitting at computers, men and women came forward to recount evils beyond imagining – women and girls locked up in schools and suffering repeated anal, oral and vaginal rape, people having their tongues cut off, or being burnt alive as human torches as they 'screamed like cats'.

By time the Tribunal closed in December 2017, it had heard more than 5000 witnesses. Of the 161 indicted, 90 war criminals had been convicted.

Scheveningen, the Dutch prison on the North Sea where they were locked up, was said to be so cushy it had been described as half-jail half-spa with personal trainers, cooking facilities and week-long family visits. But at least the perpetrators had been tracked down and were locked up. No longer would dictators live out their autumn years in villas in the South of France.

Seventy-eight of the 161 on the list had been indicted for sexual violence. More than half the convictions included responsibility for sexual violence. But this was a fraction considering the Tribunal received reports of more than 20,000 rapes.

While judges in the Rwanda Tribunal created the precedent that rape could be prosecuted as part of genocide, the precedent for Yugoslavia went further, ruling that the systematic rape and enslavement could be treated as torture and a weapon to destroy lives – and therefore as a war crime.

'Rape was used by members of the Bosnian Serb armed forces as an instrument of terror,' declared Judge Florence Mumba of Zambia who presided over the first conviction.

It had taken years to track the perpetrators down and of course this didn't in any way make up for the fact that these atrocities had been allowed to happen, but, in my mind, the Hague Tribunal had done a good job in holding to account those who commit crimes against humanity and making clear there could be no impunity.

Then I went for a coffee in a Sarajevo hotel and Resad pointed out a man in a dark suit at a nearby table. 'Look, there's a war criminal,' he said.

'My hobbies are smoking and hunting war criminals,' laughed Bakira Hasecić in her husky voice as she lit up a cigarette and drew on it heavily. She also liked shopping at Primark.

She was not joking. She had tracked down well over a hundred. Twenty-nine were prosecuted in The Hague and eighty in Bosnia.

In jeans and a ribbed polo neck the colour of stormy clouds, with cropped feathery ash-blonde hair around a face unadorned by make-up, she radiated defiance.

We met at her office, the Association of Women Victims of War, on the ground floor of a communist-era apartment block on the outskirts of Sarajevo. The building was grim and grey and, like many in the city, pockmarked with bullet holes and mortar scars – known as Sarajevo roses.

Inside, the walls were plastered with photos and newspaper cuttings as well as a large map of Bosnia scattered with red dots. Each dot marked a rape camp and there were fifty-seven for somewhere between 20,000 and 50,000 women were subjected to rape in the Bosnian War.

One of those dots marked Visegrád, Bakira's hometown in southeastern Bosnia where she used to work for the local council.

'You have probably heard of our bridge,' she said. She was referring to its imposing sixteenth-century bridge of eleven pumice-
stone arches spanning between the mountains, which was built on
the orders of the Ottoman ruler Grand Vizier Mehmed Paša. It
was the focal point of the Nobel Prize-winning Ivo Andrić's novel
The Bridge on the Drina and for centuries had borne silent witness
to history and the intermingling of the town's mix of Muslims,
Orthodox, Jews and Catholics. Even Andrić never imagined that
those still turquoise waters would run red as the people of Visegrád
turned on each other and the bridge became a slaughterhouse
from which bodies were tossed.

Nor did Bakira. 'Almost two thirds of the population
were Bosnian Muslims and until 1992 we never had any
problems,' she said. 'I would say 90 per cent of my closest friends
were Serbs.

'In 1992, when the war started, I was thirty-nine, happily
married with two daughters of sixteen and nineteen. We worked
hard and lived in a house on the river. We were quite well-off; we'd
built a hairdressing salon for my eldest daughter. Then at the
beginning of April, all hell broke loose and our world collapsed.

'On 6 April, the Serbs started bombing Visegrád and we fled to
Goražde as did many Muslims. But then the army went into
Visegrád and invited us to return, saying if we didn't come back
within three days we'd lose our jobs.

'My husband didn't want to go back but I'm very stubborn and
was worried what we would live off. We trusted the army. My
husband had served in it when it was the Yugoslav army, and I
never believed at that point we'd really have a war. So I insisted.

'When we got back I went to my office. There were men in
camouflage uniforms in the building. I found ten Muslim colleagues
sitting in one room so I joined them. Then the men in camouflage
came in and told us we had to leave. Just like that with no
explanation.

'A few days later, on 21 April, my husband and I were having coffee in our house, when suddenly he said, "Look!"

'Our home was very close to the famous bridge. We could see a group of five soldiers heading our way including a neighbour of ours, Veljko Planincic, a policeman I knew very well as he lived maybe 100 metres away and we had grown up together. He was a tall man with a moustache, though that day he had a beard.'

She cupped her hands under her chin to illustrate.

'All of a sudden they forced our door open and stormed upstairs. Veljko was with two men wearing camouflage with those white belts saying MP, military police. They had long hair and long beards and looked horrifying and unreal, like animals.

'When a policeman enters your house, you hope it's to protect you, but Veljko turned out to be a beast, as if he never saw us before in his life. They started by harassing us, demanding money and gold. They turned our home upside down, taking everything of value.

'We were all crying. Then they took my eldest daughter into another room saying they wanted her to show them something. I knew it was a lie. I tore myself free and rushed into the room. But it was too late. They were raping her in front of me and my husband.

'Afterwards they smashed her head with rifle butts. There was so much blood I almost thought they had cut her head off. I couldn't see anything but blood.

'We took her to the hospital. The doctors were very professional. She had beautiful long hair and they cut it off and stitched her wound.

'After that we were afraid to stay in our home. We managed to cross the bridge to one of our neighbours, a building that overlooks the river from the other side.

'That night my daughter got a fever. Her temperature was more than 40 degrees and we had no pills so we roamed the streets trying to find a pharmacy.

'That day will be with me the rest of my life. I was taken and raped three times. The first time they took me to the basement of the police station. There was a large armchair, some chairs and the room was half panelled with wood. I saw Milan Lukić and his cousin Sredoje Lukić, a policeman. Visegrád was a small town and we immediately recognised people. I knew Milan Lukić very well; we had helped his family in the past.

'He pulled out a crescent-shaped knife and told me to take off my clothes. I thought he was joking. But he was holding the knife right in front of me.

'I did what I was told, taking off my trousers and shirt until I was standing in my underwear.

'The second time was in a medical facility.

'The third time was in the high school building.

'In all these places it was not just me, but a number of women. They used multiple locations to carry out mass rape: the police station, the local sports centre, even the Institute for the Protection of Children. They called us Turks. They told us, "You are not going to give birth to Turks anymore, but Serbs."

'The third time my husband had found out where I was and was following. I heard a fight among the Serbs and they hit him.

'Afterwards I went home and then my husband came and he was crying. To this day he has never asked me what they did to me.'

By then horrific attacks were happening in towns and villages across Bosnia but Visegrád was particularly barbaric. Night after night, truckloads of Muslim men were taken down to the bridge by Serb paramilitaries. There they were shot or stabbed then tossed into the river, dead or half-dead. Some had their throats slit with pieces of glass and one was even found with a screwdriver thrust into his neck. So many bodies were thrown in that the manager of the hydroelectric plant downriver in Serbia complained they were clogging up his dam. As well as the slaughter on the bridge, hundreds of Muslims were packed into houses across Visegrád and burnt alive, including women and children grimly referred to as 'living torches'.

The carnage across Bosnia was carried out on orders from the Bosnian Serb leader Radovan Karadžić and his military counterpart General Mladić and overseen by a 'Crisis Committee', established in every Bosnian Serb community. In Visegrád this was led by Milan Lukić and his militia the White Eagles who would march into factories and drag out Muslims then line them up on the banks of the river and shoot them dead. 'Brother Serbs, it's time to finish off the Muslims,' he would bellow from a megaphone.

'These courts have heard many accounts but even the most seasoned judges and prosecutors pause at the mention of crimes perpetrated in Visegrád,' said one of the judges in The Hague. 'Crimes which reached an unprecedented peak of capricious cruelty not seen anywhere else.'

Visegrád was also the location for one of the most infamous rape camps, at a spa hotel called Vilina Vlas, where Lukić's gang kept Muslim women and girls. There they were raped all night every night to the point of madness, and sometimes suicide, jumping through glass balconies. Of 200 women kept there, Bakira believed that perhaps only ten or eleven survived.

She and her family managed to escape after their ordeal and headed west along the Drina river to Goražde, one of six Muslim enclaves supposed to be under protection of UN peacekeepers. 'We never dared hope we'd survive and have the opportunity to tell our stories,' she said.

By the end of the war she had lost twenty members of her family, fifty if you included her husband's side. One of them was her sister who was raped repeatedly in Vlasenica, another town which saw thousands of Muslims rounded up in a camp or killed. 'When they were done with her they killed her,' she said. 'Her body was found in 1998, different parts in three different mass graves.'

Bakira's hunt for war criminals started after she led a trip of returnees back to Visegrád in 1998 to visit their homes and graves of relatives.

'The town was so destroyed that the only way I could recognise my house was by my father's burnt-out motorbike outside,' she said.

But she kept going back. 'I have no connection with Sarajevo, I live here in a kind of fog,' she explained. 'I want to live in Visegrád.

'We were escorted by international forces such as Italians but there would also be an escort of Serb police. There were always girls in the convoy who would recognise some of them as being perpetrators. Some of the mothers would faint seeing the men who raped their daughters.

'As we visited our homes we'd be insulted by these police – they'd laugh in our faces and ask, "Did you come back because you wanted more? Did you come back so we could finish what we started?"

'They had already taken away from us what it was being a woman. When I saw them laughing and humiliating us, I decided we needed to break the silence. If we didn't talk about what we went through, and if they are not punished, what could we expect from their children but the same or even greater evil?

'In those days even Milan Lukić was often still in the town, dividing his time between there and Belgrade. He had been indicted [in 1998] but his cousin was chief of police for Serbia so he was protected.*

---

* He fled to Brazil in 2002.

'To start with, I was thinking about revenge for my daughters. But I had a camera with me and then I thought my revenge should be justice so I began taking photos and getting statements from the mothers, then sending them to the office of the ICTY. I realised our biggest revenge was prosecution of these people.'

In 2003 she set up the Association of Women Victims. To be a member you had to have been raped. Bakira was the first woman to tell her story in detail publicly. 'It was extremely difficult for me to share my story the first time but each time one of us appeared on TV more women would join,' she said. 'Now we have 35,000 members. We created a database which has everything, date and place of rape, age of the girl, social status, ethnicity – our members are not just Muslims but also Croats and Serbs. But no one speaks for the women who were raped and subsequently murdered; we only know about them through the statements of those who were taken with them and survived.

'And it wasn't just women. Since 2006 when men heard about us, they also broke the silence. We have seventy-three municipalities in Bosnia Herzegovina where women reported rape and twenty-three where men did.'

As in Rwanda, the aim of the rape was threefold – to humiliate the enemy's women, traumatise the Bosnian population and force them to leave, and also to impregnate women with Serbian babies to change the demographic balance.

'We have records of sixty-two children who were born as a result of rape but many don't say and there were a huge number of women who ended their pregnancies even at a very late stage so as not to bring their child into the family.'

Many of those who survived were left in orphanages where their origin was concealed from them and were known as 'invisible children'. For those who did know, it was an almost impossible burden. In October 2019 a play called *In the Name of the Father* was performed in Sarajevo in which the voices of the invisible children were heard through loudspeakers. 'I thought my mother hated me because I was the most horrible experience in her life,' came the voice of Ajna Jusnic, the first to be registered as born of rape.

Scotch-taped to the wall along the corridor to Bakira's office were dozens of photos of middle-aged men. 'It's not just getting people to tell their stories,' she said. 'We're chasing war criminals.

'We act as police and investigators,' she explained. 'We do a lot of field work. Some of my women are working secretly. When the prosecutor says he can't initiate a case because he can't locate the accused, I find women in the same place as the war criminal and take his photo then take that to the prosecutor and say, "Look, there he is in front of his house." He tells me, "What you did is illegal." I say, "Charge me, Mr Prosecutor!"'

Of those they had caught so far, twenty-nine had been prosecuted in The Hague and eighty in Bosnia.

'We women have to do it, because it's not in the interest of the actual police – so many of them are war criminals!'

The first time Bakira testified at The Hague, she had to borrow smart clothes, having lost everything in the war. Then she was thrown into jail the day she was due to leave Bosnia. She managed to get out.

'Unfortunately, I have to be so aggressive because no one really cares,' she shrugged. 'The government would like to forget about this rape, to erase it from our minds.'

It was the bravery of women like Bakira who testified intimate details in front of the very men who had caused them such pain which ensured that rape was prosecuted as a war crime in The Hague, as in the Rwanda Tribunal.

'When you are in court and see the perpetrator, you remember things you never mentioned before,' she said. 'I know from my own case how stressful it is.'

The first breakthrough came on 22 February 2001 when the Tribunal convicted three Bosnian Serbs for 'rape, enslavement and torture' in the small eastern town of Foca.

Survivors testified in graphic detail how hundreds of women and children as young as twelve were abducted in the summer of 1992 by the three men and held in sports halls and 'rape houses'. There they were repeatedly raped vaginally, anally and orally, and forced to dance naked with guns pointed at them.

'The three accused are not ordinary soldiers whose morals were merely loosened by the hardships of war,' Judge Florence Mumba told the court. 'They thrived in the dark atmosphere of the dehumanisation of those believed to be enemies.'

Dragoljub Kunarac, forty, was said to have been involved in a 'nightmarish scheme of sexual exploitation' and was sentenced to twenty-eight years for rape and torture. Radomir Kovač, thirty-nine, was sentenced to twenty years for similar crimes. The third defendant, Zoran Vuković, forty-five, was given twelve years because prosecutors were able to produce less evidence in his case. He was, nevertheless, convicted of raping and torturing a fifteen-year-old Muslim girl who was about the same age as his own daughter.

'You abused and ravaged Muslim women because of their ethnicity and from among their number you picked whomsoever you fancied,' Judge Mumba told them. 'You have shown the most glaring disrespect for the women's dignity and their fundamental human rights on a scale that far surpasses even what one might call the average seriousness of rapes during wartime.'

In Bakira's own case, however, only one of her tormentors was behind bars – and not for rape. Her first rapist Milan Lukić was arrested in Buenos Aires in 2005 and sentenced to life in 2009 for the murder of more than 133 civilians, of whom 120 were crammed into two houses and burnt alive, while his cousin Sredoje was given twenty-seven years.

'I was called as witness and gave testimony but I can't say justice was served,' she said. 'I had to go through all the reconstruction and re-traumatisation for which I took tablets and tablets to calm myself – then he wasn't prosecuted for rape, only for the killings.'

The prosecution moved to amend the indictments against the cousins to include crimes of sexual violence including rape, enslavement and torture, and cited the Akayesu case from Rwanda. But the Tribunal declined the motion on the grounds that this would unduly prejudice the accused.

Bakira was furious. 'We had fifty or sixty women who testified they were raped by Lukić but the Chief Prosecutor said they [the cousins] were arrested too late and that there were plenty of other charges to get him on more easily.

'Some women said it's fine, he's gone for life, but others like me were deeply offended because the individual act against us was not recognised and that matters.'

Bakira and others protested outside the international tribunal's offices in Sarajevo but to no avail. It's a woman she holds responsible. 'I blame Carla Del Ponte [the then Chief Prosecutor] – she wanted to shorten the case because the court was winding up.'

Since the Hague Tribunal closed at the end of 2017, cases have been heard in the courts in Bosnia.

'We have not stopped hunting war criminals,' said Bakira. 'It's a race against time as every day survivors and perpetrators are dying.'

But while in The Hague a special support department was created for the women, providing allowances for childcare to enable them to travel, as well as psychological help, she says locally there is not much understanding. 'Our politicians and prosecutors have no sense of what it's like,' she said. 'They just say, "Hello, how are you? Here's the toilet. Do you want a glass of water?" That's not the kind of support we are looking for.

'The courts don't help. We have women who were raped fifty or a hundred times by twenty different perpetrators. Instead of just giving one statement with everything as we did in The Hague, she has to testify each time one of these men is tried and go through the whole thing all over again. A woman should be allowed to say things the way she wants, tell the story how she wants.

'We've had ten women commit suicide, and many gone abroad. We have so many who are in our database yet couldn't find the strength to go to court. But I think that if you don't testify it's as if it never happened. These men have taken away all that was beautiful in us. There is no magic wand to erase what happened and end this suffering. Trust me, when I got the first bar of soap after I was raped I was washing myself to the point I bled.

'But when you see the perpetrator sentenced that's the best. I enjoy when I see them handcuffed, then I know they can't do anything, they have no knife, no rifle. Now criminals run away from me, not the other way around. I was in the front row for the conviction of Mladić. I got into an argument with a man who came with a flag to support him.

'In Bosnia it's better to be a perpetrator than a victim. The perpetrators' defence are paid by the state while we have to pay our own legal costs. And there's still no compensation for victims.

'Even if the verdict says the perpetrator must pay a certain amount, they usually sign over everything to their family so officially they have no money. And if the case goes to civil court the victim has to disclose their identity which no one wants.

'There's only one case I know of where money was paid. The perpetrator was living in Denmark and came to Bosnia because his father died. We found out and he was arrested at the moment he was putting the body in the grave, then convicted for war rape. He paid the victim and also paid to not serve his sentence, he washed his name for 43,000 euros. But the law has now changed so war criminals can't pay off their sentence. Now we are trying to change it to get compensation awarded.'

Bakira's movement received no state help and was dependent on donations. One of her biggest complaints was the lack of support for the economic empowerment of these women. 'Some organisations have millions but we've seen none of it – as far as I can see it goes on conferences and hotel accommodation. Not to us, the women who send the message to the world that what happened to us should not happen anywhere else.'

She and her colleagues were taking huge risks. There had been three attempts on her life, and her house and car in Visegrád had been vandalised. The police, she said, did nothing. 'When I called the police to report shooting on my house, they told me it was gunfire at a wedding.

'My family used to say this is too dangerous but when they saw how the war criminals are lying in court, denying what they did, they told me you must continue to stop this.

'I'm not afraid. They don't understand the more they do this, the more strength they give me. If they kill me there will be thousands of Bakiras after me. They can't kill all of us. Somebody is going to survive and say what happened.

'The biggest thing is not to let them see they really did kill everything inside of you. When they stole all our gold, somehow I managed to keep one ring, and when my Amila was getting married I took it off and gave it to her. Then later when we went back to visit our neighbourhood, we went to my neighbours and borrowed their jewellery and on each finger put three or four rings to show they didn't manage to hurt me even financially. Those police were surprised: How did Bakira get all this gold? I did that for months, for some kind of revenge.'

I wondered about the effect on her.

'I used to have nightmares and tried both individual and group-therapy sessions but I think I've sorted it out in myself.

Sometimes I stumble but it's usually when I am let down by our judicial system. And when I go to the field and travel round the country and hear those men cursing at me, that gives me strength.'

Growing potatoes kept her sane, she added. 'I live in Sarajevo but every weekend I go to Visegrád and have a huge garden and grow potatoes, carrots and beans. I want to be myself on my own land.

'Today my children are alive and I'm a very proud wife, mother and grandmother. I have five grandchildren, two at university, one working as a nurse and the youngest two at school. I try to make joy for them, to give to my grandchildren what I couldn't give to my children because of the war.

'My eldest granddaughter is nineteen, the same age as my daughter when she was raped, and I'm trying to keep her out of it. But when Mladić was on trial and the TV showed me arguing with the man, she came home and said everyone at university told me how lucky I am to have such a brave grandmother.'

While Bakira and her army of women had managed to hunt down many of the rapists, she had been less successful in her own case.

'Of my rapists, only Lukić has been convicted,' she sighed. 'The second was apparently killed in the war and the third is hiding in Serbia.

'But my main mission is to find Veljko Planincic because he was the one who brought them to my house so my daughter was raped. I've worked so much on this case.'

She took out her phone and opened a Facebook page in his name with photos of him with a blonde woman and children blowing out candles on a birthday cake.

'Everyone knows where he is – in Russia. He got married there so I found some photos of what he did in the war and sent them to his wife on Facebook. I am living for the day he is extradited from Russia. Just to see him in court, then I can die.'

For a long time Bakira did not talk about what happened to her daughter. 'Then we were doing a documentary in 2015 and without thinking I said my daughter was raped. When I got home my husband was crying. He said you told your own story but why did you mention Amila?

'My daughter blames me for what happened to her,' she added. 'She constantly told me if you hadn't insisted on returning to Visegrád and the war, we would never have gone through this.'

So stressed was Amila that sometimes she would faint five times in a day. 'We did medical tests and they said it was stress and lack of iron,' said Bakira. 'The iron was easy but ...

'One day we had group therapy and my Amila stood up and said what happened was my fault for returning – she spat it in my face in front of all these women.

'I tried to explain that at that time I thought it was the right thing to do. I needed to keep the job. I told her, "You have children and know you have to provide for them." Only then did she realise and forgave me.'

While we were talking her phone rang. She answered and exchanged a few words, clearly disturbed, then sighed. 'That was my husband,' she said. 'They are showing the documentary on TV again and he told me he took our daughter out. He also says if we had never returned none of this would have happened. We don't talk about it anymore ...'

The tragic thing was that ethnic cleansing seemed to have worked. The Dayton Accords which ended the war had divided Bosnia into two 'entities' – the predominantly Muslim and Croat Federation of Bosnia Herzegovina, and Republika Srpska, the overwhelmingly Serb-dominated Serb Republic. The idea was to guarantee peace, but to many Muslims scared to go back to homelands that were now Serb-controlled, it seemed to have legalised a line drawn in blood.

The President of Republika Srpska, Milorad Dodik, was an unavowed Serb nationalist who denied that what had happened at Srebrenica was a genocide, or that Serb forces had kept Sarajevo under siege, and he banned the teaching of either in schools. In 2016 he even held a referendum to make a national holiday of the day in January 1992 when Bosnian Serbs declared independence, triggering the war. Now he wanted a referendum on seceding from the rest of the country.

Bakira's hometown of Visegrád had become a Serb town and part of Republika Srpska. Streets were half empty – the population was about half the 25,000 it was when war started. The 2013 census showed it was only 10 per cent Muslim compared to two thirds before the war and the municipal assembly has only one Muslim member. There was no memorial for rape victims, but local authorities unveiled a monument to the pro-Serb Russian volunteers during the war, many of whom were involved in the raping. They also ordered the word genocide chiselled off a memorial to the dead in the town's crowded Muslim graveyard.

They had even reopened the notorious Vilina Vlas Spa Hotel that was used as a rape camp by Bakira's rapist Milan Lukić. Unsuspecting tourists enter a lobby that had had to be hosed clean of blood in 1992, and swim in a pool where people were executed. Yet the biggest complaint on Trip Advisor was dirty rooms.

Lukić remained in jail and was transferred to Estonia. His memoir was launched in 2011 in a room in the Serbian Orthodox Church in Belgrade. Other convicts who had served their time in The Hague were welcomed home as heroes by Croatian and Serbian politicians. Vojislav Šešelj, sixty-three, the leader of the far right Serb nationalist party, became a reality-TV star after returning to Serbia in 2014 following almost twelve years in jail facing trial for war crimes. When his acquittal was overturned in 2018, he boasted, 'I am proud of all crimes attributed to me and ready to repeat them. We will never give up the idea of a Greater Serbia.'

8

This Is What a Genocide Looks Like

Srebrenica

On a table in a corridor was the Book of Belongings. Inside were photographs of mundane items – buttons, belt buckles, watches, wallets, a 'Made in Portugal' label, a toy car. For years, this was almost the only way to identify remains of those killed in the worst massacre in Europe since the Second World War, so mutilated were the bodies.

After the war, mothers and wives of men and boys who had disappeared would come and silently leaf through the pages, one photograph after another, torn between wanting to end the uncertainty and praying not to recognise anything.

The women were from Srebrenica, where on 11 July 1995 around 8300 Muslim men and boys were loaded onto trucks by Serbian soldiers then shot and bludgeoned to death in meadows, football fields, farms and factories and dumped in mass graves. The firing squads were killing at such a rate that one member who later confessed at The Hague, Dražen Erdemović, told of asking to sit down because he was so tired.

I was shown the Book of Belongings in a white warehouse in a small business park in the city of Tuzla on the Drina river, deep in Republika Srpska. The other side of the river is Serbia. Russian volunteers used to go there and take potshots, says Resad. The journey there in March 2018 across the mountains from Sarajevo had been magical, like driving through Narnia, with snowy forests and wooden chalets. But talking to Bakira had left me uneasy and the book was a stark reminder of the evils that had gone on.

From the outside the warehouse looked unremarkable. A small plaque by the door said International Commission of Missing Persons. Inside was the world's biggest DNA identification project.

I was let in by a no-nonsense woman in jeans called Dragana Vučetić, known as the Bone Lady. She led me into a room on the right with a strange musty smell. Inside were row upon row of metal shelves lined with white sacks, each scrawled with a number. On the top of the shelves were a series of large brown paper bags. On the floor two skeletons were laid out on long metal trays, the bones a brackish brown. Inside the white sacks were bones, while the brown bags were filled with remnants of clothing.

Dragana Vučetić with body parts still to be identified

Dragana was the senior forensic anthropologist and matter-of-fact about her gruesome task. She explained that the bodies of those killed from Srebrenica were first buried in mass graves but Serbs then dug them up and moved them elsewhere to try and stop them being found. 'They used big diggers so many of the bodies were destroyed and bones scattered in different places. One individual we found in fifteen different locations in four different mass graves. Only in 10 per cent of cases do we find complete bodies.'

They had found bones in more than 500 locations. 'Putting them together is like a puzzle,' she said. 'First, we wash them, then I lay them out in anatomical position and check the bones are all consistent in age and size. If we find skull fragments we try and glue them together. Then I do a skeleton inventory.'

She handed me a printed page almost like a children's colour-in sheet, only the picture was of a human skeleton. Bones left white denoted 'present bones', those coloured red were 'absent' and yellow 'partially present'.

I noticed that the skeletons on the trays had many bones missing and others were crumbled almost to dust. Five ribs, six fingers, one tibia …

Dragana betrayed no emotion. Other staff told me when they opened up sacks of newly exhumed body parts, often still with skin and hair, the smell could be so overpowering that they would vomit.

The Institute opened in 1997 and many bodies were so badly decomposed that it identified just 140 victims in its first five years. Aside from identifying marks like scars and dentures, as well as age and size, this was mainly through the Book of Belongings.

Occasionally there were other clues – some bones were embedded with shards of green glass, indications they had been executed near a bottling plant.

Then in 2002 they started using DNA testing. That year they had 501 official identifications.

DNA was taken from larger bones such as the femur or tibia in the presence of the prosecutor then sent to a lab in The Hague. Results took two or three months and were then cross-referenced with blood samples from families of the missing – they now had more than 70,000 in their database.

It has been such a success that they had identified 6708 victims – more than 80 per cent of the missing. Most were men – just thirteen or fourteen women – and the youngest just thirteen. In about half the cases one could see how they died, with clearly visible holes from bullet wounds or crushed skulls.

The sacks still on the shelves contained about 800 bodies they haven't identified including 92 where they have found no DNA match.

'DNA is 100 per cent accurate but the problem is we don't do every bone and not all families have given blood,' explained Dragana.

'Every year we are finding less because the bones have deteriorated. Locations are based on witnesses or satellite images. The last mass grave found was in 2016 which had 55 body parts from 18 individuals.'

They were still getting cases, three in the first three months of 2018. The two skeletons on the floor were from Kozluk, a military farm where around 500 men were executed.

Some were surface burials where people fell in the forest trying to escape while on the so-called Death March. These were usually found by people out walking dogs. Dragana told me of one man, Ramiz Nukic, who they call 'the bone hunter', who had discovered more than 250 bodies. He walked his dog in the forest for twenty miles every day looking for his father, two brothers and uncle, and finally he found part of his father, but not the others.

Once identified, a doctor signs the death certificate and the family must decide what to do with the remains. Most bury them at Potočari cemetery in Srebrenica on 11 July, the anniversary of the massacre.

In 2017, another sixty-six were buried. But some families refused. 'In this facility we have forty officially identified where the families don't want to bury because they are still missing bits,' says Dragana. 'We have others where they just bury a bone.'

Often they find more bones of those already buried, in which case they exhume them and rebury. In 2017 they exhumed 550 to add extra bones and 150 exhumations were planned for 2018.

The forensic evidence gathered by the Institute had been critical in some of the trials in The Hague. Its methods of identification were being employed in other conflicts where many went missing, such as Iraq and some staff transferred. The Bosnian project was winding down, with funding squeezed and the number of employees in Tuzla reduced to eight from twenty.

For those who still had missing sons or husbands this was very distressing. 'For the families it's important we continue; they don't want us to give up,' said Dragana.

'Apart from the bodies still to identify, we have 3000 bags of clothing and also more than 12,000 small body bags with bones or fragments too small to identify.'

I imagine what it must be like to spend day after day, year after year, mapping a human genocide. 'I deal only with the bones,' she shrugged. 'I don't know the names or the stories.'

She pointed at the metal tray.

Afterwards I found out she is a Serb.

The drive from Tuzla to Srebrenica was a strange mixture of abandoned houses and newly built ones. This valley was where men and boys were bussed to their executions or shot dead in the hills trying to escape. We call it the Valley of Death, says Aida, my purple-haired interpreter.

In Potočari cemetery just outside Srebrenica the graves rose and fell like waves, one white needle-shaped stone after another across the hillside. On one someone had left a single white rose. A small clump of yellow primroses grew in front of another where the snow had melted.

Across the road were large white hangars and you could make out the letters DutchBat on the gatepost. This was where the 700-strong Dutch battalion were stationed who were supposed to protect the people of Srebrenica, which the UN had designated a safe zone.

They failed to do not only this when General Mladić's forces seized the town in July 1995 but also to protect the 20,000 to 30,000 civilians who fled to the compound seeking refuge. A few thousand were allowed in to start but then the gate closed and eventually all of them were forced out to the mercy of the Serbs, who began dividing them up as the blue-helmeted Dutch soldiers looked on. It's hard not to picture the people there, the women screaming as they were ordered to the left, along with the elderly and young children, while their husbands and sons were sent to the right.

The hangars had been converted into a museum of disturbing stories. 'My son's hand was pulled from mine,' said one woman in a video. 'He begged me to look after his backpack as they dragged him away. He never came back.'

Once the men had been taken away, there were more screams as young women were raped by Serb soldiers.

I warmed to Dr Branka Antic-Stauber straight away. She had a reassuring smile and a kindly face framed by a dark bob streaked with grey, and she ran an organisation called Snaga Zene, which translates as Girl Power.

She welcomed me into her cosy office in Tuzla and offered me tea made from camomile and thyme grown by women of Srebrenica, for, like Bakira, they too have found working with the earth to be nature's way of healing. She drank hers from a Father Christmas mug.

Dr Branka was working in 2001 with a paediatrician colleague to treat infectious diseases in the collective centres in Tuzla where women and children had been taken. They were shocked to hear that some of the women were returning to Srebrenica.

'We decided to go and see for ourselves,' she said. 'I had never been there but felt I knew it from talking to all the women. They used to talk about the balconies and roses but when we got there the whole place was destroyed, everything was black and grey. Then we saw smoke coming from the chimney of one of those destroyed houses so we went in and found six women huddled in a corridor in coats and scarves around a woodstove – it was November and freezing.'

'What are you doing here?' she asked them. 'Aren't you cold, aren't you afraid?'

One of the women said, 'We're not afraid at all because there is nothing to be afraid of anymore – we came to look for our dead children and we've been dead for a long time. Only our bodies are present and a person who came and killed those wouldn't make any difference.'

Tears started falling from her eyes and she got a tissue. 'Something about that reply really got to me as a woman, as a mother, as a doctor, and I decided to try and help. We couldn't solve all the problems they had, we couldn't give them their children back or undo what had happened to them, but at least we could talk to them and try to build something new and I felt something from the universe would give us strength.'

Ever since she had gone there every two weeks. The original six women returnees had swelled to more than 300 as well as their families.

'They are simple women, barely educated, but I think they can serve as a great example,' she said. 'We've always had wars and will again but if those who have lived through them can get out and speak about it, maybe we will learn.

'In twenty years I've never heard any of them say they want revenge – they just want answers and for this to never happen to anyone else.'

She struggled for a long while, she said, on how to help them. 'Rape trauma is always very difficult to work with. It affects the mental, physical and intimate health. But the women of Srebrenica not only have the trauma of what they had suffered – rapes and murders of loved ones – but also were expelled from their homes, had to live in collective centres, and then the re-traumatisation of funerals and burials every year as bodies are found.

'We tried various approaches but after five years there was no progress; everything was still dark. Then I realised the women were trying to tell us something. They had lost their husbands and sons yet returned to the land as if Mother Earth was calling them. So we started horticultural therapy and that changed everything.'

Just as Safina Lohani in Bangladesh had found, Dr Branka realised it was important for the women to have some economic power to regain control of their lives. She came up with the idea of growing roses and secured a donation of 3000 cuttings from Holland.

'The idea was for the women to grow and sell them in the shop at the Potočari memorial,' she said. 'But when they grew they didn't cut them. They told me we're sitting drinking coffee and enjoying the beauty and the perfume in our gardens!'

Eventually she managed to get 35,000 seedlings, so there was enough for farms as well as the women's gardens. They were running three rose farms and had branched out to the herbal tea we were drinking. Not only did the gardening serve as occupational therapy but it provided funds for her work.

Although the rose-growing had helped the women's healing, most still suffered physical problems, she said. 'Women who suffered sexual violence either don't go to gynaecologists at all because they are scared something may happen to them or they go there all the time. Some have developed cervical cancer, a lot have thyroid-gland disorder because the thyroid is the organ most affected by stress, and have low insulin levels triggering diabetes.'

She still met every Friday with survivors. 'Even though it has been a long time, the stories are still very vivid. They start crying and shaking. I never stop being shocked.'

Just the week before my visit, a woman had told her a story which she said gave her chills. 'She told me she was pregnant when she was raped and her eight-year-old daughter was made to watch. She was raped by several men in front of her daughter then afterwards the rapists asked the girl to wash their penises and the mum's genitalia. Afterwards the woman gave birth prematurely at thirty-four weeks and her baby boy was born blind. As for her daughter, she never finished school and became very promiscuous and had five children with three different men.

'That was hard to hear,' said Dr Branka. 'That man caused so much damage. The woman could cope with her own trauma but the blind son and the damaged daughter …

'She didn't talk about her rape for years because after that happened their home was burnt down, so they had nowhere to live, and she struggled to support the children. So with all this going on to say she had been raped seemed less important. Many don't tell their story for years because of the shame.'

It was twenty-five years before Enesa told anyone her story. Her reddish hair was pulled back in a short ponytail, her eyes red-rimmed, and she kept licking her lips and rubbing her hands. At fifty-nine she looked wrung out by life.

She lived in Tuzla but was originally from Srebrenica and was living between Srebrenica and Potočari with her husband and two children when the war started. 'On 16 April 1992 what happened to me, happened in my house,' she started. 'Srebrenica was meant to be a safe haven protected by the UN but it was already clear we Muslims would need to leave and so we were all keeping guard. Every night we would stay in different houses, several families together. That particular night I was in a third house with friends and children. The electricity and water had been cut off by the Serbs and it was just days before we would be forced out altogether.

'It was semi-dark, the first dark, when I realised we didn't have enough water. I picked up two five-litre bottles and told my friend I'd go to the spring to fetch some. I also wanted to go and get my children some spare clothes from our house. So I went to fetch the water then left the bottles at the entrance to my house while I popped in. The house was unlocked. As I entered the hallway, I was grabbed from behind. A man's hand came over my mouth then another man appeared wearing a mask and calling me *balinka*, which is a very bad name for a Muslim, and demanding to know where our gold and money was. They were in uniforms. I was shaking and screaming. I was wearing a dark-red house dress which tied like a bathrobe, and after I said there was no gold or money, they pulled it off and did what they did in the way they wanted from the front and back. One was raping me and the other said, "I'd like some too." I was on the ground then another came and suddenly I felt sharp pain in my left breast and I didn't know what it was. I fainted. When I came round I was lying in blood and bleeding from my left breast and right hand. Half of my nipple was bitten away. I took my robe and tried to remove the blood from the floor then went to my cupboard to get clothes. Then my two-year-old son came into the house and asked, "Mummy, what was it?"'

She started crying. 'We had been in the middle of building another storey on our house so I told him I'd fallen on the steps which were unfinished. He took me by the hand and back to my friend's house.

'I put bandages on my arm and didn't tell anyone what happened. The following day we were told we had to leave so on the 17th we left with other people and came to Tuzla and registered as refugees. On the way there were soldiers at checkpoints and our van was stopped by men using the same bad words and asking for gold and silver and money.

'I had both my children in my arms. They were shaking, terrified. When we all said we had nothing, the soldiers started checking us roughly. My daughter had tiny gold earrings which were a gift from my mother and he ripped them out. She was screaming and I was trying to calm her, and the soldier said you should feel lucky because we haven't slaughtered you.

'All we had left were blankets. For more than a year we lived in Maidan sports hall. My husband remained in Srebrenica and found another woman and stayed there four years. He somehow survived then left for Sarajevo and died there in 2002.

'Then a year after we came to Tuzla I realised my son was not well. He wasn't growing and his thyroid and other functions had stopped. Finally, when he was nine, he was diagnosed with complete hormonal dysfunction because of stress. Now he gets hormone shots to replace them – he walks and talks but is completely dependent on the shots and I don't get any help from the state – just 55 euros a month, so I work cleaning homes and offices but his medicines are very expensive ... Now they are saying there is insufficient copper in his body and his liver has almost stopped working and doctors are arguing over what to do ...'

She looked at me in despair.

'What about your own health?' I ask.

'Don't ask,' she replied. 'Blood pressure, stress, heart ... My doctor tells me I can't look after my son if I don't look after myself.'

In all those years she had told nobody what had happened to her until the previous year.

'I had several parallel struggles,' she explained. 'One was shame for what happened. Also I feared if I started talking about it then it would happen again. Then I wanted to kill myself then I thought about cutting out my female parts. Then there was the illness of my son so I was busy fighting for him.

'Every time I was about to speak to someone, I didn't know who to talk to, then something would happen to my son – he would have a seizure. Last time I couldn't find all the medicines he needed and he fell down, his eyes white and spitting foam, and me and my daughter were so lost we couldn't remember the emergency number. Another time about nine years ago I was ready to speak and my son ended up in hospital.'

Things changed for her when she moved the previous year and met a neighbour in another apartment who had also been raped. 'We talked about our experiences and I finally told her. I'd been dreaming about my mother who was killed in Srebrenica in 1993 by a mortar shell and she kept asking me, "Baby, what do you want to tell me?" I think in the end I just felt so tired, that's why I told. My neighbour told me to come to Dr Branka.

'I didn't feel any better after talking about it but am now in therapy,' she added.

Dr Branka patted her hand. 'It's a crucial step to acknowledge it happened,' she said.

'My children don't know,' said Enesa. 'I am giving my daughter hints, she knows something is going on but … I don't know why I feel ashamed.

'I'm never going to that house ever again. Even when I go for the memorial service it takes me three or four months to recover. I have a sister who returned to Srebrenica but I can't visit her.'

I asked Enesa if she had found love again after her husband.

'No,' she almost shuddered. 'I can't imagine. I was thirty-three when I was raped and the blood that came out of me that day was the last blood.'

Branka told me this was not the first time she had heard this. 'I also had a girl raped at twenty-two who never again had a period,' she said. 'The stress causes hormones to rise to abnormal levels and everything stops because the adrenalin and cortisol produced blocks all others.'

She had become curious about what men got from war rape and had researched the chemical processes in the brain. 'How can a person who is not motivated by desire even get an erection?' she asked. 'Can hate or fear or revenge do this? Oxytocin, the hormone which both men and women produce, which is responsible for sexuality and arousal and reaches high levels during both – some people call it the cuddle hormone – is also produced in fear so perhaps that's one of the explanations. But it's not acceptable, men choosing to attack something which is the symbol of love and new life. Why are they deliberately choosing to attack that?'

'Whatever is the worst punishment, the men should face,' said Enesa. She blew her nose then checked her watch and said she must go to her cleaning job. I asked if I could hug her. Some of the women don't like being touched but she smiled and buried herself in my jumper before slipping away.

She seemed so fragile, I told Branka I felt scared that talking about it had made things worse. 'It's not possible to heal from this forever,' she said, 'but it helps to speak about it as soon as possible and to share the story with someone compassionate. What I have seen definitely helps their healing is when perpetrators get punished because that gives the victim confirmation by authority she was not the one at fault for what happened to her and that she's innocent.

'The problem is only a few have been convicted. My association has participated in eight cases where women went to court but only two got convictions. There was one case with a group of eleven men who went into homes taking girls and ended up with fifty-six girls. But of those eleven, only three were declared guilty. Three were declared not guilty and the others set free on lack of evidence. That case took three years, the women repeatedly having to go to court and testify, and we needed to prepare them over and over again. They went through all of that painful suffering to get justice only to hear their perpetrators declared not guilty. After that they felt there was no point in speaking up and told the other women we should all keep silent.

'I tell the women, "If you remain silent, it's as if nothing happened. There are no perpetrators." I told them, "Yes, those men were declared not guilty but they were singled out in court for three years, their names are public, their families and friends have heard. Don't you think people will wonder?"

'But when you look at how long rape trials go on and how few convictions there are, you can't escape the feeling that something else is going on – that the government is considering war rape as something not serious. This needs political will and recognition by every single political leader, regardless of their ethnic background.'

Listening to Enesa left me lost for words. We came out to darkness. I realised we hadn't eaten since leaving Srebrenica after breakfast so told our driver to head to a nearby shopping mall. Inside, the lights seemed too bright, the people too noisy. We sat down in a pizza place and, as usual in Bosnia, everyone around was smoking, including Aida and the driver.

On the way back to Sarajevo, they started bickering like an old married couple even though they had only met two days before. I asked the problem. 'He says he's a romantic and he dreams of going to Cuba,' complained Aida. 'I'm telling him why don't you just go? Don't wait. You never know what life might throw at you.'

9

The Hunting Hour

Berlin

For many of us the first time we heard of rape being used as a weapon of war was in the 1990s during the fighting in Bosnia. As the first news reports emerged of rape camps, there were shockwaves. How could something like this happen in the heart of Europe?

Yet it wasn't new at all. On a crisp October day of yellowing trees and blue skies, I stepped off the S-Bahn at Treptower Park in what used to be East Berlin, headed down the steps and along the river Spree with its tourist cafés and glass-roofed sightseeing boats. A series of signposts brought me to a grey stone arch and a pathway which led to a statue of a grieving Mother Russia. I followed the direction of her gaze along an avenue of weeping birch to emerge onto a platform between two vast red granite flags decorated with hammer and sickle.

It was hard not to gasp. Nobody does monumental like the Stalinists and the largest Soviet war memorial outside the former Soviet Union is overwhelming, not least because of the sheer unexpectedness of it. In front of me stretched a long sunken garden with a line of enormous stone sarcophaguses either side, each carved with a scene of war or liberation, one with Lenin's disembodied face floating over the soldiers. At the other end, on a grass mound, towered a majestic figure, starkly silhouetted against the pale blue sky like a declaration.

A bronze statue of a Soviet soldier stood atop a crushed swastika, holding a sword in one hand and cradling a small German girl in the other. It is massive – 36 feet high and weighing about 70 tons.

The effect was silencing and was meant to be. Treptower Park is the final resting place for 7000 of the 80,000 Soviet troops killed in the spring of 1945 in the Battle for Berlin, the last major offensive in Europe of World War Two.

I sat on a bench under the yellow trees and thought of all the sons and husbands and fathers buried here who never went home, as well as their mothers, wives and daughters left bereft. People were out enjoying the autumn sunshine, jogging, walking dogs and pushchairs. A group of tourists went by on a bicycle tour. The park was just off a busy road, yet the atmosphere was hushed.

After a while I climbed the steps to the base of the statue and peered inside. Long-stemmed red roses and carnations lay scattered on the ground under a mural of a group of people in bright red and gold mosaic like a religious fresco. Above was an inscription in Russian and German declaring, THE SOVIET PEOPLE SAVED EUROPEAN CIVILISATION FROM FASCISM.

The cost was almost unfathomable. Between 1941 and 1945, 30 million men and women served in the Soviet military, mostly conscripts into what seemed almost certain defeat. Two and a half million soldiers were captured in the first five months of the war and more than eight million killed by the end.

Back on my bench I stared at the towering soldier carrying the girl. Far from the heroic image it is intended to convey, many German women call this memorial the Tomb of the Unknown Rapist.

For what the carved-stone scenes of battle and liberation do not tell is that the Red Army assaulted hundreds of thousands of women as they fought their way to the German capital. As many as one in three women in Berlin were raped, an estimated 100,000, and 'at least two million' overall, according to the historian Antony Beevor who called it the 'greatest phenomenon of mass rape in history'.

Shocked by what he found as he trawled through diaries, soldiers' letters, and communist-regime records for his book *Berlin: The Downfall, 1945,* he wrote: 'In many ways the fate of the women and the girls in Berlin is far worse than that of the soldiers starving and suffering in Stalingrad.'

The rapes began as soon as Stalin's troops entered East Prussia and Silesia in January 1944. British, French, American and Canadian troops also raped German women but the scale was different. In many towns and villages 'every female, aged from eight to eighty, was raped', recounted Natalya Gesse, a Soviet war correspondent who witnessed the Red Army in action. 'It was an army of rapists.'

The writer Alexander Solzhenitsyn who was then a young captain, went on to describe the horror in his narrative poem *Prussian Nights*:

The little daughter's on the mattress
Dead. How many have been on it?
A platoon, a company perhaps?

But most said nothing. Soldiers who refused to take part in these drunken orgies were treated with suspicion.

Technically, rape in the Red Army was punishable by death; in fact, officers often stood by during gang rapes, or made sure every man had his turn. Was it a policy, a weapon of war? 'Yes and no,' says Beevor. 'It's incredibly complex. There wasn't ever an order to go out and rape but there was a background atmosphere of vengeance and often subliminal psychology.'

The Russians by then had suffered years of atrocities following the launch of Operation Barbarossa, the Nazi invasion of the Soviet Union in 1941 which aimed to wipe out Slavs to make room for Aryans and secure more food sources. As many as 27 million inhabitants of the Soviet Union are believed to have died during the war, including more than three million who were deliberately starved in German POW camps under the so-called Hunger Plan.

Humiliating German women was one means of Russian retaliation for treating them as an inferior race – the sexuality of the women making them the easiest target. After years of being fed anti-German propaganda, Red Army soldiers probably did not see their victims as human.

Beevor believes it may also have been a reaction to humiliation from their own officers – what he calls 'the knock-on theory of oppression'. And plenty of vodka and schnapps to help fuel the rage. When they couldn't perform, they used the bottles instead.

'It was just pure violence,' he told me. 'They were raping eighty- or ninety-year-old women to seven-year-old girls. There was no selection at all.'

Often rape was accompanied by mutilation and murder. The images of the corpses on Nazi newsreels were so horrendous that many German women initially assumed they were a fabrication of the Goebbels propaganda machine.

As word spread of what was happening, there were waves of pre-emptive suicides as the Russians approached, as well as parents killing their own children before killing themselves. In one northern town of Demmin alone, 600 people killed themselves in spring 1945, according to German documentary-maker Florian Huber who wrote a book about the estimated hundreds of thousands who took their own lives.

In Berlin soldiers would down vodka and go on hunting parties, flicking their torches to choose their victims. Women learnt to hide at night during the 'hunting hour' or spread ashes and iodine on their faces to make themselves unattractive – much as the Yazidi girls did years later in the Galaxy Cinema. Many spoke of nights filled with screams because most of the windows had been blown out in the bombing. Among them were Jewish women who had already suffered under Nazi camps and had imagined the Soviet troops as their liberators.

And the rapes were carried out not only against Germans but also the Soviets' own allies in Hungary, Romania, Poland and Yugoslavia. When the Yugoslav communist Milovan Djilas protested, Stalin retorted: 'Can't he understand it if a soldier who has crossed thousands of kilometres through blood and fire and death has fun with a woman or takes some trifle?'

That 'fun' would be something from which the women would never recover. Thousands died, according to records from Berlin hospitals, mostly of suicide. Many were infected by venereal disease. Those who fell pregnant killed the babies.

They were even raping their own women – Russian and Ukrainians who had been taken to Germany as slave labour.

Beevor recounts how shaken he was to be told by a German victim that women who tried to commit suicide after gang rape only managed to maim themselves by cutting their wrists the wrong way. So horrendous were the stories that he would wake in the night for days afterwards.

Yet this was rarely talked about after the war. Certainly not in the USSR, where it was called the Great Patriotic War and return-ing soldiers were seen as heroes, though there was a sick joke circulating in 1945 about Ivan returning from war to his wife where she has saved up a bottle of vodka to celebrate. He cannot get it up and orders her, 'Now, put up a fight.'

Nor in Germany, where men who returned home recoiled from hearing the accounts of the women they had failed to protect. A

German woman wrote an anonymous memoir *Eine Frau in Berlin* describing herself as 'a pale-faced blonde always dressed in the same winter coat' and recounting how she was gang-raped by Soviet soldiers and eventually sought out a Russian officer to sleep with as a 'wolf to keep away the pack'. When it was published in 1953, the book was widely reviled and she was accused of 'besmirching the honour of German women'. It quickly went out of print.

US President Harry Truman only found out years later that the lakeside villa, where he stayed in July 1945 during the Potsdam conference with Churchill and Stalin to partition the post-war world, had just a few weeks earlier been a scene of horror.

He had been told that the yellow stucco villa was owned by the head of the Nazi movie industry who had been sent to Siberia. He remarked in his diary that, 'As all others it was stripped of everything by the Russians – not even a tin spoon left.'

Years later he got a letter from the wealthy publisher Hans Dietrich Muller Grote who told him it was in fact the house of his father Gustav Muller Grote, also a publisher, and had long been a gathering place for writers and artists.

'At the end of the war my parents were still living there,' he wrote. 'Some of my sisters moved there with their children as the suburb seemed to offer more security from bombings … In the beginning of May, the Russians arrived. Ten weeks before you entered this house, its tenants were living in constant fright and fear. By day and by night plundering Russian soldiers went in and out, raping my sisters before their own parents and children, beating up my old parents …'*

It took more than half a century for people to take notice. When the anonymous Berlin woman's memoir was reprinted in 2003, the

---

* Quoted in David McCullough, *Truman* (New York: Simon & Schuster, 1992).

year after Antony Beevor's revelations, it became a bestseller. By then she was dead. Another harrowing account, *Warum war ich bloss ein Mädchen? (Why Did I Have to Be a Girl)*, was published in 2010 by Gabi Köpp, the first woman to talk publicly of what she had suffered. Köpp was just fifteen when she was grabbed by a Soviet soldier in January 1945 as she fled in the snow, and endured fourteen days of hell, being raped again and again and flinching under a table at the words 'Where's little Gabi?' Her own mother told her not to tell anyone when she finally escaped and they were reunited. Köpp said she had difficulty sleeping for the rest of her life and never knew romantic love. She died shortly after her book came out.*

In the Deutsch-Russisches Museum in Berlin, formerly known as the Surrender Museum, with its Kapitulation Hall where the German Wehrmacht signed its surrender to the Allied Powers at midnight on 8 May 1945, there are room after room detailing German atrocities. Yet I struggled to find any mention of Red Army violations of women. Finally, after asking the guide twice, he pointed me to a small exhibit in room nine marked *Ubergriffe* or Abuses.

Next to a few handwritten reports of rape was a typed card stating:

> *The Red Army sent reports of crimes against German civilians to the political and military leadership in Moscow. On 20 April 1945, the Supreme Commander of Soviet troops ordered they be stopped to make the fighting and later occupation easier.*

When I studied the Second World War at school in the 1980s, my textbooks said nothing of the mass rape – indeed it seemed a war

---

* Interview with Kopp in *Der Spiegel*, 26 February 2010.

of men. Even my son's much more recent history books had no mention.

No one apologised; no one was prosecuted.

Indeed, to this day it is a taboo subject in Russia, the rapes dismissed as a myth, western propaganda against the Red Army, or what today might be termed fake news. When Beevor's book came out, Grigori Karasin, the then Russian ambassador to London, accused him of 'lies, slander and blasphemy' and the book was banned from Russian schools and colleges.

In 2014 President Vladimir Putin signed a law stating that anyone who denigrates Russia's record in the Second World War could face heavy fines and five years in prison. Beevor suspects the records he used may have been removed from the archives.

In the Polish city of Gdansk, city records estimate that up to 40 per cent of women were raped, according to leading daily *Gazeta Wyborcza*. In 2013 a young art student in Gdansk called Jerzy Szumczyk erected a statue of a Russian soldier kneeling between the legs of a heavily pregnant woman, holding down her hair with one hand and a pistol in her mouth with his other. He named it *Komm, Frau*, meaning 'Come here, woman', one of the few German phrases the Red Army soldiers knew and which all German women dreaded. The statue was torn down within a few hours amid furious Russian complaints.

Silence, impunity, denial – when you looked at the history it was not surprising that in everywhere I was covering from Afghanistan to Zimbabwe women were being raped by state security forces. How was it that rape, a crime universally condemned, could be disregarded and trivialised when it occurred in war?

I said at the start of this chapter that Bosnia was the first war in which there was widespread international media coverage of the mass rapes that were happening. Yet when I started looking around, there were plenty of representations. You only had to visit room eighteen of the National Gallery in London and look at *The Rape of the Sabine Women* by Peter Paul Rubens – a tangle of semi-naked women with anguished expressions, skirts lifted and breasts exposed, being grabbed by Roman soldiers as Romulus watches on from a dais and directs the action.

They represent the story told by the Roman historian Livy, of how after Romulus founded Rome in 753 BC, he worried about the shortage of women to ensure its future. He came up with the wheeze of inviting the neighbouring Sabine tribe to a feast in honour of Neptune then abducting their women.

Rome you could say was founded on rape. The same subject inspired a painting by Nicolas Poussin in the New York Metropolitan Museum and a marble sculpture by Giambologna in the open-aired Loggia dei Lanzi at the side of the Uffizi Gallery in Florence. The sculpture comprises three intertwined bodies, one of them a woman writhing upwards while desperately trying to escape the clutches of a younger man, who pushes away an older man below, presumably her father.

When tourists stop to admire the sculptor's mastery in capturing in stone such fluidity of movement, how many think about what it is really representing? Far from a condemnation, in some ways that whole sculpture terrace feels like a celebration of rape of women.

Next to *The Rape of the Sabine Women* is *The Rape of Polyxena* by Pio Fedi, which shows a Greek warrior who may or may not be Achilles, his left arm clutching Polyxena, youngest daughter of the King of Troy, her breasts exposed. In his right his sword is raised to beat back Queen Hecuba, who is at his feet, clinging desperately to her daughter. Under his feet is her dead son Hector.

Achilles is said to have fallen for Polyxena when he glimpsed her fetching water and she had offered herself in exchange for the return of her brother Hector's body. She learnt the secret of his vulnerable heel, enabling her brother Paris to kill him with an arrow and bring an end to the war. Rather than showing her as a heroine, the statue shows her being abducted to be sacrificed on his tomb.

Also on the terrace is Cellini's triumphant bronze of Perseus with sword, holding the severed head of Medusa with its coils of hissing snakes for hair, transformed by Athena to punish her for being raped by Poseidon.

Ovid described Medusa as a beautiful maiden who was the only mortal of three sisters known as the Gorgons. Her beauty caught the eye of the sea god who proceeded to rape her in the sacred temple of Athena. Furious at the desecration of her temple, Athena transformed Medusa into a monster with the deadly ability to turn whoever looked upon her face to stone. Poseidon, meanwhile, received no punishment, which some see as an early example of victim-blaming.

The use of rape in war 'has existed for as long as there has been conflict', declared a report by United Nations Women in 1998.

The word rape comes from the Middle English *rapen, rappen* – to abduct, ravish, snatch. It originates from the Latin *rapere* which means to steal, seize or carry away, as if women were property, which is exactly what men thought for so many centuries.

Herodotus wrote of the gang rape of women by the Persians in their wars against the Greeks in the fifth century BC: 'A few Phoenicians were chased and caught near the mountains and some women were raped successively by so many Persian soldiers that they died.'

The Bible too makes clear in the Old Testament that rape was standard practice in its accounts of the battles of the Israelites. Deuteronomy 21.10–14 states: 'When you go out to war against your enemies … and you see among the captives a beautiful woman, and you desire to take her … you may go in to her and be her husband.'

Moses appears to be ordering the rape of 32,000 virgins while fighting the Midianites when in Numbers 31 he is quoted as saying, 'Now therefore kill every male among the little ones, and kill every woman that has known man by lying with him. But all the women children, that have not known a man by lying with him, keep alive for yourselves.'

Nor was it just in ancient times. Vikings were also known for rape and pillage, as were Genghis Khan and his Mongols and pretty much everyone through the Middle Ages and beyond.

Wartime diaries, letters home and military records from the American Civil War leave little doubt that many southern women were raped, both white and black. 'Heard from home,' wrote John Williams of the 7th Tennessee Regiment in his diary in the spring of 1863. 'The Yankees has been through there. Seems to be their object to commit rape on every Negro woman they can find.'*

The final months of the war saw General William Sherman's notorious March to the Sea, leading his 60,000 battle-hardened Union troops in a swathe across the south from a burning Atlanta, through Georgia and the Carolinas, to finally capture the port of Savannah to hand to President Lincoln in December 1864 in time for Christmas. On the way they left a trail of destruction, burning homes to demoralise the Confederates. According to one southern newspaper they also left in their tracks 'hundreds of violated women and deflowered maidens'.†

* * *

---

* Quoted in Crystal Feimster, *Southern Horrors: Women and the Politics of Rape and Lynching* (London: Harvard University Press, 2009).

† Quoted in Matthew Carr, *Sherman's Ghosts: Soldiers, Civilians, and the American Way of War* (New York: New Press, 2015).

Perhaps the first use of rape as a specific weapon of war to spread terror was in the Spanish Civil War. This began in July 1936 after an alliance of centrist and leftist parties narrowly won the elections and took power, releasing political prisoners and encouraging peasants to seize land.

The right watched with mounting alarm in what was a deeply divided country. Deciding enough was enough, General Francisco Franco, then chief of the general staff, raised a rebel fascist army in Spanish Morocco that was flown in German transport planes across the straits of Gibraltar set on toppling the Republican government in Madrid.

The war was soon seen as an ideological battleground between left and right, drawing in leftist volunteers from around the world to join the international brigades, as well as writers and intellectuals Ernest Hemingway, Martha Gellhorn, John Dos Passos, George Orwell and W. H. Auden and photographers like Robert Capa and Gerda Taro, some of whom engaged in passionate love affairs with the war as backdrop.

Hundreds of thousands of Spaniards were killed during the three-year war. Far less well known is the scale of deliberate and systematic persecution of women.

The Moroccan *regulares* of Franco's Army of Africa operated as the shock troops of the Nationalists. They were encouraged by Franco's officers to inflict horrific atrocities on Republican women as they headed toward Madrid. 'Not just rape but appalling evisceration of peasant women of Andalucia and Estremadura,' says Beevor who wrote a book on the war.

Wives, mothers, sisters and daughters of those leftists executed or exiled would be raped as retribution and humiliated by having their heads shaved and forced to drink castor oil which acted as a laxative so they would publicly soil themselves. Sometimes, after raping women, they would brand the breasts of their women with the yoke and phalanx of arrows, the Falangist symbol.

After the capture of any town or village, troops were given two hours during which they could loot and rape.

Women who had been politically active would be locked up in filthy overcrowded jails where they too would be raped. Some would then be executed by firing squad. Those who came out alive would be left with lifelong physical and psychological problems. Having lost all they owned, and their menfolk been killed, many were forced into prostitution to survive.

'Systematic rape by the columns of Moroccan troops was part of the plan to instil terror,' according to British historian Paul Preston, whose spine-chilling book *The Spanish Holocaust* did more than any previous to uncover what really went on in this dark period.

The extent to which the abuse of women was official policy was evident from the speeches of General Gonzalo Queipo de Llano, the military leader who effectively ruled southern Spain. Preston points out that his radio broadcasts were 'larded with sexual references' and 'describing scenes of rape with a coarse relish that encouraged his militias to repeat such scenes'.*

In one Queipo de Llano declared: 'Our brave Legionarios and Regulares have shown the red cowards what it means to be a man. And incidentally the wives of the reds too. These Communist and Anarchist women, after all, have made themselves fair game by their doctrine of free love. And now they have at least made the acquaintance of real men, and not milksops of militiamen. Kicking their legs about and squealing won't save them.'

After Franco died of old age in 1975, paving a return to democracy, Spain did all it could to blot out its past. In 1977 Parliament agreed a Pact of Forgetting and passed an amnesty law to ensure no one could be held to account. There were no purges or Truth

---

* Paul Preston, *The Spanish Holocaust: Inquisition and Extermination in Twentieth-Century Spain* (London: HarperPress, 2013), p. 149.

Commission and nothing in the history books. General de Llano, responsible for the execution of 54,000 people in Seville, including the poet Federico García Lorca, was buried in a special chapel in the city's Basilica de La Macarena.

Not long after the start of the Spanish Civil War was the Rape of Nanking, the atrocities committed by the Imperial Japanese Army in an attack that destroyed Nanjing, then capital of China, during the Second Sino-Japanese War. In a six-week-long massacre from December 1937 to January 1938, Japanese troops went door to door searching for girls as young as ten, raping so many – estimates range from 20–80,000. Many were then killed, left 'in the street with their legs splayed open, orifices pierced with wooden rods, twigs and weeds', according to accounts from the time.*

The mass rapes in Nanking so horrified the world that Emperor Hirohito became alarmed about its damage to Japan's image. Yet, far from refraining, his Imperial Army went on to abduct thousands of women and girls from China, Korea and across South East Asia during the Second World War. They interned them in military brothels in occupied territories as what they called 'comfort women', but who were basically sex slaves.

A 1938 directive of the Japanese Department of War advocated regulated sex in 'comfort stations' 'to boost the spirit of the troops, keep law and order and prevent rape and venereal disease'.

Girls as young as twelve were rounded up on the streets all over South East Asia, and kidnapped or convinced to travel to what they thought were nursing units or jobs in factories, or purchased from their parents as indentured servants. Instead they were sent to brothels to provide sexual services to Japanese soldiers, sometimes as many as fifty a day, and held for months or even years.

---

* Iris Chang, *The Rape of Nanking: The Forgotten Holocaust* (New York: Basic Books, 1997).

An estimated 50–200,000 comfort women were forced to serve the three million Japanese troops. No one knows how many exactly, as Japanese officials destroyed documents after the war. Many were killed by retreating troops. Many of the women died of sexually transmitted infections or complications from their violent treatment at the hands of Japanese soldiers; others committed suicide.

In 1993, the UN's Global Tribunal on Violations of Women's Human Rights estimated that at the end of the Second World War, 90 per cent of the 'comfort women' had died. Those who survived became societal outcasts, referred to as 'Japanese hand-me-downs'.

In Japan there was silence as officials insisted the comfort stations never existed or that the women were paid prostitutes. But gradually more and more brave survivors came forward.

It took almost fifty years until in 1993 Japan officially acknowledged what had happened with an apology from Prime Minister Morihiro Hosokawa. Even then one of his successors Shinzō Abe criticised him and only in 2015 was an agreement reached with South Korea to finally pay $8.8 million in reparations to the surviving women, by then numbering less than fifty.

The issue has still not gone away – South Korea asked for a stronger apology from its old colonial power and women continue to gather every Wednesday by a statue outside the Japanese embassy in Seoul to demand 'Apologise!' and the rewriting of history textbooks.

Japan, it seemed, remains in denial. Since 2014, editors at NHK, the Japanese state broadcaster, have been banned from using the term sex slaves and must instead describe them as 'people referred to as war-time comfort women'.

In October 2018 the Japanese city of Osaka overturned sixty years of being twinned with San Francisco in protest of a statue that had been erected in Chinatown depicting comfort women.

* * *

The Russians and Japanese were not the only soldiers raping during the Second World War, of course – the British, French, Americans and Canadians were also at it, but on a far smaller scale. In Italy, Moroccan mercenary troops fought with Free French Forces on terms that included 'license to rape and plunder in enemy territory'.

Also largely swept under the carpet of history was the rape during the Vietnam War which raged from 1961 until 1973. Thousands of anguished books have been written about the debacle in which 58,000 Americans perished and forty times as many Vietnamese, yet there is barely a mention of the rape by both American and Vietnamese soldiers – and indeed the French before them.

One of the most notorious incidents of the war was the My Lai Massacre of March 1968 in which American GIs killed 400 unarmed villagers including children, as exposed in a series of graphic photographs. But there were also multiple rapes that hardly got a line in any of the reporting.

A later inquiry headed by General William Peers* into the massacre included detailed eyewitness accounts of twenty acts of rape on women and girls aged between ten and forty-five. Many of the assaults were gang rape and involved sexual torture and not one infantryman sought to halt it. Yet no one was prosecuted for it.

The slightest tear in the carpet was revealed in the eighteen-hour documentary series on the Vietnam War by Ken Burns and Lynn Novick, screened in 2017. A key episode, 'Things Fall Apart',† focuses on the Tet Offensive, a shock series of attacks in a hundred towns and cities across southern Vietnam by the North Vietnamese army (NVA) and Vietcong, launched during the Lunar

---

* Peers Commission completed 1970 and published 1974.

† Episode six, 'Things Fall Apart', *The Vietnam War* by Ken Burns and Lynn Novick, PBS 2017.

New Year festival in January 1968, which became one of the turning points of the war.

Its longest and bloodiest battle was fought in the streets of Hue, one of the country's loveliest cities and former Imperial capital. Almost overnight the NVA and Vietcong captured most of the city either side of the Perfume River, leaving US troops under siege in a compound of the Military Assistance Command, Vietnam, or MACV, in the walled Citadel, north of the river.

Nineteen-year-old Marine Corporal Bill Ehrhart was at the end of his twelve-month tour and preparing to go home. But when his company was ordered to relieve the besieged American compound, he volunteered to go with them.

To get to it involved weeks of brutal block-by-block battles to retake surrounding neighbourhoods. 'It was ugly, ugly fighting,' he said. 'We literally had to clear houses a room at a time, a floor at a time then on to the next.

'It felt like every NVA in the world was trying to kill me and my pals,' he added. 'I was scared utterly witless but it was the greatest adrenaline high I'd ever experienced.'

The ancient city was left in ruins. Thousands of people died and tens of thousands lost their homes. Surviving civilians were herded into the university to escape the grenades being tossed into their living rooms.

It was there something happened that Ehrhart said haunts him even more than the killings. 'One of the guys came in and says I found this girl who will fuck us all for C rations. I thought wait, we're in the middle of this big battle and I'm gonna go and … but I'm nineteen, my buddies gonna go … I demonstrated to myself how little courage I had, I have lived with it ever since. I did it because I wasn't going to say you guys, we shouldn't do something like this.

'Even more than the killings it's the thing I'm most ashamed of when I think back … I think because my mother's a woman, my wife's a woman, my daughter's a woman.

'Somebody gets shot that's not a good thing, you see somebody running away, well they could have been a VC, but that woman, no … I had every opportunity to say no.'

In neighbouring Cambodia, the Khmer Rouge slaughtered thousands of Cambodians between 1975 and 1979. Doctors, teachers, lawyers and anyone with education were cast as traitors in the new Cambodia, which the Khmer Rouge leader Pol Pot wanted to drag back to 'year zero'. Having soft hands or wearing glasses were enough to warrant execution. In less than four years, his Maoist regime murdered two million Cambodians, a quarter of the country's population, many of them at mass-execution sites known as the 'killing fields'. Once again, much less reported, was the fact that they also raped women, who were forced to marry strangers in mass weddings without customary Buddhist rituals, and to consummate at gunpoint. Afterwards a Khmer Rouge cadre would stand outside huts to make sure the couple were having sex and they would be ordered to produce a child for the party.

Elsewhere, Turkish troops participating in the 1974 invasion and occupation of Cyprus were notorious for the widespread rape of women and girls. In one instance, twenty-five girls who reported their rapes by Turkish soldiers to Turkish officers were then raped again by those officers.

When Saddam Hussein's soldiers and secret police invaded Kuwait in 1990, they looted shops and homes, set fire to oil wells, smeared excrement across the floors of the royal palace, and scratched out the name Kuwait to try and erase the country's identity. Much less reported at the time, they also raped thousands of Kuwaiti women and Filipino housemaids.

*　*　*

'War happens to people one by one,' wrote Martha Gellhorn, in her book *The Face of War* in 1959. But it happens in different ways and where death may not be the worst thing.

The more I read, researched and talked to women, the more I wondered about everything I had learnt in history.

10

Then There Was Silence

Buenos Aires

María José Lavalle Lemos was ten and watching Disney cartoons at a friend's house in the beach resort of Mar del Plata where she lived, in the summer of 1987, when the local judge arrived and took her to his office. Teresa González de Rubén, the police sergeant she knew as Mummy, was waiting.

'Your mummy has something to tell you,' began the judge, Juan Ramos Padilla. 'I was confused and thinking about why I couldn't have stayed at my friend's for ice cream,' said María José. 'I had no idea what was going to happen.'

She was told that the people she had always known as Mummy and Daddy were not her parents. She had been born in a clandestine torture centre not a local hospital. Her real parents were among *los desaparecidos*, thousands abducted by secret police after a military junta seized power in March 1976, and taken to detention centres where most were tortured or killed. The woman who had brought her up and registered her as her own daughter had been a guard in the torture centre in Banfield where her real parents disappeared.

For María José the next three days after the revelations at Judge Padilla's office were a void. 'Everything I thought was true was not,' she told me when we met five years later. 'I didn't know who I was anymore.'

She was taken to hospital for a blood test then looked after in a local hotel while the samples were scrutinised. On the third morning the results came through, revealing with 99.88 per cent certainty that she was the lost daughter of Mónica and Gustavo Antonio Lavalle, who had been dragged from their home in Buenos Aires, along with their fifteen-month-old baby María Laura, in the early hours of 21 July 1977, and later killed. Mónica had been eight months pregnant when she was abducted.

The couple, who ran a leather workshop, were both committed members of the union of artisan workers. Mónica had been involved in student politics at university where she studied geology and Gustavo was also an activist. So popular were they in their community that a street would later be named after them.

To the military regime they were left-wing 'subversives' – among thousands of unionists, lawyers and students snatched from their homes or the streets by masked men as they left their offices, stepped off buses, or even from high schools.

Five days after the Lavalles' disappearance, an anonymous call to Gustavo's parents led to little María Laura being found abandoned, suffering from malnutrition. But nothing more was heard. To their families it was as if the earth had swallowed the couple up. All records of their fate were destroyed.

During the seven years of military dictatorship from 1976 to 1983, thousands of Argentinian men and women were 'disappeared' in what became known as the Dirty War – 13,000 according to official sources, more like 30,000 say human rights organisations.

Sports clubs, bus garages, military schools, even a hippodrome, were turned into around 600 detention centres where those picked up were taken and tortured, often to death. Corpses were disposed of in secret dumping grounds while many others were herded onto planes and hurled to their deaths in the River Plata or the Atlantic Ocean.

Around 30 per cent of those abducted were women and some, like Mónica, were pregnant. They were kept alive until they had given birth in special rooms in the detention centres then loaded onto one of the so-called death flights. The babies were either given to childless couples who had no idea of their origins, or, more chillingly, brought up by the very military or secret police who had murdered their mothers.

A couple of years after Mónica's disappearance, her mother Haydee Vallino de Lemos met a woman who had also been in the Banfield detention centre. She told her that Mónica had given birth there to a baby girl.

'I knew Mónica was pregnant when she was taken and often imagined there had been a child,' said Haydee. 'But I didn't know how to begin finding her.'

She joined other mothers of the disappeared who had begun marching in silence at 3.30 every Thursday afternoon under the palms and jacaranda trees of the Plaza de Mayo in Buenos Aires. It was a symbolic choice – the square was named after the May revolution which led the way to independence from Spain, and was overlooked by the Cathedral, headquarters of the powerful Catholic Church, and the Casa Rosada, Argentina's pink Presidential Palace from which Eva Perón once used to address adoring crowds.

The first march on 30 April 1977 started with just fourteen women. They had to march in pairs as three counted as an illegal gathering, so they walked round and round the pyramid in the centre. Inspired by the idea of wearing babies' nappies on their heads they began wearing white headscarves and embroidered them with the names of their missing children.

Initially no one listened. Many just hurried past. The Madres de Plaza de Mayo were harassed by the police and denounced by the junta as 'crazy women'. Their families begged them to stop, fearful for their safety. Three of the group's leaders were kidnapped and murdered along with two French nuns who had been helping them.

Yet the numbers of mothers marching grew. Among these were some like Haydee who had discovered that their abducted daughters had given birth. They formed a separate group called the Abuelas or Grandmothers.

Another early member was Estela Barnes de Carlotto, a former high-school principal in La Plata who made finding these stolen children – *niños desaparecidos* – her life mission and in 1989 became President of the Abuelas. She is a glamorous woman with a cloud of ash-blonde hair, immaculate make-up and stylish clothes she makes herself (her mother had been a fashion designer). We met in her small office filled with soft toys and photographs of children like María José who had been located.

'We are all over sixty and mostly just housewives with no political experience or militancy but we all share the knowledge that we have been robbed, not only of our children but our grandchildren,' she told me. 'Those predators thought we women were weak and would stay at home crying in fear but they were wrong.'

On the wall behind her was a black-and-white photograph of her stunning eldest daughter Laura standing in front of a crashing sea, resembling Joan Baez with her smoky black eyes and long hair.

Laura was a history student at La Plata university and an activist, she said, 'with a strong personality and sense of right'. She had been abducted along with her boyfriend Walmir Montoya in November 1977 and transported to a clandestine detention centre on the outskirts of La Plata. The centre was in an old radio station and nicknamed La Cacha after a cartoon witch who abducted small children.

'We were very naive then; we didn't know the military were killing people,' said Estela. Then Laura's body turned up in August

1978, face smashed by a rifle and riddled with bullets. She stopped and looked down for a moment. 'In some ways we were fortunate as most parents were not even given a body to bury.'

There was something else Estela had not known. Her daughter had been three months pregnant when she was kidnapped. Two years after her death, Estela met a female lawyer who was one of the few survivors of La Cacha. She learnt that Laura had given birth before she was murdered, to a boy she called Guido, delivered while she was handcuffed to a stretcher. 'I knew she had been at La Cacha but not what happened to the baby,' said Estela. 'He was my grandson, he had been stolen, and I was determined to find him.'

It seemed an impossible task. Laura's boyfriend Walmir had also been killed. In the early days the search mostly ran into dead ends. The grandmothers had to operate in secrecy. They were constantly followed, received threatening phone calls and sometimes were arrested. 'It was real 007 stuff,' said Estela. 'Imagine: we're looking for children whose names we don't know, nor their appearance, whereabouts or date of birth.'

They relied mostly on anonymous tip-offs – calls or letters from people who informed on neighbours acting suspiciously or who moved away suddenly. Estela's phone rang incessantly.

'There can be all sorts of clues,' said Haydee. 'It could be they worked in the regime and then appeared with a baby after showing no signs of pregnancy, or that they are dark while the child is fair, or they treat the child badly. They often act shiftily and are usually not liked because of their military connections.'

The courage and dignity of these women in the face of such suffering captured international attention and brought funds for an investigating team.

Once the military regime ended, following its ill-fated 1982 invasion of the British-held Falkland Islands, the search became easier, as did the advent of DNA testing a few years later. The new civilian President Raúl Alfonsín sanctioned the establishment of a

National Bank of Genetic Data in 1987 that contained samples of blood from all the grandparents. Once a child such as María José was found, data could then be used to prove his or her match with their legitimate family.

At the time of my first visit in 1992, they had located fifty of the children, of whom half had been returned to their biological families. Thirteen remained with their adoptive families but were in contact with their real ones; five were being fought over in court; and seven had been killed. But Estela believed the real number to be far more, given that 30,000 people disappeared.

As I talked to María José and her grandmother Haydee, I learned of the difficulty for everyone involved. To fund the search, Haydee had been forced to sell her wedding ring and television. Her house was broken into and ransacked – an act she believed was meant to threaten her – leaving her only memories and one crumpled black-and-white photograph of Mónica and Gustavo.

The other grandparents, Gustavo's parents, refused to acknowledge that the couple was missing – like many Argentinians, they tried to ignore the repression. Worse still, disapproving of Haydee's involvement with Las Abuelas, they also restricted her access to Mónica's other daughter, María Laura, whom they were bringing up.

When María José's adoptive parents heard that the Abuelas were on their trail they moved four times. María José was scarcely allowed out. But each time they moved tip-offs would come from suspicious neighbours. One of these ended up with Judge Padilla, who discovered that Teresa González had worked in the Banfield detention centre from 1976–8 where many of the missing had been taken.

At first González denied she had taken María José. But after being detained, she admitted that the girl was not hers and she had worked in the centre where she was born. 'In fact, she seemed almost relieved, as if she had discharged a ten-year lie,' said Judge

Padilla. When the judge told Haydee, she knew the age and location fitted but hardly dared hope it was her granddaughter. She was lucky. María José was only the second child to be found.

Judge Padilla was unsure what to do. 'It was all new and I didn't know what was best for the child,' he said. 'It seemed to me a terrible suffering for a child to suddenly discover that the people she assumed were her parents were not. I spoke with psychiatrists and was unconvinced. Finally, my twelve-year-old son said, "Look Daddy, truth is truth." I realised then it was better for a child to know the truth, however painful, than be lied to.'

María José was silent and withdrawn during counselling sessions with the judge and psychiatrist. 'At first I thought I'd rather go back to the people who brought me up because I was frightened. I had always been with them,' she said.

María Laura was also struggling to come to terms with the discovery that she had a younger sister. But the pair bore a striking resemblance. Eventually they were left alone together. After forty minutes of silence, the judge heard voices, then giggles, and finally whoops of laughter. The two came out holding up their arms – they had discovered each had a moon-shaped birthmark in the same place.

'It seemed as if we had always been together,' said María Laura. 'As soon as I met my granny and my sister I didn't want to go back,' said María José.

González's confession made the case simpler. Within a week of her discovery María José had chosen to live with her grandmother and her sister decided to leave their other grandparents and join her.

Haydee told me she was overjoyed, at the age of seventy-two to be living with her two granddaughters. They had both been brought up as only children and often had terrible fights but were adapting. Through the Abuelas they had access to counselling to help them adjust.

Her flat in Buenos Aires was small and she had little to spare for luxuries such as those María José had enjoyed with her abductors. 'They treated me well but it was all a lie,' she said.

'A child can be given beautiful clothes and toys but if she has been robbed of her identity she has lost the most precious thing,' said Haydee. 'It's worse than being a slave; at least a slave has history.'

Years later, at a trial in 2018 of officers who wörked at the San Justo Brigade detention centre where the couple were first held, the girls' aunt Adriana, elder sister of the murdered Gustavo, told the court how traumatic it had been for everyone. Throughout her childhood María Laura had nightmares and been 'scared of loud noises, sirens and people in uniform' while for María José 'it was hard to suddenly incorporate herself into a family of strangers and one where there was an empty space where her parents should have been'.*

For the other grandmothers the search went on. Although their demands for access to police records were denied, the initial post-military years seemed positive. Unlike other Latin American countries emerging from dictatorship, Argentina quickly started bringing to account those behind the Dirty War. The 1985 Trial of the Juntas was the world's first major trial for war crimes since Nuremberg and 833 people testified including Estela. It ended with the prosecutor declaring *Nunca más* – Never again!

But, the following year, fearing another coup, President Alfonsín declared that the country needed to look to the future, not the past, and issued the Full Stop Law to end investigations and prosecutions. This was followed by the Law of Due Obedience granting amnesty to all junior and middle-ranking officers who had

---

* 'Declararon las hermanas Lavalle Lemos', *El Teclado*, 29 August 2018.

followed orders. In 1990, his successor President Carlos Menem pardoned those who had been convicted.

The future once again seemed dark. The Mothers Organisation split, divided between those who thought they should work with the state or not. For Estela, as President of Las Abuelas, her only tool, aside from brave persistence, was publicity. She told me she hoped that when children still living with foster parents got older, they might start asking questions about their past, get suspicious and approach her office. But there were cases when children they suspected to be stolen refused to be tested.

None of the 'parents' who had to return children were willing to speak. But a friend of Teresa González said 'she wanted to give María José a chance of life. Surely it's better that she was saved and brought up in security than left to die in the camp?'

Alicia Lo Giúdice, a psychiatrist who counselled some of the returned children, told me 'they don't accept they stole the children. They say they adopted them. Maybe they even believe it.'

The grandparents were less sympathetic. Some saw it as a macabre form of war booty, others a form of brainwashing – the ultimate victory over opponents they wished to crush. 'It's as though having killed the parents, the repressors then wanted to control the destiny of the children,' said Estela.

In summing up María José's case, Judge Padilla compared the little girl to 'a pet animal which is treated with affection but with the sole objective of giving pleasure to the owner'.

The thought of torturers keeping their pregnant captives alive to give birth then taking the children was so sinister that it seemed like something from a dystopian novel. Indeed, the Canadian writer Margaret Atwood wrote that Argentina 'provided some of the real-life practices I included in *The Handmaid's Tale*'.*

---

* Foreword to Ana Correa, *Somos Belén* (Buenos Aires: Planeta Argentina, 2019).

How could people do such a thing? And what of the doctors or midwives who delivered the babies and priests who baptised them, all of whom were complicit? Yet, some repressors clearly saw what they had done in ideological terms as saving the children from communists and handing them over to a 'proper Catholic family' so they would not have the 'godless' leftist beliefs of their parents.

'Subversive parents educate their children for subversion. That has to be prevented,'* said General Ramón Juan Alberto Camps, chief of police for Buenos Aires province from 1976–8. He explained that the leaders of the Dirty War were afraid that children of the disappeared would grow up hating the army because of the fate of their parents and develop into a new generation of subversives.

Over the years the grandmothers' detective work would locate more children and help convict dozens of torturers as cases once more began to be heard.

Estela, however, still did not find hers. Her husband died, her hair turned white and her face grew lined, though she was as elegant – and forceful – as ever. At the age of eighty-four, in 2014, she still insisted she would never give up. 'There is a powerful force driving from inside – it is love that is driving us, love for our children and grandchildren.'

Among those impressed by her dedication was a music student called Ignacio Hurban who was watching TV one day, and saw her being interviewed. 'I thought what a shame: this woman has been spending her whole life searching and may never find her grandchild.'†

---

* Interview with Santiago Aroca, *Tiempo*, Madrid, 9 November 1983.

† Uki Goñi, 'A Grandmother's 36-Year Hunt for the Child Stolen by the Argentinian Junta', *Observer*, 7 June 2015.

His own parents were farm workers in the small rural town of Olavarría, 220 miles from Buenos Aires, working for a wealthy local landowner Francisco Aguilar. Sometimes, as he grew older, he thought it odd that he bore no physical resemblance to them and that he had a very different outlook on life.

Ignacio studied at a conservatory in Buenos Aires and became a jazz musician, playing piano in his own band. He married and moved back to Olavarría where he started recording albums and running a music school. Life was going well. The couple had just bought a new car and were thinking of starting a family. Then a dinner to celebrate his thirty-sixth birthday in June 2014 changed everything.

One of the guests was a local woman who was a friend of the daughter of Aguilar, the landowner. She told Ignacio's wife that baby Ignacio had appeared as if from nowhere at the height of the dictatorship.

For Ignacio it was an enormous shock. He decided to go and search for his biological family. He went to the Abuelas who arranged for a blood test and the results were sent to the National Bank of Genetic Data. In August 2014, just days after, he got the result. He was the missing grandson of Estela.

He later said he'd hoped it was her, remembering that interview he had seen years before on TV. The pair appeared at a press conference with matching cheek-to-cheek beams. Estela had become a national treasure, and it was as if the whole country shared their joy. 'I could hug my grandson,' she said. 'He doesn't look like my daughter but I know in his blood he is her. It was like I got them both back.'

Ignacio Hurban changed his name to Ignacio Montoya Carlotto. But the parents who had raised him then faced a legal process. Every time a child is found the judiciary gets involved.

'The people who raised my grandson committed a serious crime, a crime against humanity,' said Estela. 'But there are extenuating circumstances in that they were simple farm people who couldn't have children under the control of a domineering master who one day brought them a baby and said don't ask questions and never tell anyone he is not your son.'

Even having found her own grandson, Estela did not stop. Ignacio was the 114th missing child to be identified. By 2018, when she turned eighty-eight, the number had risen to 129. 'As long as I am alive, I will keep searching for the missing grandchildren and for truth and justice,' she told me.

The incubation rooms were on the top floor. Three windowless rooms, each with an operating table and a few medical instruments.

As Argentina tries to come to terms with its gruesome past, some of its torture centres have recently been turned into monuments, memorial gardens or museums. Often, like Garage Olimpo, the former terminal of the number 5 bus in Buenos Aires, these were jarringly sited in the middle of residential areas.

Largest and most notorious was ESMA, the Escuela Superior de Mecánica de la Armada (Navy Mechanics School), where 5000 people were taken and tortured. Only about 200 are known to have survived. 'It's our Auschwitz,' said an Argentinian friend.

The Navy had reluctantly left and in 2015 it had been opened as a museum. The main entrance led to a grand white colonnaded building in a large leafy campus on a busy road in the north of the city, not far from the domestic airport. Beyond was the officers' mess, the Casino de Oficiales, a four-storey cream building with dark green shutters where the torture had taken place. A glass front had been erected, printed with black-and-white faces of the victims so they wouldn't come in contact with the building. I was struck by how young they all were.

It was here that students, activists, journalists and union members were brought, their heads covered in hoods and their ankles and wrists shackled so they could only shuffle. Once inside they were assigned numbers and taken to the eaves, what was called the *Capucha* or the Hood, where they were kept lying on the floor in coffin-like indentations in the floor with their heads covered. Buckets served as toilets.

Every so often their numbers would be called and they would be escorted to the basement where the torture took place. There was little to see but plenty to imagine: the beatings, cigarette burns, electric shocks with cattle prods set to the highest setting and often to the genitals, and 'submarines' – waterboarding.

Battered and limping, the prisoners would then be brought up again, past the officers' bedrooms on the first and second floors, to the eaves. There was something particularly sinister about these men carrying out the torture in the same building as where they ate, lived and socialised, with prisoners in their hoods and shackles being brought up and down past their doors while they slept. You could even make out bloody handprints on a wall.

On Wednesdays some prisoners would then be told to get ready for the *traslados* or transfers. In fact, these were death flights. They were taken to the airport, drugged and put on military planes, then tossed from the air into the sea or River Plata. Some bodies washed up in Uruguay.

One of the truck drivers ordered to load people on planes recounted in a trial how he had asked, 'Where are you taking them?' to an officer. 'They go to the fog of nowhere – *la niebla de ninguna parte*,' came the reply.

Astonishingly, while this was going on, Argentina had held the World Cup in 1978, hosting teams and fans from Scotland to Sweden (England had failed to qualify), and winning the title. The Monumental Stadium where the final was held against Holland was only just over a mile from ESMA and officers including

Captain Jorge Acosta, the head of ESMA, celebrated the victory by kissing women they had just tortured. According to one survivor, 'Acosta entered the room, shouting we won, we won!'*

Now at least, unlike in most places I had been, justice was being served. In a hall on the ground floor a series of projections flashed up on the walls with the faces and names of convicted perpetrators – *Los Condenados*.

The amnesty laws were struck down by the Supreme Court in 2005 at the urging of President Néstor Kirchner. This meant prosecutions of those who carried out the murderous repression could again start.

Between 2006 and 2018, 3010 military officers were charged with crimes against humanity. Trials involving those in ESMA had so many perpetrators and victims that they were known as mega-trials. The third mega-trial ran from 2012–17 and was the largest trial in Argentine history, with 54 people standing trial for crimes against 789 victims. By 2019, 862 people had been convicted, 530 had died and 715 were still on trial. Those jailed included pilots of the death flights. At each trial parents of the missing came bearing blown-up black-and-white photographs of their lost sons and daughters. When sentences were declared, crowds cheered.

Among the survivors of ESMA was Graciela García Romero. With brown eyes and feathery brown hair, dressed in black jeans and boots and a blue puffer jacket, she looked younger than the late sixties I knew her to be, and managed to seem both feisty and wounded. In November 2018 she came to meet me at a café in my hotel on Calle San Martín at 3 p.m. on a Friday afternoon.

---

* Testimony from Graciela Daleo in ESMA 2 trial, case 1270, 29 April 2010.

Before we started talking, she took me outside. 'Look,' she said. Two doors down, outside number 700, she stopped at a blue door next to the entrance to the Teatro Payró. 'This is where I was kidnapped,' she said. 'It was also 3 p.m. on a Friday.

'It was 15 October 1976 and I was walking with my friend Diana Garcia when suddenly I felt arms around my neck and body. I shouted out but no one did anything. Six or seven men in plain clothes with pistols had grabbed us and dragged us onto the main street, Avenida Córdoba. They threw me into a white car and took me to ESMA. I never saw Diana again.'

I stared at her. Of all the places in Buenos Aires I could have asked her to come, what a horrible coincidence.

A young Graciela before her abduction

She laughed off my apologies and we went back in and ordered cappuccinos. She told me she had just read Nadia Murad's book about being a Yazidi sex slave. 'I realised that's what happened to us,' she said. 'We too were sex slaves.'

She began to tell me her story. Nicknamed *la Negrita*, Graciela had been a militant with the Montoneros, a leftist urban guerrilla group, initially created to bring back the exiled former President Juan Perón. In the early 1970s when he disowned them, they focused on attacking international business interests, bombing the Buenos Aires Sheraton, and kidnapping executives – they still retain the record for the world's highest ransom, $60 million for the Born brothers. When the military seized power, the Montoneros switched to armed struggle to try to overthrow the regime.

Graciela had joined the movement through a boyfriend and was provided a pistol, though she never used it. She was in her mid-twenties when she was picked up by the secret police and taken to ESMA. There she was hooded and taken to the *Capucha* where they were guarded by what she calls the *Verdes*, after the colour of their uniform and because they were young students at the college. 'We had to pee and defecate into a foul-smelling bucket and if we managed to use the real bathroom there was always one of the Verdes watching, commenting on our bodies.'

She was taken to the basement where there were a number of cells off a passageway they referred to as 'the Avenue of Happiness'. There she was interrogated, stripped naked and slapped in the face. Sometimes she was tied to a stretcher and they carried out a mock execution. It was no empty threat – piles of inert bodies were stacked up on the floor.

Initially they told her she might be sent to a 'rehab farm' in the south. Then she learnt of the *traslados*. 'We realised when people were taken on those flights, their shoes were left behind. Every Wednesday from early in the day you could feel the tension as people waited to see who would be taken, whose number would be called.'

After a couple of weeks, she was taken out one evening to a farmhouse with some other female prisoners. 'A group of naval officers were sitting at a table eating proper food,' she recalled. 'All we got at ESMA was stale bread, occasional rotten meat and boiled maté, so we all took the opportunity to eat. Then this captain came down and joined us who called himself Ariada and who started talking about western Christian civilisation, about Aristotle and Plato. I didn't open my mouth as I didn't know what I was doing there. Then they played records. After that the man who called himself Ariada asked each officer, "Which girl do you prefer?" It felt like they were playing with us.'

Later, she would discover he was Captain Jorge Eduardo Acosta, the intelligence officer who ran ESMA, and was known as *El Tigre*, the Tiger. All the officers referred to each other by animal nicknames like Crow, Piranha and Puma.

Back in ESMA she was moved to what they called a *camarote*, a small cubicle with its windows blocked off, sharing with another female prisoner.

Several times she was visited by a drunken officer called Antonio Pernías, who was known as the Rat. Once he placed a freshly baked croissant on her bed, demanding a blow job in return. 'I managed to fend him off but it was a warning of what was to come,' she said.

One day she was taken out with three other female prisoners to meet Acosta's chief advisor, Francis Whamond, a retired naval captain. 'What toiletries do you want?' he asked. 'We didn't understand. He said we had to bathe so did we want shampoo, soap and deodorant? We thought he had gone mad. But in fact, they were preparing us for them.

'After we had washed, he took the four of us downstairs. I was taken to Acosta's office. It was dim light. He was wearing a light-blue T-shirt and had some cake in front of him.

'He asked me if I wanted a slice and I said yes. I was crazy hungry. He talked and talked. Then he said, "Tomorrow, I'm going to get you out of here."

'The next day he put me in a car and I was taken to an apartment they used for these things. The building was in Calle Olleros in an elegant area of Belgrano, and there was no power so he was annoyed as there were many floors. He kept saying, "Why is there no light?" I took advantage and said I was unwell. He said it doesn't matter and we started walking up maybe eight or ten flights. Finally, we got to the flat which was almost empty apart from a double bed.

'The apartment was used by naval officers for sex and they called it the Guadalcanal after a famous battle in World War Two.

'That was the first of many times they took me to that building or another one. They would leave me whole weekends there locked in, waiting for Acosta to come and rape me. If I tried to resist he would threaten to put me on one of the *traslados*.'

Back at ESMA, she began to dread the words '544 downstairs!'

'Every time a guard said it, I shrank inside,' she said. 544 was the number assigned to her and meant she would be taken for one of the officers to come and rape her.

In some ways Acosta treated her as his girlfriend. 'He brought clothes and made me dress up and put on make-up and took me to one of the best restaurants in the city for dinner. He took me dancing at a famous nightclub.

'I found him repellent,' she said. 'He was in his mid-thirties, he had light eyes, a high voice and weak lower lip and claimed he spoke to Jesus every night.'

One night he even took her to see her family. 'It was late, they were in their pyjamas. Everyone hugged me and cried. Acosta sat next to me and said the military were defenders of the western world and Christianity and he had set out to rescue young people like me and my family needed to cooperate with this rehabilitation. He asked my two sisters what they were doing. One was a lawyer, the other a philosophy student at the university. He asked her why are you going to that faculty of "zurdos" [lefties]?

'Later, he told my father they had to move house and summoned my lawyer sister to ESMA. He told her, "It's easy to enter this place but difficult to leave."

'What they did to us was perverse. It was psychological and biological destruction. We were slaves who could be killed any time. After two years in that situation I just wanted to die in that camarote.'

The only escape was sleep. 'Some compañeras when they were brought back from the apartments would get sleeping tablets from the nurse and sleep all day. Because when you opened your eyes you would again see the nightmare.' But Graciela suffered insomnia.

In December 1978, she was one of a group of women released. But it was what was called *libertad vigilada* – she was forced to work at the Foreign Ministry, where they could keep their eye on her and to return to ESMA at night. She would be taken there by car by the Verdes.

Each Wednesday as people were summoned for the death flights, she waited to hear her number. 'A group of intelligence officers would choose the fates of those they had taken, putting their thumbs up or down at different names as if we were gladiators in Roman times.'

As more and more women were killed, including ones with whom she had shared her camarote, she asked Acosta why she had been saved and not the others. 'Because Jesus said so,' he told her.

After a while she was moved on to do press work with another detainee and later, during the Falklands war, at the ministry of social welfare. Only after that, was she finally released.

Why didn't she escape, I wondered, when she was working at those places?

'We had no papers so we couldn't leave,' she said. 'And I was fearful for my family, my two other sisters. Acosta knew all about them.

'During that time, they twice took me to see Acosta. The last time I dared tell him I didn't want to see him anymore. I didn't care if he killed me.'

'Be careful with women, Negrita,' he replied. 'They can hurt.'

She had not told him she was in a same-sex relationship. 'It was clear then he was tapping my phone.'

For years afterwards, Graciela said nothing about what she had been through. 'We had been raped but we were accused of being collaborators, as if I had been the girlfriend of Acosta. We were like ticking timebombs. No one wanted to associate with us.'

It was, she said, 'the start of thirty years of pain'.

Graciela in 2018 outside the door where she was abducted in 1976

She began work as a photographer and archivist but for a long time she lived in isolation. 'I didn't want to see any of my friends,' she said. 'I slept with the light on.'

Eventually a colleague recommended she went to a group that met every Wednesday to compile lists of people seen at ESMA to try and document the disappeared. 'The day after I was always sick,' she said.

I was astonished by Graciela's story. At neither Olimpo or ESMA was there any mention of specific treatment of women, apart from the birthing. Yet the way she described it, rape of women prisoners and keeping them in what was described as 'forceful co-existence' was widespread. 'I think all the women in ESMA were raped,' she said.

While the search for the missing by the mothers and grand-mothers like Estela became a heroic symbol of resistance in the new democracy, women like Graciela who had been forced to sleep with their torturers were seen as taboo.

To try to understand, and learn what efforts were being made to try and get justice, I met Lorena Balardini, a sociologist who was part of a team looking at sexual violence cases at the Office of the Prosecutor General that had been set up in 2014. Prior to that she had been at the Centre for Legal and Social Studies (CELS) in the legal team pursuing cases against the dictatorship.

'The first time I heard about rape in the detention centres was in 2007 while attending the first ESMA trial,' she said.

That first trial was very short with just one defendant, a coast-guard officer Héctor Febres, accused of mass torture and execu-tions of the new mothers. In ESMA he had been known as Gordo Selva – Fat Jungle – because of his extreme torture methods. The night before sentencing, he was found dead in his cell of apparent cyanide poisoning – following a dinner with his wife and adult children. There were rumours he had been killed by the military to silence him.

Lorena told me how during the trial she and her boss Caroline Varsky, a well-known human rights lawyer, had watched a woman called Josefa Prada testify about her time in ESMA. 'She was being very emotional and the prosecutor was asking about fellow captives and this victim was trying to talk about how she felt. At one point she said I remember that day because it was the day I was raped, and she talked about how she felt destroyed inside.

'We were all very shocked – we'd never heard anything like it. Then the prosecutor, who was female, just said, "Okay", and went on to the next question.

'Caroline was very angry and went to speak to the victim. We decided we needed to do something because the women were talking and the state officials were not listening. We wanted to help them be heard. So we started talking to the women. The excuse had been that women were not talking about it but this wasn't true – when you had conversations with them, they were talking about it and wanted to do something.'

In fact, they realised, women had been speaking up about this from the very start – it was just that no one was listening. 'In the Juntas Trial in 1985 in which nine commanders were tried, there was a victim who said I was raped, and the prosecutor just ignored this. He literally said, "Don't lose the wood for the trees. We need to focus on the torture and murder."'

That woman was Elena Alfaro who had fled to Paris where I went to see her. She was two months pregnant when armed men stormed into her house in Buenos Aires around midnight on 19 April 1977, just a few days before her twenty-fifth birthday, and dragged her from her bed.

Her partner Luis Fabbri, with whom she shared the house, had been picked up on the street a few hours earlier. The couple had met when she was studying orthodontics and he was studying law, and it was because of his activism they were picked up. He worked in the local council where he was a journalist and union representative.

'They looted the house and threw me to the floor of their vehicle, bound my eyes and took me to what they called an infirmary. But it was a series of torture cells and I could hear the screams and groans of others who I would get to know.

'They took me to another room, tied my hands and feet to a table with a metal frame they called the grill where they tortured me with a cattle prod, ignoring my cries that I was pregnant and they would kill my son.

'My partner was in the adjoining room and they wanted him to hear. Later they brought him to me and he had been tortured so badly he was almost destroyed.'

They were in a clandestine detention centre known as El Vesubio, a farm outside Buenos Aires. Its code name Empresa El Vesubio – the Vesuvio Company – was a reference to the volcanic forces they would unleash on detainees. Conditions were horrendous. 'We were kept in *cuchas* or kennels, small brick-walled rooms,' she recalled.

She saw her husband a few more times, then on 23 May he was one of sixteen transferred, taken to a house in Buenos Aires and shot dead.

For Elena the nightmare was just beginning. A beautiful woman who had once been voted Reina del Trigo – Queen of the Cornfields – in La Pampa, she caught the eye of the camp commander Durán Sáenz. On a national holiday, 20 June, he took her to his room and raped her. 'He left me in his room, naked, tied to the bed with no food and drink [until the following night],' she later testified. 'I was four months pregnant and my pregnancy was obvious. It was a sadistic thing raping pregnant women … We women were used for nothing other than men's pleasure and sin like a barbaric rite.

'I became the property of Durán Sáenz,' she added. 'It's important to use the right words. I didn't have a "sexual relationship" with him. To have sex with someone implies consent.'

Rape was common at El Vesubio, she said. She was also raped by Lieutenant Colonel Franco Luque, a notorious drunk and womaniser. Guards regularly groped female prisoners and kept a guinea pig which they would put between the legs of women they had tied to poles and stripped naked.

When her son was born in November 1977, she begged to keep him. Shortly after, the commander released them both to live with her aunt in La Plata but her movements were controlled. 'They were watching me the whole time,' she said. Sáenz continued to visit her and when he moved to the US, his brother then came and raped her.

Eventually, in March 1982, Elena fled to Paris with her son. 'I pretended we were going on holiday to Europe to get out. It was very hard, I spoke no French. But I didn't want to go to Spain because of Franco.'

She learnt French and studied medical research as well as becoming a women's rights activist. By the time I met her in 2018 she was visiting schools, to talk about her experience.

In the 1985 trial, she testified in front of six judges, describing her own rape and that of six women. Three were also kept in Sáenz's harem and later disappeared, one a seventeen-year-old schoolgirl. 'We as women were in a situation where we were totally at the mercy of any force or any man who happened to be there,' she said. 'To be raped there was a very common thing.'

Yet the presiding judge Dr Jorge Valerga Aráoz made no comment. Instead, he asked her, 'Did you notice any foreigners among the detainees in El Vesubio?'

Defence lawyers portrayed her as promiscuous and a traitor. People whispered she had survived because she had gone to bed with the military. 'It was like I'd thrown a stone at the whole thing,

centuries and centuries of patriarchy,' she told me. 'No one listened
to me. Instead they used it to denounce and defame me. The military blackened my name.'

But it wasn't just the military. She also blamed the Abuelas.
'They want it to be all about them – for them it became a
business.'

As Caroline Varsky and Lorena started collecting testimonies,
they soon realised that these were not isolated cases. They heard
of one commander who kept a harem and raped them daily. Some
women were raped after torture when they could hardly walk.
There were also many cases of sexual slavery as happened with
Graciela and Elena.

Many women had not come forward because they did not want
their families to know what had happened or were worried about
being cast as a traitor even though what had happened to them
was humiliating and morally degrading and if they had refused to
subject themselves to the officers, they would have been killed.

'We don't know how many victims there are of state terrorism
and don't know the exact number who suffered sexual violence,
but we discovered tens of victims in each detention centre,' said
Lorena. 'We came to the conclusion this was something that
happened all over the country in detention centres, in houses, in
military facilities.

'So, we contested the view from the 1980s that the sexual
violence was just something that happened, that the men just lost
their minds because the girls were so beautiful. Instead, like the
stealing of babies, this was part of a systematic plan to destroy the
humanity of the victim, another technique like torture but different in its essence.

'It was clear to us that if a woman said she suffered sexual
violence then the charge should be that, not just part of the

torture. We fought a lot for these crimes to be regarded as independent.'

But they found it was not easy to change this attitude. Where they had come forward, rape victims were sometimes not believed. So many years had passed there was no physical evidence in most cases. Often the identity of the perpetrator was not known.

'This was also true of torture and in that case the prosecutor would blame the head of the detention centre or chain of command,' said Lorena. 'But with rape they wouldn't do that as they said it wasn't the commander of the centre who had the desire.'

Among the women Lorena and Caroline met as they collected testimonies was Graciela, at one of the weekly meetings on ESMA. They asked her if she would be prepared to press charges against Captain Jorge Acosta.

She agreed, testifying in 2007, then again in the second ESMA trial which began in 2009. With eighty-six cases, this was much larger than the first one. Worried that witnesses and perpetrators would die off, while survivors were having to testify over and over again in different trials and so being repeatedly traumatised, human rights groups had been pressing for one big trial to show the systematic nature of the repression.

Among the accused was Acosta. On 23 June 2009, the judge charged Acosta with rape – the first time that the rape of a detainee had been deemed an independent crime. Federal judge Sergio Torres declared, 'Sexual subjugations were not isolated cases but performed systematically as part of the clandestine plan of repression and extermination.'

Another officer at ESMA, Captain Raúl Scheller, known as the Penguin, told investigators that Acosta had ordered men to seize and rape female prisoners.

Acosta was unapologetic. 'Human rights violations are unavoidable during war,' he said.

Graciela told the court, 'All these days before coming to testify, I thought over time it had diminished but I see no. Reliving all these years does not diminish the experience but makes it ever more terrible, serious and unforgivable.'

The upper chamber decided, however, that what happened to Graciela wasn't rape but torture. Though Acosta and eleven other death squad members from ESMA were eventually given life sentences in October 2011, these were for killing and torture not rape.*

Lorena was horrified. 'I think Graciela should be proud of what she did but in terms of what happened legally it was a failure. We encouraged her to go to court and make a claim and she testified many times.'

During the trial so many witnesses had testified about rape and sexual assault that the lawyers' closing arguments included a special chapter on sexual violence which Lorena compiled.

'We then asked the lower court to take all these testimonies to start a new case on sexual violence,' she said. 'That was a nightmare, it took like four years – if I'm a victim and have given testimony that's very hard, I shouldn't have to go again and ask for trials.'

Despite the court's refusal to include rape charges in her case, Graciela told me she was glad she testified. 'Talking to the judges was the beginning of my rehabilitation,' she said. 'For so many years society did not want to listen. Also, we had been defamed because we had survived and were seen as in a situation of privilege even if we didn't choose it. But now we could tell our side of

---

* In July 2012 Acosta received a further thirty years for baby snatching and in November 2017 a further life sentence for the death flights. As of December 2019 he remains in jail.

the story. The right word for what we went through is terror. I am alive by accident. I will always carry this mark. But seeing the life sentences at long last, after all they did to us, truly, it gives you your life back.'

She was still in therapy, but happy in a relationship, and just before we met had been on a trip to Japan with two other survivors, where she had met some of the surviving comfort women from the Second World War and shared experiences. 'They want to break down decades of imperial silence and get concrete judicial recourse,' she said.

Reading about what had happened to the Yazidis had brought it all back. 'They were in a desert in Iraq, we were in one of Latin America's most important cities, but it was the same. They kidnapped me and kept me in the same clandestine state as those girls, and it was the same anguish for the families whose daughters were missing.'

The first conviction for sexual violence during Argentina's dictatorship came in 2010, some thirty-three years after the crime was committed.

The perpetrator was a former air-force sergeant, Gregorio Rafael Molina, who had been in charge of a torture centre known as La Cueva, the Rathole, in a disused radar station on an air-force base in Mar del Plata.

With his deep voice and moustache, he fancied himself as the actor Charles Bronson and demanded to be known by that name. He called his harem 'Charlie's Angels' after the popular TV series, but to them he was known as the Toad because of his pockmarked skin.

Accusations of what he had done to women first emerged in the Trial of the Juntas and were again repeated in the Truth Commission but ignored.

Among his victims was Marta García Candeloro, a psychologist, who was kidnapped on 13 June 1977 in the city of Neuquén in western Argentina, along with her husband Dr Jorge Candeloro, a well-known labour lawyer.

The couple were flown to the base in Mar del Plata where she later described being frogmarched through a door in a grass mound, down twenty or thirty concrete steps, to hear the sound of large metal doors slamming, then a hubbub of people and echoing voices.

This was the large underground camp over which Molina reigned, raping almost every woman who came through.

Marta recalled: 'One of the men asked me, "Oh, so you're a psychologist. A whore like all shrinks. Here, you'll learn what's good for you," and he set about punching me in the stomach. Hell began there …'

In the Trial of the Juntas, she spoke of the last time she ever heard her husband's voice, fifteen days after their abduction. 'They always took him first then me. This time they did the opposite. In the middle of my interrogation they brought in my husband, telling him if he wouldn't talk, they would kill me. They began to apply electric shocks to me so he would hear my cries and he called out to me, "My love, I love you, I never dreamt they would bring you to this." This enraged them. The last words were cut short as they were applying the electric prod to him. They untied me and threw me into my cell. His interrogation was never-ending. All at once there was a single piercing heart-rending shriek. It still resounds in my ears. I will never be able to forget it. It was his last cry. Then there was silence.'

She had testified for eight hours but not talked of rape. 'Among all the horror in the concentration camps, rape seemed secondary,' she later explained. 'With my husband's death, with everything that happened in there, all the horror, rape was displaced.'

When the justice process reopened in 2007, this time she and another survivor pressed charges for rape. Initially the court dismissed the charge but the appeals court of Mar del Plata over-turned that decision and added the rape charges, and three years later it came to court.

Marta's harrowing account of being raped by Molina three times in 1977 had everyone in tears, including the judges, one of whom was a woman. In three hours of testimony Marta told how he came to her drunk, after she emerged from a torture session, and said 'after so much pain I'm going to give you pleasure'.

He put his Colt 45 pistol on her breasts, mixing the blood from the wounds inflicted by torture with his semen. 'It was hard to understand, even harder to forget,' she said.

In June 2010 he was sentenced to life for several crimes includ-ing two killings, thirty-six kidnaps and torture, five counts of aggravated rape and one of attempted rape of two victims – he died in prison hospital in July 2012. As the first ruling in Argentina which considered rape a crime against humanity, it opened the field for more prosecutions. But many other chambers decided it wasn't correct to change charges of torture to those of sexual violence.

By 2019 there had been twenty-six rulings on sexual violence. In the fourth ESMA mega-trial which began in 2018 with nine officers accused of crimes against 936 victims, prosecutors asked that crimes of sexual violence be considered separately.

More and more women were coming forward. 'Many decided to talk in the last few years because they felt safe – before they were worried or in denial or forced by their families to be silent,' said Lorena. 'Now we have many testimonies in trials all over the coun-try mentioning sexual crimes.'

There were also men coming forward to talk of being sexually abused.

There were still problems. 'First the victim herself has to say I want prosecution for sexual violence and many don't know that

– it's absurd. They believe if they are telling a state officer in a case, the prosecutor will do something. Then there is still the idea that a sexual crime is something a perpetrator commits because he has a sexual desire or need. The problem wasn't that our courts don't have the tools, but the judge was saying there was a systematic plan of repression of political opponents and rape wasn't part of that.

'It's important for the women themselves that the sexual violence is recognised,' she added. 'From the very beginning when I heard Josefa speaking in the trial in 2007, it was clear it was different to torture, it didn't feel the same. Women would say to us when I was beaten, it hurt, I felt very small, but when they raped me, they destroyed me: it was as if they had killed something.'

She had another point, which was something I too had found unsettling. 'In Argentina these women victims were mostly middle-class, educated and urban with access to lawyers and therapists, privileged women who had jobs and could fight, but they still don't get justice so there is something really, really wrong about the system.

'It's not like poor rural women who don't even have water – these are women who can buy all their water bottled in supermarkets but still can't get justice. Look at Graciela, she had a gun, she was a strong political activist, she was raped systematically by a man and tells the court, yet the court decided she wasn't raped, she was tortured? If we can't achieve justice, what hope is there for women in less developed parts of the world?'

On my last night in Buenos Aires I went to the grand Beaux-Arts-style Post Office Tower which had been converted into a cavernous cultural centre. There I joined a public tango lesson on the lower ground floor. Dozens of couples of all ages were dancing under a forest of coloured bunting hanging from the ceiling. Can there be a more passionate dance on earth? It took me a while to build the nerve to join in. As I watched the women flung around by the men, heads tossed back and forth, legs kicking up then tangling round each other, it seemed a portrait of the machismo of this country.

In some of the couples, however, women were leading men. That afternoon I had taken part in a roundtable with an impressive group of female journalists. Everyone was talking about the recent campaign to legalise abortion. It was illegal in Argentina except in the case of rape or where the mother's life was in danger, and there were an estimated 345,000 clandestine abortions a year. The lower house had passed the bill that summer but the Senate had rejected it so they were trying again.

Every week a sea of women gathered outside parliament, and in cities round the country, demanding the right to choice. They also highlighted Argentina's shocking rate of femicide, which saw one woman killed every thirty hours on average – something many blamed on the country's widespread impunity.

All were wearing green headscarves in homage to the Mothers and Grandmothers of the Plaza de Mayo. I noticed that some of the women I had been chatting to, and at the tango class, had green handkerchiefs tied to their bags. Headscarves had become so symbolic that there was even a word for it – *pañuelización.*

The grandmothers had not given up their struggle. Then in their eighties and nineties, some were in wheelchairs, some with walking frames or sticks, but every Thursday at 3.30 p.m., they still walked round and round Plaza de Mayo, wearing headscarves embroidered with names and holding placards with faded photographs of young men and women. In almost forty-two years, they had never missed a week.

11

The Beekeeper of Aleppo

Dohuk, Northern Iraq

I had never thought of beekeeping as anything to do with women's rights or derring-do until I met Abdullah Shrim.

A slight grey-haired man of forty-three in metal-rimmed glasses and crumpled grey suit, he perched owl-like on the edge of the sofa in the dim lounge of the Dilshad Palace hotel, between a garish statue of Long John Silver and a fish tank encrusted with dirt.

Abdullah Shrim and his bees before ISIS

Nothing about his dress or demeanour suggested the word hero. Indeed, he was the sort of person you wouldn't notice on the street. Yet when I went to camps in northern Iraq in early 2018 to meet Yazidi girls who had managed to escape from their ISIS tormentors, and when I asked who had helped rescue them, one after another said, Shrim.

'Before ISIS came I was a beekeeper and trader, keeping my hives in Sinjar and selling my honey in Aleppo,' he told me. 'Women growing up in these areas don't have rights – when someone has a son in the Middle East there are parties and songs and people bring sweets, but if it's a daughter they don't do anything and when she grows up and gets married she doesn't have any ideas or opinions, just what her family says.

'But while I was raising the bees and saw how well their society functioned with a Queen Bee at the centre, I wondered why our world should be different. So I began researching different countries in the world where women are rulers. And when ISIS came and killed and stole our women, I decided to do something.'

Those captured included fifty-six members of his own family. Yet he insisted, 'It wasn't because of my family I got involved. It really was because of the bees. Everything was destroyed in Sinjar and now I just have a few hives, but when I am with the bees it lifts my mood.'

The first girl he rescued, back on 27 October 2014, was his niece. 'She was being held by a man in Raqqa and she called me. I got in touch with some of the traders I used to work with and asked how I could get her out.

'They told me the only way is through cigarette smugglers. Under ISIS, cigarettes were haram or forbidden but they still wanted them. We Yazidis were also haram to them. So, the traders said, if you want to get them out, you have to do it like cigarettes. But girls will be more expensive.

'I'd never done anything like this before, never worked with smugglers or crossed borders illegally so I was terrified.'

Through his trading network he found a Kurdish driver in the area of his niece who managed to pick her up at a time her captor was praying and take her to the border. 'This gave me confidence it could be done,' he said. By the time I met him, three and a half years later, he had rescued 367 women and girls from the clutches of the Caliphate.

He was helped by the fact that, surprisingly, many of the kidnapped Yazidis had managed to keep their phones and had been able to keep in touch with their families. But over time that changed, said Shrim. 'Rescues became more complicated as Kurds left ISIS areas and I had to use Arab drivers. They also were charging more, from $1000 to as much as $40,000.

'For each rescue I develop a plan with my son who is an engineer,' he explained. 'In one case where eight Yazidi women and children were in a heavily guarded house, we sent in coffins and a funeral car, pretending two of their children had died and needed to be buried.'

That almost led to disaster when ISIS guards insisted they would go along and dig the graves. 'I thought the children were going to be buried alive,' he said. 'We managed to get them all out when the men went for their tools.'

The hardest part was getting the girls out of the house – if they were caught trying to escape, they would be tortured. Often he rented safe houses where contacts could watch comings and goings, or to which he could move the girls so they would not be passing through checkpoints when the alarm was raised. He even rented a bakery to deliver bread as a way to check if the girls were still in houses.

'We tried so many things,' he said. 'We got women to distribute clothes to other women, as then they could enter the house and see their faces uncovered.'

It was dangerous work. Five men and a young woman working with the network in Syria were executed by ISIS after being caught. Shrim received frequent threats. 'They sent me a photo of me here in Dohuk to say we can kill you wherever we want. One girl I rescued told me ISIS have your picture and say we're going to kill him whenever we see him.'

He shrugged. 'My life is not more important than the tears of my niece or the other girls I have liberated.'

Since the Caliphate started crumbling in 2017 and ISIS lost control of Mosul then Raqqa, it had actually got harder to get girls out, as many had been moved to Turkey where, he said, authorities were refusing to cooperate. Some were thought to have been sold on to prostitution rings in Europe. Shrim believed perhaps a thousand were still alive but many were dead.

The last girl he had freed was another niece, Khitab, abducted when she was only nine. He had got her out just three days before we met, from the northern Syrian city of Idlib where she was being held by Jabhat al-Nusra, the Islamist group affiliated to al Qaeda. 'She was sold to so many men. She was tortured,' he says, shaking his head.

He had tried to rescue her before using an ambulance but on the way out they were stopped and Khitab recaptured. 'They tortured her so many times after that,' he said.

This time she was being held near Idlib General Hospital so he instructed her to go there when her captor went out for Friday prayers and stand outside holding a white bag. 'I told her to wait for a man to come and say, "I am Abdullah."'

He and his wife were waiting in a minibus across the border. He showed me a photograph on his phone of them all happily reunited.

Shrim longed for the days when he and his wife could go back to Sinjar and his quiet life of keeping bees. Throughout our meeting his phone did not stop buzzing. Every time he rescued someone, the families of those still missing would contact him to see if the new arrival had any fresh information about other girls. He kept names and dates and photos of all the girls. 'I will keep helping to free women and children as long as I can,' he said.

He was not the only Yazidi who had given up waiting for the world to help and decided to take things into their own hands. There was a kind of underground railroad involving at least three other groups including Shaker Jeffrey, the young Yazidi who had translated for me in Germany.

Another evening I met Khaleel al-Dakhi and his wife, Ameena Saeed. Khaleel was a lawyer and Ameena had been one of two Yazidi MPs in the Iraqi parliament until she quit in protest in 2014 at the failure to protect her people.

They both looked exhausted – not only did they have a young baby, but they were up till late every night trying to track down the missing. Khaleel took three phones from his pocket and laid them on the table.

'At the beginning we just collected names, ages and villages of the kidnapped,' he explained. 'We were a group of volunteers – lawyers, policemen, a member of the Yazidi prince's family – and our plan was to document who was missing and what we knew about them, because this thing seemed bigger than us and we thought there would be some government somewhere who would help these girls be rescued.

'We gave the information to the Iraqi government, the Kurdish authorities, embassies, the US military, but no one did anything. After a month we had no answer except for Barzani's office [the Kurdish Prime Minister] which told us they would provide some funds. So we realised we would have to do it ourselves.'

The couple had then rescued 265 girls though one rescue went tragically awry in May 2015. They were trying to bring out a big group so had to leave one lot of thirteen in a safe house overnight while they escorted out the first group. But the first group got lost trying to walk to a peshmerga checkpoint in the dark, and by the time he got back to the second group, one girl had panicked and left. She was caught by ISIS and told them where the others were. 'Only one of those has been found,' said Khaleel. 'The rest are missing or killed.'

Despite the danger and difficulties, they refused to give up. The couple had two daughters of their own, an eight-year-old and a baby of five months. 'I have a dream that my daughters be educated and have a future,' said Khaleel. 'These families have the same dreams. These girls hadn't done anything wrong and deserve a future.'

While many saw rescuers like Ameena, Khaleel and Shrim as heroes, comparing them to the underground resistance in the war, others accused them of profiting or argued that the money paid helped finance ISIS. Shrim looked mortified at the idea he might profit and insisted he had never paid ISIS. Instead he asked, 'If it was your mother or daughter and you could get them back from this horror by paying $10,000 wouldn't you?'

Among those who owed her life to Shrim was Turko, a feisty woman living with her five children in one of a few tents dotted on a stretch of wasteland outside a Yazidi camp in Khanke, about forty-five minutes from the Kurdish city of Dohuk.

When Iraqi Prime Minister Haider al-Abadi announced in December 2017 that ISIS had been driven out of Iraq and the war was over, I had presumed that the Yazidis would be returning to their beloved home of Sinjar. Instead, 350,000 of them – about 80 per cent of the population – were still in camps across northern Iraq. It was a bleak life behind a wire fence, muddy fields lined with row after row of white tubular tents that were too cold in the winter and too hot in the summer. Occasionally, one of the stoves would blow over and fire would sweep through, destroying what few possessions they had.

Khanke camp was home to more than 16,000 Yazidis. Turko preferred to live outside, she said, because the camp with all its barbed wire felt like a prison. Her tent was surprisingly cosy, with a double bed, a TV, a gas heater to keep out the chill, and piles of bright pink quilts and cushions – but it was still a tent far from home.

She sat on a cushion on the floor, cradling two adorable five-month-old twins, her apple-cheeked face framed by a cascade of glossy auburn hair, and she began her story.

'My husband and brother had been away working in Kurdistan when ISIS fighters came into our village Herdan in August 2014

and took all us young women. They took me and our three daughters who were then three, six and eight and moved us from place to place.

'We ended up in Raqqa, captives of a Saudi ISIS commander called Haider who forced the girls to study Koran. He was forcing me to have sex with him, hurting me, and I feared he would do the same to my girls.'

She tried to escape but the house was guarded. 'He told me, "If you don't stop trying to run away, I will take your daughters." Anyone who tried to run away he would electrocute.

'ISIS was cutting off heads and he made us go and watch, even the children. They would hang the headless corpses for days and we would pass them on the way to the mosque and back.

'One night when he was forcing himself on me, I told him, "One day you will all be finished." He threw me and my daughters in a filthy cellar for three months where we could not wash and were given little food.

'I didn't care about myself; if it was just me I would have committed suicide,' she said, crying. 'But I was with my daughters. When we got out we were in such a bad state they took us to hospital. We had typhoid.'

Later, back with her Saudi captor, Turko concluded there was no hope. 'All that torture and rape – death was better for us,' she said. 'I tried to kill us all, I poured fuel over us and was about to set fire but one of my daughters stopped me.'

Sometime after that, in November 2016, the Saudi was away in Mosul fighting the Iraqi forces which had launched a campaign to recapture the city. 'He had left me some money for food so I paid a Syrian woman to borrow her ID, put on a niqab like an ISIS wife, then went to an office which had Wi-Fi and sent a WhatsApp to my brother. It was very dangerous. If they'd caught me they would have burnt me alive in a big cage but I was desperate because of my daughters.'

Her brother called Shrim and gave him Turko's location and personal information such as her date of birth as proof of life. Shrim told him to tell their mother to collect money – $32,000 – for Turko and her daughters from the kidnap office set up by the Kurdish government.

He then put Turko in touch with an Arab smuggler. She explained where the house was, near a downed plane, and when the Saudi usually went out. One day, when an airstrike began, the smuggler told her it was their chance to run.

But her daughters didn't want to leave. 'They had been brainwashed, particularly the eldest Rehan,' she said. 'On our way to escape she was screaming, "Don't take us back to the infidels!" They were all angry and complaining we're not praying or fasting so we won't go to Paradise.'

Once outside Raqqa, Turko and the girls had to walk for four days, occasionally hiding among reeds to rest, with no food or drink, except once when they came across a water tank. At one point Turko tripped and hurt her ankle so the smuggler carried her. 'It was very scary, always thinking we would be captured,' she said.

Finally, they came to a Kurdish village in Kobane in northern Syria and they were safe. 'I shouted whoo-hoo!' she laughed. 'I was super happy.'

The next morning they woke at dawn and prostrated themselves to pray like Muslims. One of the other Yazidis asked, 'What are you doing? You're not in the Islamic State anymore!'

'Look at us!' said Turko. She showed me a video on her phone of her and her three daughters by a river bank all clad in black hijab.

After two and a half years in captivity, coming back had not been easy. 'I was so happy to see my husband but also not happy because of what had happened and not knowing if he would accept me,' she said. 'It's been over one year now and still I can't look at him normally.'

Her daughters were so indoctrinated that they regarded their fellow Yazidis as infidels. 'The girls are still always talking about religion and think of themselves as Muslims. I told them Muslims are cutting off hands and heads of people and they reply, "They deserve it." They won't talk to their uncle or cousins, they say they are infidels.'

Shrim laughed bitterly when I asked him about this. 'Turko asked me if her husband still prayed – she too was brainwashed.'

He explained that often when the women come back they had been so brainwashed they believed ISIS ruled the world. Some even tried to make contact with their captors.

Like most Yazidi women I spoke to, Turko was terrified of going back to Sinjar. Instead she wanted to leave the country. 'Just take us out of Iraq because Iraqi people did this to us,' she pleaded.

It was clear that escaping ISIS was not the end of their problems. Just inside Khanke camp were a few trailers where the Free Yazidi Foundation held yoga and art sessions for women, as well as trauma counselling. A yoga class was underway and I was invited along. Inside, a group of girls was sitting on the floor. Tacked on the walls were drawings of flowers and eyes as well as a pencil sketch of four girls in hijab chained together. Every member of the class, including the instructor Zainab, was a survivor of being kept as a sex slave by ISIS fighters, raped and sold over and over. As Zainab told them to breathe 'slow and deep', they squirmed and fidgeted.

I thought it was me putting them off and slipped out. But Yesim Arikut-Treece, a British trauma psychologist working with them, explained that one of the class, Khalida, twenty, had hung herself the previous week.

Suicide was common among the women. Many of the girls were physically damaged by repeated rape. Some couldn't face going out. A lot of the men had turned to drinking and there were high levels of domestic abuse. Large numbers of Yazidi families were in debt because they borrowed thousands of dollars to rescue daughters – one man I met, Abdullah, had spent $70,000 to recover his seven children.

They could not go home, explained Sevvi Hassan, a woman clad in a gauzy white long-sleeved, long-skirted Puritanical dress that was typical of many older Yazidis. She told me she was forty-five but she looked twenty years older and she had recently come back from Sinjar after trying to return home. 'Everything was rubble,' she said. 'Our house had no door or roof or windows, there was no water or electricity and no people, just ghosts. We'd been well-off with orchards of pomegranates, figs, olives and grapes and ninety sheep and thirty goats but everything was gone.'

Nor was it safe. Different militia contested the area. Worst of all she said, were the dark memories. Her eldest daughter Zeena, a twenty-eight-year-old mother of four, was so traumatised that she poured fuel over herself and set fire. 'She kept thinking ISIS was coming back to take her again and the children. Only one side of her face remains unscathed.'

Khanke alone had seen four girls commit suicide and thirteen attempts. Pari Ibrahim, the young US-based Yazidi lawyer who started the Free Yazidi Foundation after losing forty members of her own family, told me she'd heard there were around ten Yazidis committing suicide every week.

'I wanted to open a trauma clinic for the women but I knew this would be a stigma,' said Pari. 'In the Middle East people get called crazy if they have mental health problems.'

So she opened a women's centre which would be a safe space for survivors to meet, and secured funding from Women for Women International, the UN and the British government, to employ a trauma psychologist. The first one was a British grandmother from Dorset called Ginny Dobson. Within the first couple of days she had ninety sessions with women.

Some were reluctant to attend the centre, including Zainab, the freckle-faced strawberry-haired yoga instructor, who had been abducted along with all her five sisters. She was the last one to escape and when she finally got out, the others had been taken to Germany while her parents and brothers were nowhere to be found. 'I felt like it made no difference to the world if I existed or not,' she said. But she was persuaded to go along to a graduation ceremony after which she agreed to do an English course then met Ginny. Within months she was transformed, said Pari, 'from being a woman who sat in an unfinished building all alone to someone shining'.

Pari had warned me before I went that many Yazidis were fed up with telling their stories to journalists who just wanted to know about the horror, like vultures feasting on their misery. They no longer saw the point of talking as international outrage had not translated into rebuilding their homeland or delivering justice for what they suffered. They were particularly upset about a recent BBC documentary where a filmmaker had persuaded one of the rescued girls in Khanke to accompany them to Mosul to find the house where she had been held and repeatedly raped, and then brought her face to face with an ISIS prisoner.

'Please don't portray them as sex slaves. They were humans first,' said Pari.

It was in Khanke where I met Naima, the girl whose name had been drawn out of a bowl and been passed to twelve different men. She wanted to talk for she had fought back.

'All the time those ISIS men were forcing me to have sex, the hurt and pain made me stronger,' she said. 'The choice was death or accept. But I thought one day it will be my turn and they will be in my situation.'

She had just turned eighteen and was at home in Khanesor on 3 August 2014 when the news spread that ISIS had come to Sinjar. 'Everyone fled to the mountain. But we had no food or water in the mountain, and heard that they were going to block the way into Syria, so we decided to escape before they cut it off.

'We were two families in two cars – about twenty of us squashed in, my uncle's family and my parents, my grandmother and my four sisters and five brothers. But when we got to the old American checkpoint at Dugre, two cars were blocking the road, full of ISIS fighters in black with guns. "Give us your gold and girls without headscarves!" they demanded.

'We were scared then we heard bombing so they made us get back in our cars. There were about thirty cars all crammed with Yazidis like us, but they were being escorted by ISIS pick-ups – two in the beginning, one in the middle and two at the end. We thought about trying to get away and go back to the mountain but we'd heard some people had tried and been shot and killed.

'We stopped in Shiloh where they separated the men from the women. Then we heard the sound of shooting and some of the women started to scream.

'I went to look but the men were just sitting. Then they put men and women in separate cars. My mother, brother and sister managed to escape as did my grandmother and another brother as their drivers were Yazidi.

'I was with my cousin. My little sister Maha, who was six, was crying and went with my eldest brother. They drove us to Sinjar city. On the way we saw terrible things, dead bodies, cars on fire. They took us to an administrative building which was full of girls and women and then brought my little sister there. Around 8 p.m. a mullah came and started reading the Koran and said we will take some photos then you can go home. But they never took us home. I asked, "Where are the men?"

'For the next twenty days they moved us from one place to another then eventually to Badush prison which was full of women and girls. They stripped us of any jewellery or money. There was almost no food, it was horrible. It smelt of sweat and vomit and menstrual blood. I felt sick. Every day men would come and choose a girl. The first time the men took me, I froze. I did not know what rape was before that day.

'We could hear bombing coming nearer so they took us to another school then to Qasr al Gharib in Tal Afar, an old Shia village where all the residents had fled, and which they were using for people who had converted. I found my brothers and uncle. They told me that ISIS had put a dagger on one side and a Koran on the other and told them: "If you choose the Koran you convert to Islam and will see your family; if you choose the dagger you will be killed."

'We were in that village for four months. They would come and take the women or girls they liked and the boys for slave labour and training. They also took the sheep and goats to Mosul to feed their men.

'One day a bus came and they took a group of us to Mosul to Galaxy Cinema, a big hall with columns and tiled floors that was used for weddings. At the entrance were lots of men's sandals. It was like a market of girls. We were separated into ugly and beautiful. We messed up our hair and rubbed dirt and ashes in our faces as it was better not to be beautiful.

'After a week some men from Raqqa came and took me, my six-year-old sister and our cousin. Once we got there, I was separated from them and put in a house with ten girls all about my age, and lots of children, even a baby, so it was very noisy. One day an Iraqi called Abu Ali came and took me to his house. I was happy to be away from the noise but then he left me in an ISIS training centre full of girls and women.

'A mullah came and told me to say the Shahadah [the first of the five pillars of Islam] to prove I had converted. I started saying,

"There is no God but Allah and Muhammad is his messenger …" but he pulled out his gun. "Please kill me," I begged, "because then I will be free." I was happy because I thought this would be the end of all this. But he said, "As you have converted, no one can hurt you." Then he told me to go and wash myself. After that they took the group of us to Mosul. That's when they put our names in the bottle and started the selling on.'

It was when she was with her fifth 'owner', Faisal the bomb maker, that she decided to fight back.

'One day he told me "You are a bitch." I asked him, "Do you know the meaning of bitch? Do you think I'm doing something I like?"

'The day he sold me to Abu Badr, he told me, "Make yourself ready and walk slowly in case you fall." I said, "How I walk is not your business." It was the last day of December 2015 and it was cold and wet and he went outside without shoes. I walked to the car then I went back to him and said, "Faisal, one day you're going to be punished for what you have done." As the car left, he started to cry and I felt happy. He might have the guns but he was crying, not me.

'I was with Abu Badr for twenty-four days. He raped me of course. I was sold many times but the worst experience was with this man because he told me the wife of his friend Abu Sahib was sick and he was taking me to her. But when we got to Abu Sahib's place, there was nothing wrong with his wife. They put me in a room and that night Abu Sahib came to me. I told him, "I am not yours, I am Abu Badr's." I belonged to Abu Badr and it was haram for anyone else to touch me. He tried to force himself on me but I was shouting and screaming and eventually his wife came.

'The next morning he took me to another ISIS centre and raped me there. I was kept in that centre under guard and in the afternoon Abu Badr came. I asked him if he had sold me but he said no, so I told him what Abu Sahib had done.

'Then Abu Sahib came back and said he was taking me. I refused, saying Abu Badr hasn't sold me, and started shouting. He told me to be quiet but I said no, I want everyone to know. "You ISIS say you bring Islam but what you are doing is against Islam, you don't even obey your own rules and you even rape pregnant women."

'He tried to force me but I had a knife I'd managed to get from his kitchen. The guard came and took it then they locked me in. I punched the window to break the glass and tried to slash my wrists to kill myself but then the guard came and took the glass.

'Eventually after twenty-four days I was sold again, for $10,200 to Abu Haman whose real name was Ahmed Hasoum, and was another specialist in bombs and explosives. I was with him for eight months in Mosul in a place near the famous restaurant Jendul.

'I was a slave but had some control,' she continued. 'Once I made an emir cry. One of my friends was with him. She had two kids and the man wasn't bringing any food. Those boys when they saw food on TV, they'd cry, "Mum, we need this." For a month we had no tea or cooking oil and for one whole week just stale bread.

'Then this emir Abu Walid came and was sitting on the sofa, his big body all spread out like they did, and when I asked, "Why don't you bring food? The restaurant is nearby," he said because you are just throwing the food away. Then he spat on me. I told him, "Imagine these were your kids pleading for food and you couldn't give it. If it was the other way round, I wouldn't put you in this situation." Then I said, "Come with me," and held his hand and showed him we are eating this dry, very hard bread.

'He started to cry, then came back with cakes and biscuits. That made me happy, that I made an emir cry. They did a lot of bad things to me but when I could make myself the hero of the situation I felt happy.'

I wondered if her family had tried to rescue her using Shrim or one of the others. 'They didn't know where I was,' she said. 'Once

I managed to get the phone and call my father and was speaking Kurdish to him but as I was giving the address, the man took the phone from me.'

In October 2016, while she was with Abu Haman in Mosul, western forces started bombing to try and recapture the city from ISIS. 'It was scary but we knew it meant people outside were trying to do something finally.

'Then one of Abu Haman's friends Haudi came and said the house was in danger, it could be bombed any time, so I should go with him. He took me to his house and I stayed there ten days.

'Abu Haman is dead,' she said suddenly in English, laughing harshly.

'He died in the bombing – I was happy he was dead but it turned out he had written a will. It said I should be sold for $6000 and the money go to his family.

'So I was sold to Abu Ali al-Rashidi and he took me to his house. I was wearing niqab so couldn't see where we went. I was with him twenty-four hours, he did the same with me, then the next morning at 10 a.m. he took me to the house of his friend Nashwan and said I will leave you here while I go to fight.

'Then Nashwan came but I knew I didn't belong to him so I sat far away from him. He said, "Abu Ali didn't tell you?"

'"Tell me what?" I asked.

'He said, "Abu Ali sold you for $5000."

'These ISIS were passing us on like sweets, selling us without even telling us. I stayed three months with Nashwan and the same thing. Then he died in the bombing but he had also written a will saying I should be sold and the money go to his family.

'The bombing was getting more intense but I was happy as they had started to clear ISIS out of the left bank of the Tigris which divides the city. Then they were bombing the bridges so we on the western side were cut off.'

'Weren't you scared?' I asked.

'No. The bombs didn't scare me, the only thing that scared me was that if my owner died another one would come and take me. After Nashwan was killed I was sold to Hamad. I with him twelve days then he sold me to a pharmacist. I stayed with him one month, he did the same thing.

'All the time the bombing was coming closer. He took me to an ISIS family full of ISIS women and girls. They had heard that the Iraqi army would do the same with them as their men did with us Yazidi women and were scared. They told me, "If the Iraq army come and ask you say we are all Yazidi taken by ISIS." Suddenly everyone wanted to be Yazidi! One even asked me if you have a handsome brother please give him to me. So I realised the tables were turning, they were scared and that was good.

'Then he sold me again for $5000 to Abdullah whose real name was Tawfiq Hattam al Hossaini, a Sunni from Tal Afar. I was five months with him, he did the same things ...'

I was astonished at her recall of all the detail. 'The one thing I could do was know all their names so what they did would not be forgotten,' she explained. 'Now I am out I am writing everything in a book with everyone's name.'

I couldn't help wondering how she had avoided getting pregnant in all these three years with all these men.

'You can say we used a natural way, if you get my meaning,' she shrugged. 'Also ISIS didn't want us to have children. Sometimes they gave girls contraceptives or Egyptian tablets or used condoms though not with me.

'ISIS forced me to go to doctors twice. I didn't want to go because I was scared. I was hurting a lot from all the bruising inside. The doctor told me you have a urinary tract infection and strong inflammation inside so don't let anyone have sex with you for ten days but still they did ...

'Abdullah also died!' Again she laughed that hollow laugh. 'He was the last one and after he died I stayed with his sister and brother. Those last six months were very difficult because there was so much bombing in the Old City where we were. The house was hit more than once and some of the family were injured.'

One day in January 2017, Abdullah's sister gave Naima her phone and asked her to call her father and ask for help. 'She told me to tell him these people don't have anything to do with ISIS. Instead I told him, "Forgive me anything I did and if I survive I will come back."'

'It was the first time I had spoken to anyone from my family for six months. In the whole time of captivity after being separated from my brothers and sister, I had been in touch just four times.

'One morning we moved to an underground shelter. Bombs were coming one after another and we could hear gunfire, warplanes, every kind of weapon. There were about sixty people, including three old men. One of the old men said, "The Iraqi army are nearby, we will go to them." ISIS were getting clothes and things ready and also burning anything that identified them as ISIS – photos, IDs, memory sticks, everything …

'We went out from underground around 7 p.m. on the evening of 3 July. It was a shock, I didn't recognise anything, I couldn't see any normal house, everything was destroyed and it was like a mountain of dust.

'There was bombing going on all the time and we walked for a while and saw some Iraqi army but that area was not completely free from ISIS so they were busy attacking.

'The Iraqi soldiers were trying to show us the way to go. There was an ISIS fighter with a long beard lying dead, his face covered in dust and blood and I had to jump over him. In my mind I thought maybe he's still alive and might cut me. But I felt I had to do it. It was a good feeling, I felt stronger after I did it. Seeing their dead bodies was like what they did to us.

'We walked through the rubble till almost 9 p.m. when we got to a clinic where people who fled were gathering. I had escaped from Abdullah's sister but was with another family who had a small child who started to cry. I didn't know if they were an ISIS family or just people from Mosul but I had a bottle of water so I took the baby and gave him some.

'I told them I am Yazidi and they said, "When we meet Iraqi army, please tell them this family looked after me and are nothing to do with ISIS." I said okay, then I gave back their baby and ran away.

'A little further I saw an Iraqi soldier and told him in a whisper, "I'm Yazidi." He said, "Really?" I said yes. He asked my name. "I'm Naima," I said.

'I knew he might think I was just an ISIS wife trying to escape. He put me in a bus of people fleeing the city. Before the bus left, an Iraqi soldier came and asked, "Is Naima here?" He asked for contacts of my family. I gave him my father's phone number and he called and asked, "Do you have a daughter captured by ISIS?"

'When my father said yes, he told him, "She is with us and safe," then gave me the phone. It was the first time I had heard my father's voice for six months.

'The bus was full with no space to sit and the Iraqi soldier told a man to give me his seat, saying, "She is Yazidi." So then I was more precious than them.

'The people were being taken to a camp for ISIS families but after a while the bus stopped and I was taken to an Iraqi army vehicle to go to a police station.

'They took me upstairs to the second floor as ISIS wives were being brought there, and they didn't want me to see them. The Iraqis were taking their gold and IDs and I could hear the women shouting and screaming. What happened to us happened to them. They lost everything just as we had.

'A woman living nearby came with biscuits and clean clothes for me and offered to let me stay the night at her house near the police station. As we were leaving, they were bringing in some

ISIS they had caught, blindfolded and handcuffed, and that made me happy.

'The next morning at 8 a.m. the kind woman brought me back to the second floor of the police station and told to wait by the door. Eventually, about 8.30 a.m., the door opened and there was my father. He hugged me and started to cry. I was so happy to see him but I didn't cry or laugh.

'The police then took my father to a court to sign a paper to say he wouldn't kill me. They do that with all the Yazidi girls handed over but we didn't know that and he was very offended. "What are you saying?" he asked. "She's my daughter and for three years I didn't see her."

'Finally that evening they took us to Akrab checkpoint on the border between Kurdistan and Sinjar, where one of my cousins was waiting with a taxi. We arrived about 6 a.m. It was 6 July 2017. That is the end of the story.'

Naima had told me all this in the trailer. Afterwards she walked me through the camp past rows and rows of white tents to hers with its fridge and pile of quilts, and I could see it wasn't the end at all.

'When I came back I found we couldn't go home but only to this camp and that my family was no longer complete. It's like you have a garden that's green and you leave it for a while and come back and it's brown and dry and dead.

'I'm here in the tent with my mum, dad, grandmother, two sisters and two brothers (three of my sisters are married so I am the eldest of remaining). My sisters including my little sister Maha, who is nine and a half, were also kidnapped but they were rescued from Raqqa before me. My family had paid to rescue eleven relatives from ISIS including my aunt and her children so now we owe a lot of money.

'But three of my brothers and my uncle are still missing. We've had no news. Last night I saw them in my dreams and they seemed in a very bad situation; they looked so tired. Sometimes I see young men playing football and think it's my brother.'

She showed me a picture on her phone of brothers and uncle overlaid with images of flowers and a soundtrack of romantic piano. 'I made a video about them in case anyone has seen them,' she said.

'To start with when I came back I stayed in the tent. I didn't want to go out or meet people. I felt life had stopped. I didn't talk about what had happened to me to anyone. If I did go out, I just got in arguments. When people asked, "What did they do to you?" I'd shout "What, you don't know what they did to us?"

'But I realised life just continues, it doesn't wait for war to be over, and saw that I had to change for my family's sake. The missing were my father's sons before they were my brothers. Someone took me to this Free Yazidi Foundation and they gave me a job teaching health awareness in the camp which helped.'

I asked if she had gone back home to Khanesor at all. She was quiet for a moment. 'If I went back to Sinjar it would be with a broken heart. I've been back twice, once to get my ID, and my father didn't let me see our home. The second time was with my sister and I saw it. It was very difficult, everything inside destroyed, all the doors and windows broken.'

She looked down at her hands. 'I want the worst things to happen to the men that did this to me. I want them to die not in a quick or humane way but slowly, slowly, so they know what it's like to do bad things to people.'

Not far from the camp was a mound on which stood three white conical Yazidi shrines, like pleated skirts, meant to represent the rays of the sun they worship shining down on earth. A group of women in long white dresses gathered there as the real sun went down, watching it become a swollen red orb that dissolved on the horizon beyond the fenced-off tents. With families and communities divided between camps, some Yazidi leaders feared that the community, which dates back to ancient Mesopotamia, might not even survive.

The women were praying for missing children. Like Naima's family, almost every tent I entered in Khanke had relatives missing. Though perhaps two thirds of the 7000 girls abducted had been recovered, there were still 3154 Yazidis missing, many of them women and girls.

It turned out that when the West declared victory against ISIS after driving them out of Mosul and Raqqa in 2017, they had done nothing to rescue the girls. The US-led coalition even allowed a convoy of around 3500 people to escape Raqqa, which included fighters and perhaps their enslaved girls. Later, behind all the wire and sandbag walls and checkpoints in the coalition headquarters in Baghdad, I interviewed the deputy commander, a British major

called Felix Gedney, and asked him why. 'It wasn't our plan,' he
replied, 'but the fighting was very intense and our partner forces
felt they couldn't ignore the pleas of local tribal leaders who were
very emotive.'

Shrim, the beekeeper, said he and the other rescuers were only
getting back about three a month. Not only had the girls become
harder to reach, with Turkey refusing to cooperate, but some
refused to come back because it would mean leaving their children
behind. One of his own nieces was in that situation, having had a
baby daughter in captivity. He believed some of the abducted girls
had remained inside Mosul or in camps with ISIS supporters
because they feared having to give up their children if they come
home.

The Yazidi sect is strictly closed, perhaps because there had
been so many attempts over the centuries to wipe them out. A
child must be born a Yazidi to worship as one, and adults must
marry within the religion. Women cannot date outside and, in the
past, any sexual contact with a non-believer meant banishment.
Many Yazidis repeated to me the story of a Yazidi girl who had
fallen in love with a Muslim boy a few years before and was stoned
to death.

It had been a remarkable step for the Yazidi spiritual leader
Baba Sheikh to proclaim that girls abducted by ISIS were innocent, in fact holier than other girls, and should be welcomed back.
What it did not cover was children born from ISIS captors, and so
families wouldn't accept them.

This seemed very harsh so I decided to go to Lalish, the holy
valley where he lived and where Yazidis go to be baptised. It is
where Yazidis face to pray in the daytime.

It was cold and rainy, the green hills of the Shekhan valley
shrouded in tendrils of mist. My guide was a young Yazidi called
Bader and we drove in a taxi with a golden peacock angel and two
blue-glass evil-eye amulets dangling from the driver's mirror.

Eventually we came to a checkpoint across a road that led up to a temple with three more of the white cone-shaped towers. We could drive no further. Bader told me to take off my shoes and socks as Lalish must not be contaminated by dirt from outside. It was cold and damp, and it felt odd to start with but the stone was smooth and oddly pleasant on the feet.

We walked past an arcade of shuttered shops and up some steps to a small stone building. A large old woman in a purple velvet dress with a white veil squatted in the doorway under a plastic clock, guarding a pot of what looked like earth.

Her name was Asmara and she explained that the pot contained 'holy soil' which Yazidis wrap in a small cloth and keep in their pocket or wallet for luck. She had, she said, been there for twenty years, even sleeping there, as she was from a family of pirs or holy people. 'Only our family can guard this entrance,' she said proudly.

Asmara and her pot of holy soil

Beyond her, inside the room, I could see a natural spring bubbling behind a brass rail but as a non-Yazidi I was not allowed in.

We heard giggling and crossed to the other side of the road where a group of girls were taking selfies, all in long colourful dresses as if they had raided a dressing-up cupboard. Then we walked through an arch where I was instructed not to step on the doorframe, only over it, and into a courtyard with a fig tree.

A group of men sat round a fire under a canopy. This was where Baba Sheikh held court. Beyond them was a massive marble portal with a black snake carved wriggling up the wall to the right of it. According to Yazidi legend, the snake plugged the hole when Noah's Ark was leaking and stopped it sinking, so they regard black snakes as sacred and never kill them.

Through the portal, again careful not to step on the sill, we entered a dim room with seven columns, all festooned with brightly coloured silk knots. The columns represent the seven Yazidi angels to whom they believe God entrusted the world after creation, and the knots were apparently for luck. Untying a knot releases the previous pilgrim's wish so it could be granted, then a new wish could be requested by knotting another ribbon three times.

A cool breeze was coming from some steps down which led to the holy zum zum spring where Yazidis are baptised and which they believe comes from the same source as the one in Mecca. Once again as a non-Yazidi I wasn't allowed, so I headed the other way to the main chamber with a very high ceiling, for this was the tallest dome of the temple. Inside was a stone sarcophagus covered in green velvet cloth, the burial place of Sheikh Adi Musafir, one of the founders of the Yazidi faith. Sheikh Adi, who passed away in the twelfth century, was supposed to be the earthly manifestation of the Yazidis' true ruler, Melek Tawoos, the Peacock Angel. Yazidis told me they believed he comes to Earth every year on a day called Charsema Sor or Red Wednesday, the start of their new year.

Down another set of steps brought us to a room with large amphoras of olive oil from the groves of Lalish stacked along the walls. A few Yazidis were taking turns at standing with their backs to a stone pillar and throwing a small silk bundle over their shoulders toward it. Apparently if the cloth landed on top of the pillar, their wish would be granted.

It was frustrating trying to understand the Yazidi faith. Everyone I met seemed to give me a different account of their history. I kept asking Bader questions but he was little help. 'It's all stupid, all the leaders are corrupt and just making money from people,' he said.

I had hoped Baba Sheikh would be able to explain everything but sadly his place under the canopy was empty. He was ill in Germany, said the men round the fire as I warmed my wet feet.

'The children born in captivity are innocent. Why shouldn't they be allowed back?' I asked Murad Ismael, the poetry-loving engineer who founded Yazda, the main activist group for Yazidis.

'That's a step too far,' he explained when we met for coffee in the inappropriately named Classy Hotel in Erbil.

So moved was he by the plight of the abandoned children that he even tried to adopt one, to the horror of his family, as he was unmarried. But when he went to court, he discovered the child was not an orphan at all – the man who had said he was an uncle was the father. He was angry but we both wondered how desperate people must be that they would give away their children in the hope that would mean a better life for them.

Murad had worked as an interpreter for US forces in Iraq after the 2003 invasion, enabling him to get a special visa for America. He had been studying in Houston in August 2014 when he started getting calls from terrified family and friends back in Sinjar telling him that ISIS had invaded.

He began emailing every member of Congress and journalist he could reach with photographs of desperate Yazidi children, as well as videos of people being buried on top of the mountain.

He and a group of fellow Yazidis who had also worked for the US military then flew to Washington to protest outside the White House, but they were moved on to make way for Palestinians. They stayed on, sleeping six to a room in a grimy motel in Maryland, and eventually managed to get a meeting with the State Department Office of International Religious Freedom. There, they told such horrific stories of families killed by ISIS and people starving on the mountain that they reduced Doug Padgett, a six-foot-five-inch former Navy officer, to tears.

Ismael did not expect much. 'We are a small minority living in another minority in the middle of nowhere,' he shrugged. He and his Yazidi friends had one advantage, however. Having worked with the US military, they knew how their minds worked and came up with a Three Point Plan: The US must drop food and water on the mountain, then help a Yazidi militia that had been formed in Sinjar. Finally, the Americans would persuade the Iraqi government to track the growing number of Yazidis taken captive by ISIS.

Ismael, who had a master's degree in geophysics, made maps of Sinjar on which he marked fields and water towers and stuck red octagons to mark ISIS positions and stick figures for fleeing Yazidis.

The group was overjoyed when they managed to persuade President Obama to authorise aid drops and airstrikes in Sinjar, and publicly denounce what was happening to Yazidis as a 'potential act of genocide'.

This was quickly followed by disillusion when the Americans ignored the rest of their plan and did nothing to prevent the massacre of villagers in Kocho despite their increasingly desperate warnings. Ismael even threatened to set himself on fire in front of the White House, but it was to no avail.

When their money ran out the Yazidis went back to Houston and formed Yazda. The whole experience, he said, made him feel it was no good relying on humanity.

Eventually the Germans took in 1100 women, Canada took around 700 and Australia around 300. French President Emmanuel Macron had promised to take in a hundred families. The UK and US had not taken in a single one of the Yazidi women, something he struggled to understand.

'Everyone talks about the survivors, and there was lots of media coverage but in reality they don't get help,' he said. 'We had one woman with TB and we couldn't even get her the $700 she needed for surgery.'

Sinjar remained in ruins, and it seemed no one was prepared to rebuild it. 'Being in the camps is destroying the fabric of the community,' said Ismael. 'My main fear is we have something like Palestinian refugee camps that will be here forever and people will have a sub-life.'

That was not all. To his frustration not a single perpetrator had been brought to justice and none of the mass graves exhumed. 'We've recorded more than 1400 short testimonies from women and more than 300 lengthy statements,' he said. 'We have lists of names of ISIS militants and databases if someone would take it.'

Meanwhile, thousands of ISIS captors were still at large, according to Khaleel, the lawyer turned rescuer. 'I got out one girl, Rana, aged fifteen who had been sold and resold thirteen times, and she went to Mosul to get her identity papers and saw the last man who had been holding her just walking in the street. She shouted but he covered his face and ran away.'

He and Ameena had started trying to track down some of the perpetrators themselves. One of the girls they had rescued that

January was a twenty-year-old called Bushra. She had been sold on and on and her last captor had been a seventy-year-old man in Deir Azzour.

Once she was safely back, Khaleel created a fake Facebook identity to contact the man, offering to help get her back. Bushra recorded a voice message to send him, saying that if he came to get her, she would go back with him.

The man took the bait. Khaleel showed me a video of an old man with a grey beard crying into an olive tree and begging, 'Please come back, I miss you!'

'We have managed to catch a lot of ISIS people like this,' he said.

But Ameena had started to wonder if there was any point. 'I don't feel optimistic about getting justice,' she said. 'Our own government doesn't support us, the Iraqi government doesn't help, lots of ISIS leaders are paying and going free. Seventy-three mass graves of Yazidis have been found and no one is investigating or protecting them.'

12

The Nineveh Trials

Nineveh

Once, more than two millennia ago, there was a king called Ashurbanipal, then the most powerful man on earth, who declared himself 'king of the world' and lived in a 'Palace without Rivals' said to have seventy-nine rooms. Back then, in the seventh century BC, Nineveh was the largest city on earth, surrounded by towering walls with fifteen gates, each flanked by winged bulls, and containing palaces decorated with enormous stone reliefs, temples, gardens watered by a network of canals and aqueducts, game parks and a royal library of more than 30,000 clay cuneiform tablets.

The capital of the Assyrian empire may have been one of the oldest and greatest cities on earth but it's probably best known these days for its description in the Bible as the cauldron of evil and debauchery to which God sent Jonah to warn its people to repent their sin or face annihilation.

Seeing the Nineveh sign from Mosul on the east bank of the Tigris, it was hard not to feel a thrill. Iraq is full of such names from the ancient world – Babylon, the Garden of Eden and Ur, the birthplace of Abraham, but the modern-day reality was often disappointing. There was no sign of a Hanging Garden at Babylon, while the small dead tree near where the Tigris meets the

Euphrates outside Basra was not at all how I'd envisaged the Tree of Knowledge.

All that remained of Nineveh was a tall rectangular mud bank like the ramparts of a vast fort, a mound, and one gate that had been reconstructed. Inside was a large plain with the earthworks around and a few broken columns. There was far more of it in the British Museum.

The destruction was not for once the work of ISIS – Nineveh was sacked by the Babylonians, Persians and Medes who burnt it to the ground and brought down the empire. When ISIS rolled up with their bulldozers and dynamite in 2014, there was little left, but a video shows them destroying Adad Gate which had been reconstructed as well as some of the fortification wall. They also blew up the mosque of Nebi Yunus, said to be Jonah's burial place.

The Assyrians too were a brutal lot, building pyramids of skulls of their enemies, disembowelling captives and regularly cropping off noses and ears. They commemorated their barbarity in writing and art, just as ISIS would later broadcast its own horrors on social media.

Some of the tablets excavated in the early twentieth century were inscribed with a code of law which included a surprising number on sexual relations. 'If a woman in a quarrel injure the testicle of a man, one of her fingers they shall cut off,' read one. If both were harmed then her eyes could be gouged out. There was also a death penalty for rape.

It was to see justice in action rather than destruction of antiquities that I had come to Mosul in March 2018 with my Kurdish fixer Halan, in the white Toyota he called Monica Lewinsky. All car models in Iraq have nicknames, he told me, when I expressed my astonishment. Why her, he couldn't explain. Perhaps the model dated from the time of the scandal?

Our destination was a scruffy nearby town, Tel Kaif, dominated by a terracotta brick church which had been recently rebuilt. The church was Chaldean – built by Assyrian Catholics – a reminder that the area was home to one of the world's oldest Christian communities. Christians from Mosul had fled there in July 2014 after ISIS took the city and gave them a 24-hour deadline to convert or pay protection tax, but ISIS later came there too and destroyed that church.

Next to the church was a walled compound with guards and people milling around outside. Inside, prisoners in Guantanamo-style tangerine jumpsuits were lined up in the corridors, facing the walls. This modest setting was where trials were underway of members of ISIS responsible for three years of barbaric rule over a third of the country.

I was shown into a room with a policeman on the door where three judges in black robes with white cuffs presided over an elevated bench piled high with yellow folders. Behind them was an Iraqi flag and a banner imprinted with the scales of justice. At a table beneath the judges, and slightly to the right, sat the public prosecutor and two women taking notes, while on the other side was a defence lawyer in black robes with green trim. The only audience was me and Halan, my translator.

A lanky prisoner with a shaven head and a dirty jumpsuit was in the dock. His name was Omar Abdul Qadar and he turned out to be a journalist.

The chief justice read out the details. 'You were arrested on 4 July 2017 in Noor neighbourhood of Mosul and claimed not to have joined ISIS but to be doing propaganda for them.'

'I repeat I have not joined or fought for ISIS,' said the prisoner. 'I worked at Zahoor press agency before ISIS came, then after the fall of Mosul they took it over and changed the name to Bayan. I would get people's stories. I got 125,000 dinar a month. I was like a contractor.'

'Are you saying ISIS is like a company with contractors and employees?' asked the judge.

'Yes,' replied the man.

'But you had a weapon from ISIS and were doing their propaganda.'

'I did it because I was forced to,' insisted the journalist.

The judge continued reading the statement. 'I was getting news for Bayan news agency and presenting news on their channel. I was given a gun by ISIS and helped set up three TVs in the streets to broadcast their propaganda and to distribute CDs and memory sticks …'

He stopped and peered over his glasses at the prisoner. 'You went with your brother Bashir to the mosque. Did you repeat the bayat [pledge of allegiance]?'

'There were thousands of people in the mosque for Friday prayers,' replied the prisoner. 'Everyone was reading the bayat.

'I am innocent of all accusations,' he pleaded.

The judge was unmoved. 'Omar, I accuse you of joining ISIS in Mosul in 2014, saying the bayat and helping them to spread their publications and distribute their propaganda.'

'It is not true,' repeated the journalist.

The public prosecutor then got up and read from a piece of paper. 'He confessed in initial confession that he joined ISIS with his brother on the East Bank of Mosul and said the bayat then supervised distribution of propaganda. As public prosecutor we think his initial confessions are more dependable than what he says now and he must be sentenced to death.'

The defence lawyer stood up. 'All these confessions were done under torture so I ask you to reconsider and pardon my client,' he said, then sat down.

The judge then sent everyone out to consider the verdict. Omar, the journalist, stood against the wall awaiting his fate and rubbing his hands. After a few minutes the door opened and we were all summoned back in.

The judge looked at him. 'You joined ISIS which can mean the death sentence of hanging, but we have decreased this to life sentence taking into consideration that you didn't fight. Your case will now be referred to Baghdad. Do you have anything to say?'

'I have a master's degree from business school,' said the journalist. 'I could have a middle-class salary but I was forced to work for ISIS for 125,000 dinar – do you think I would have done that by choice?'

This seemed a strange defence. 'It's not about your degree,' said the judge. 'I'm judging you according to the evidence and your confession.'

'If I'm in prison I will have no access to lawyers,' protested the prisoner.

The policeman handcuffed him and he was led away. The whole thing was over in less than half an hour. The defence lawyer told me he had been assigned by the state and not given access to any of the evidence.

At 11.20 a.m. the next prisoner was shown in. This time it was a young man of twenty-four called Harith who had been arrested in Haj Ali camp in May 2017. He was accused of working as a guard at an ISIS military post, and he signed a confession in which he had admitted to joining ISIS in September 2014, pledging the bayat, getting a gun and working at a checkpoint as well as giving information about women not behaving properly who would then be punished.

'This is not true,' he insisted twisting his hands behind his back. 'I swear to God I have not worked for ISIS.'

A similar back and forth ensued as in the first case, the defence lawyer again protesting the confession had been extracted under torture. The judge soon tired of it and sent him out.

At 11.48 a.m. he was called back in. 'We could have given you a death penalty for joining ISIS but because of your age we decreased it to fifteen years.'

'I swear I'm innocent,' he protested.

The judge was unmoved. 'We give this sentence according to what we see,' he shrugged.

I couldn't quite work out why the journalist got a heavier sentence than the guard and also wondered whether this apparent leniency was for my benefit. I'd heard from human rights groups that most people were sentenced to death.

The judges got through three cases in as many hours and the whole thing felt like an assembly line. It was hardly surprising. The Nineveh court worked only from ten in the morning to two in the afternoon four days a week and was one of just two courts for ISIS prisoners – the other in Baghdad – and there were thousands to get through. The battlefield victories against the terrorist group had led to arrests not just of fighters but also their families, and low-level functionaries like drivers and cooks.

Human Rights Watch estimated the Iraqi authorities had locked up 20,000 suspected ISIS members of whom 1350 were foreign women and children. Many were from Turkey, the Gulf, Central Asia and Tunisia, but others were from western countries, like Britain and France, which had refused to take their citizens back.

The chief judge Jamal Daoud Sinjari had initially told me he was not allowed to give interviews. But after the second case he beckoned me forward and said he could answer some questions.

He explained that this was actually a slow day – some days he got through eight cases. So far he had judged 480 prisoners of whom he said about a third had received the death penalty. But he still had more than 1000 prisoners to get through, on top of which there were another 30,000 arrest warrants. Everyone was being

tried on the same charge – terrorism – which under Iraq's coun-
ter-terrorism law carried the death penalty for anyone 'who
commits, incites, plans, finances or assists in acts of terrorism'.

This set the bar so low that it meant drivers or wives could
easily be convicted – the *New York Times* ran a story about the
Baghdad court in which fourteen women married to ISIS men had
been tried, convicted and sentenced to death in just two hours.*

Judge Sinjari said in his court he had only tried one woman so
far and he had sentenced her to hanging. 'She had been involved
since 2005 and encouraged all her brothers to be involved, and had
herself shot a police officer in the head.

'She confessed,' he added. 'A lot confess. Just yesterday a twenty-
year-old man confessed to killing twenty people – getting groups
of five at a time and shooting them in the head from behind.'

I asked about the lawyer's claim that the confessions had been
obtained through torture, something that was widely reported.

'It's not in the interest of us judges to accuse someone if they
are innocent,' he replied. 'And it's not only confessions we depend
on, there are also ISIS documents and witnesses.'

I wondered how they could issue judgments so quickly. 'We are
looking for detail to prove it's the right story and from experience
we can tell if someone is telling the truth,' he replied.

Perhaps after fifteen years of bloodshed and terrorism that had
seen an estimated 100,000 Iraqis killed, it was not surprising there
was little concern about leniency or due process. Iraq's Prime
Minister Haider al-Abadi received widespread public support
when he spoke of stepping up the pace of prosecutions.

It seemed dangerous work given that everyone kept telling me
that Mosul was still full of ISIS members and more than 160
judges and investigators had been killed in terrorist attacks in Iraq

---

* Margaret Coker and Falih Hassan, 'A 10-Minute Trial, a Death Sentence:
Iraqi Justice for ISIS Suspects', *New York Times*, 17 April 2018.

since the US invasion. I asked if the judges got special protection.

Judge Sinjari looked at the heavens and smiled. 'We have guards while we are at work but not at home,' he said. 'I have three guards but I live in Kurdistan so how can I take them back? We haven't had direct threats but we hear from others.'

I was intrigued by his name – it turned out he was himself from Sinjar though not a Yazidi. I asked if any of the prisoners he had tried had kept Yazidi sex slaves?

'Of course,' he replied. 'We've tried several who had sex slaves and one who fought over one. Others have said their emir had sex slaves.'

Why didn't he charge these men with rape or abduction?

He looked astonished. 'If there are two people fighting in the street, that's just one problem but when these terrorists join ISIS they are killing, raping, beheading so it all counts as terrorism. That carries the death penalty so there is no need to worry about the rape.'

I tried to explain that it mattered to the women who had suffered being raped, enslaved and sold.

'If a civilian raped a Yazidi girl, that's rape,' he replied, 'but if someone joined ISIS and raped a Yazidi girl, it's terrorism because he has also killed people and fought Iraqi forces.'

I tried again, pointing out that if you don't even include rape in the charges it's as if it's of no consequence, yet the women have to live with this for the rest of their lives.

He started shuffling his papers. 'Why are you westerners obsessed about Yazidis?' he asked. 'It's not only Yazidis. It is better to ask what happened to all Iraqis because many more things happened that people didn't hear about – Arabs and Christians of Sinjar were as destroyed as Yazidis. Eighty per cent of Sinjar was destroyed. In my own case a Yazidi family has taken my house!'

The interview was over. He banged his gavel and another prisoner was brought in. This time it was an older man, who managed to look distinguished even in filthy jumpsuit and lilac flip-flops. Unlike the others, this man had an audience – the public benches filled with men in long robes and red-and-white chequered headdresses. He also had his own lawyer.

The old man's name was Sheikh Rashid Khan and he was a tribal leader, from al Mowali village.

'You joined ISIS in 2015,' began the judge. 'We have a video where you took the bayat and gave a speech and also we have a three-page confession.'

The sheikh shook his head but instead of saying anything a witness was called. One of the men in headdresses went to the stand and took an oath. His story was rambling and confusing and to start with I wasn't sure if he was for the defence or prosecution.

'He is from my tribe,' said the witness. 'In summer 2015 militants came to our village with weapons and told us all to pray at the big mosque and asked us to give bayat. People refused so the militants said they hadn't been welcomed as they should. They grabbed the prisoner's hand because he was the sheikh and went to his diwan [guesthouse] and were filming him.'

Another witness came forward. 'I was tending my sheep in the fields when ISIS came the first time and put their flag on our mosque. Some villagers replaced it with the Iraqi flag and wrote anti-ISIS slogans. About ten days later I was again tending my sheep when ISIS came back and beat and killed some villagers. They called everyone to the mosque to put our hands in the air and say the bayat then they asked the sheikh to shake hands. We were surrounded by them: what could anyone do? Then they went to the sheikh's diwan and everyone sat and they hung an ISIS flag on the wall then gave the sheikh a statement and videoed him reading it.'

There were six witnesses in total, all of whom seemed to be related and all of whose accounts were contradictory. One claimed ISIS had rounded up more than 100 villagers and tortured them for five days. But all agreed the sheikh had nothing to do with ISIS and had had no choice but to read the bayat.

Finally, the judge called proceedings to a halt. 'I accuse you of joining ISIS from your own free will – is it true?' he asked.

'No, I didn't have any choice,' said the prisoner.

We were then sent out. The sheikh was placed facing the wall and began praying over and over. His witnesses all conferred with the lawyer. It wasn't clear to me how this would go though the judge was noticeably more deferential than he had been to the previous accused.

After ten minutes, the door opened and we all trailed back in. The judge announced the prisoner had been found innocent and would be released immediately. The sheikh raised his hands to the heavens and cried.

The judges started packing up. It was almost 2 p.m. When I got outside the court building, the sheikh was there with his supporters, already changed into fresh clothes and a headdress. A huge box of sweets had appeared and he handed me some. I asked about his seven months in prison. They invited us back to their village where they said there would be celebrations and 'lots of shooting', but Halan said it would not be wise.

Instead, we had lunch in Mosul, passing the ruins of the Old City where they were still pulling out corpses. It was nine months since the end of the battle which ousted ISIS, but the ancient city, which had been inhabited since the seventh century, still looked like an apocalyptic bombsite. Everywhere you looked there were staircases to nowhere, concertinaed buildings, upended concrete blocks and the occasional blackened corpse. The smell was putrid but people were reluctant to move the bodies for fear of booby traps. The UN had erected signs warning of IEDs. Someone had scrawled *Fuck ISIS* in big black letters on what was left of the Al Nuri mosque where the group's leader al-Baghdadi, dressed in black robes and turban and sporting a Rolex, had proclaimed his Caliphate.

We had coffee in a café across the road from Mosul university, which was also in ruins as it had been a base for ISIS, so was bombed by the US-led coalition and torched by the fighters as they left. Its library was once regarded as among the finest in the Middle East with a million books but had been left a charred husk.

The café owner told us a book drive was underway so we crossed over. As we neared, I was surprised to hear a violin playing and recognised the tune – the theme music from *Last of the Mohicans*.

The violinist, playing amid the ruins, was Mohammad Ahmad, a twenty-nine-year-old law student, who told me that under ISIS he had played with a wooden clothes peg on the bridge to mute the sound and with the air conditioner on. 'If ISIS had heard they would have killed me,' he said.

Once they came to his house to search and he buried his two violins in the garden. 'My dad forgot and watered the plants so destroyed one,' he laughed.

Though they found nothing they arrested him anyway and kept him for a month, beating him and making him kneel while they threatened to shoot him. 'It was like living in hell,' he said. 'Now I play in all the places that were destroyed in the hope that people will hear and feel life has begun again, whatever they went through.'

Before I left Mosul, there was something I wanted to see. Many of the Yazidi girls I had met had talked about being kept in the slave market in the Galaxy Cinema.

Mohammad, the violinist, thought it was by Al Ghābāt forest on the eastern bank of the Tigris, which before the ISIS occupation had been a popular picnic spot, so we climbed into Monica Lewinsky and headed there. It seemed as if life was starting to come back, a few families out and about, the air scented with the fruity aroma of shisha pipes, and restaurants grilling the local red carp which Mosul used to be famous for. I wasn't sure about eating the fish having seen the rotting corpses in the Old City just over the other side.

We drove back and forth along the bank but no one seemed to know where it was. People kept directing us to a strange fibreglass pirate ship that used to be a nightclub and clearly wasn't the place the girls had described. Eventually we consulted Google.

Away from the river bank was a large pyramid-shaped hotel

which once had a casino and ISIS had converted into a hotel for their commanders, prompting wags to dub it the Shariaton. Across the road was a field of pulverised rubble. A guard confirmed it was all that remained of the Galaxy after an airstrike. I wandered through the ruins. Whatever had hit it had done a thorough job. Everything was smashed, apart from a few floor tiles. Some of the debris had blue paint. The only sign that women had ever been there were a few tiny scraps of fabric. The air seemed heavy and still. What must it have been like to stand there as human merchandise as the ISIS fighters came through, lifting their scarves to check their faces and fondling their breasts, rejecting this one for being too dark or too 'used', taking that one for being young and pretty.

I remembered the words of Zainab, the yoga instructor in the trailer at Khanke, who had been held in Galaxy Cinema. 'I think the world has forgotten already,' she told me. 'But tell them, if you think they will listen.'

Listening to such heartbreaking stories, one question preyed repeatedly on my mind. What enjoyment could men get from abusing women in such a way?

'There is nothing sexual about rape,' insisted Dr Mukwege, the Nobel Prize-winning doctor, whose hospital in Congo had treated some 55,000 victims. In her 1975 book on rape, Susan Brownmiller also dismissed the idea that it is anything to do with desire or satisfying the male libido, describing it instead as an assertion of power. '[Rape] is nothing more or less than a conscious process of intimidation by which all men keep all women in a state of fear,' she wrote.

Are men somehow hardwired to hurt women? And if so, how have we mothers created that person? It's a question the feminist writer Eve Ensler asked, and tried to answer, in her book *The*

Apology, where she assumes the voice of her father Arthur who abused her from the age of five. 'All along I made you feel like you were the one who had done something terribly wrong,' she imagines him saying.

There is of course a difference between the perpetrators of sexual violence in war and those who commit acts of sexual violence in times of peace. Inger Skjelsbæk, a psychologist from the Peace Research Institute in Oslo, has done extensive research in this field and points out that 'the setting of war represents an extreme break with the norms and values that guide peaceful coexistence between people(s) – as illustrated by the very fact that killing is permissible under certain conditions in war.

'However,' she continues, 'there is a clear distinction between killing and committing acts of sexual violence in war: killing can be legitimised under certain conditions, whereas sexual violence cannot. Nevertheless, it is possible to regard sexual violence in war as part of a repertoire of actions that appear permissible because the circumstances of war are extraordinary and because such behaviour elicits no consequences, punishment, or condemnation from the military leadership.'

Uncovering the horrendous scale of Soviet rapes in Berlin in 1945 led the historian Antony Beevor to wonder if there is a dark area of male sexuality which can emerge all too easily in war when there are no social and disciplinary restraints. Are all men inherent rapists unleashed in the chaos of war? 'To what degree would men with weapons and without any fear of justice or retribution do the same thing in these circumstances?' he muses, when I ask him about it. 'We just don't know.'

He points out that the feminist doctrine that rape is purely about violence and power is flawed because it defines the crime purely from the victim's point of view. 'It fails utterly to probe the range of male instincts and motives – revenge on the enemy, a desire to humiliate the enemy, a need to wipe away his own humiliations at the hands of his own superiors and of course sheer sexual opportunism because he has a gun in his hands and can pick his victim.'

Indeed many believe that rape is inevitable in war, whether it's opportunistic or fuelled by the determination to humiliate the enemy and the intoxication of triumph. Wars are after all a place of high testosterone, of young men proving themselves and asserting their masculinity. Army barracks have long been notorious for misogynistic language, derogatory terms used for women, and *Playboy* pin-ups.

But, why then was there such different levels between different armies during the Second World War? The British army 'raped the least by a long way', according to Beevor, who believes it may be partly due to military culture, rather than the often cited 'bromide in the tea'.

He points out there is also the grey area of wartime prostitution, women forced by starvation and desperation into sex. American soldiers were sometimes described as 'Russians with well-pressed trousers' who didn't need to rape to get sex because they had so many cigarettes to distribute, these being valuable currency.

And it does not happen in every war. There have for example been few reports of sexual violence in the conflict between Israel and the Palestinians. Elisabeth Jean Wood, professor of politics at Yale, believes that rape is not inevitable in war. She carried out a study of civil wars in twenty African countries between 2000 and 2009 and found that 59 per cent of 177 armed actors were not reported to have engaged in rape or other sexual violence.*

So why do some armed groups commit massive wartime rape and not others? Dara Kay Cohen, a professor of public policy at Harvard University, conducted a case study of the civil war in

---

* E. J. Wood, 'Armed Groups and Sexual Violence: When Is Wartime Rape Rare?', *Politics & Society* 37, 2009.

Sierra Leone where rape was common, and came up with a theory of what she calls 'combatant socialisation'.*

Pointing out that gang rape is much more common in war than in peacetime, she argued that armed groups use wartime rape as a socialisation tool. 'Combatant groups that recruit new members through forcible means, such as abduction or press-ganging, must create a coherent fighting force out of a collection of strangers, many of whom were abused in order to compel them to join … Rape – especially gang rape – enables groups with forcibly recruited fighters to create bonds of loyalty and esteem from initial circumstances of fear and mistrust.'

Presumably there are other factors such as how long men are away from home fighting, and the attitudes to women in their countries – many of the worst places were countries with high rates of domestic violence or where marital rape is not considered an offence. They often had few women in parliament and other positions of power. Or was this a matter of the chicken and the egg?

Although in some of the conflicts I look at in this book, fighters were encouraged or even instructed to rape, it was clear in many cases the perpetrator had a choice. As Inger Skjelsbæk asked: 'What message does the person send by committing rape as opposed to, for example, cutting off a limb?'

Interestingly, whereas the #MeToo movement focused on perpetrators, when people look at rape in war they have tended to focus on the victims. But listening only to victims has done almost nothing to end sexual violence, which suggests that understanding the perpetrators may be useful.

'I've been working on sexual violence all these years,' Eve Ensler said when we met. 'I'm wondering where the men are? This isn't our issue, we don't rape ourselves. It's a men's issue.'

---

* Dara Kay Cohen, 'Explaining Rape during Civil War', *American Political Science Review*, Harvard University, August 2013.

Inger Skjelsbæk told me that when she started out in the 1990s researching sexual violence, she spent a year contacting some of those convicted for rape from the war in Bosnia. From the twenty or so she contacted she got only two responses. 'One contacted me through his lawyer and said we could meet if I paid a lot of money. The other said I could come to Germany and visit him in jail only if we didn't talk about the rapes.'

So instead she turned to the sentencing judgments and looked at the narratives of perpetrators and lawyers. 'I was surprised to find they construed the rape as something normal that happens in war,' she said. 'Some of the perpetrators even talked as if by committing these rapes they were being chivalrous because they were not killing the women. Sex was construed as something not violent in the heads of these perpetrators.'

Some even talked as if rape was part of love relationships in war. In one case there was a long discussion about whether girls were actually in love with their perpetrators because one girl had drawn a love heart on a postcard.

The only way to answer the question seemed to be to talk to the perpetrators themselves. So a few months later, I returned to Erbil, where many of the ISIS fighters had been in custody since the fall of Mosul and where Kurdish intelligence had agreed to give me access.

On a grey rainy Monday morning before Christmas, I left my hotel, passing a surprising number of Christmas trees and inflatable Santas, for I had been staying in the Christian area around St Joseph's Cathedral, the headquarters of the Chaldean church. Many of those in Mosul and the Nineveh Plains who fled the ISIS onslaught came here and many more had fled the country – Iraq's Christian community was thought to have been reduced to just 300,000, compared to 1.2 million under Saddam.

We headed along the 60 Metre Road (the Kurds are unimagina-tive in naming their ring roads so there was also 30 Metre Road, 40 Metre Road, 90 Metre and 120 Metre), and eventually came to a long cream wall and a checkpoint manned by peshmerga. Inside, in a former tobacco factory, was the prison, run by Asayish, the Kurdish intelligence, where 1502 men accused of being members of ISIS had been taken after the fall of the Caliphate, mostly Iraqi. Of these, 277 had been transferred to the courts in Nineveh and 576 to those in Baghdad, leaving 649.

A general in khaki sweater and pants who did not give his name showed me into a conference room with a long shiny mahogany table and high-backed black leather chairs, and set out with bottles of water and hand sanitiser. The walls were papered with cream satin wallpaper and there was a large flat-screen TV as well as a glass-doored fridge full of bottles of Coca-Cola. We were joined by a pale-faced man with a brush of black hair and a quizzical expres-sion, wearing a long black mac over a white shirt and red tie. He was introduced only as captain, and was presumably an intelli-gence officer.

'Start off softly and then they might talk,' recommended the general. This did not seem the moment to tell him I had been doing my job for thirty years.

The first prisoner to be brought in was a sallow-skinned fellow in a grey sweater and brown bomber jacket with sticking-out earlobes and calloused worker's hands. As he sat down opposite me and my interpreter, his eyes darted back and forth like a lizard. His name was Salahaddin, he told us, he was 37 and from Shirkat, a town known for supporting ISIS. There, he worked on his family farm, growing tomatoes, cotton and watermelon.

Speaking in flat tones, he described a miserable life, starting with being imprisoned as a toddler along with all his family by Saddam. His father and five uncles had been hanged in 1988, when he was just six, during the Anfal military campaign when thousands of Kurdish villages were destroyed and men of fighting age slaughtered by the Ba'athist regime.

When Saddam was toppled in 2003 in the US-led invasion, Salahaddin said, 'I was so happy he was gone.' Afterwards, he received a state pension as compensation for what they had suffered. 'It was a good life then, friends all looking after each other, and we would go to Tikrit, Baghdad and Kirkuk for picnics.'

But within a year, as the new Shia government began suppressing the Sunnis who had ruled for so long, his elder brother became very religious. 'He had a friend he was always talking about religion with and was brainwashed. He joined AQI [al Qaeda in Iraq] and became a commander.'

Later, after the group's leader Abu Musab al-Zarqawi was killed in a US airstrike in 2006, and the movement went underground to re-emerge as ISIS, the brother became an ISIS commander known as Abu Anas.

'I wasn't a fan,' claimed Salahaddin. 'I didn't even used to pray, but I couldn't talk to my brother because I was scared of him. If you said anything, he got very angry.'

A half smile played on the captain's face.

His middle brother also joined. 'In his case it was for money,' he said.

Then, on 15 October 2016, he was having breakfast in the garden around 7 a.m. when the sky started vibrating, there was a loud bang and then smoke everywhere. The airstrike had scored a direct hit on his house next door. He ran to see what had happened.

'It had been flattened,' he said. 'All the neighbours came to help get out survivors.'

He clambered through the wreckage to find his mother, wife and four-year-old son all dead as well as four of his brother's children. The only survivors were his daughter and his brother's wife and daughter.

'After that I joined ISIS too because I was so upset,' he said. 'I went to West Mosul, swore the bayat [oath of allegiance] and was based in the al Salaam hospital as a security guard.'

ISIS was at its peak controlling 34,000 square kilometres and ten million people, making money from smuggling oil and cultural relics, as well as imposing taxes. Salahaddin was provided an AK47 and went on operations. 'They paid me 200,000 dinars a month,' he said.

At this point I asked about the Yazidi girls. His eyes flickered a little more. 'They used to be with the big members of ISIS,' he said, 'not ordinary fighters like me. My brother had one, not me.

'It was hard to get a Yazidi girl because they always cried and you had to pay. They would sell them for as much as $10,000 or $20,000. My brother bought one for $4000. He had an ownership certificate. Her name was Suzanne, she was maybe thirteen or fourteen, she was beautiful and so young. She had two young sisters and I tried to buy them but I didn't have enough money.'

Were you encouraged to take Yazidi women? I asked.

'Yes,' he replied. 'They told us it was part of Shariat to take sabaya [slaves]. There was a guy called Nafar who used to sell from his house. Sometimes I stayed there and he had four or five girls. I didn't sleep with them because I treated them like humans.'

He seemed to know an awful lot about it.

'When my brother got killed in April 2017 I had to look after his wife and the girl. They were in the Old City with my daughter. I looked after Suzanne as if she were my brother's daughter. It was wrong to have this Yazidi girl.'

Salahaddin was in Mosul right till the end as the hospital was one of the last hold-outs. 'Al-Salam hospital was a big operation. First we drove back the Iraqi forces but then came airstrike after airstrike and we got stuck inside the doctors' houses and surrounded. My brother's wife called and said the Iraqi army took Suzanne.'

The battle for Mosul lasted nine months, longer than the battle for Stalingrad, with intensive bombardment from US, British and other allied planes, and street-to-street fighting in the narrow alleys. The Old City finally fell in early July 2017, the beginning of the end of the Caliphate.

'I escaped and swam across the [Tigris] river from west to east then tried to get to Erbil with my wife and daughter but was arrested on 1 August 2017,' said Salahaddin. 'I was kept one night with the peshmerga then have been here ever since waiting to go to court.'

This was confusing as previously he had said that his wife had been killed in the airstrike.

'I got another wife in 2016 and she was in West Mosul with my brother's wife and the Yazidi,' he said.

It was one of a number of contradictions. I suppose getting Muslim men to talk about raping women to a western female journalist was never going to be easy, particularly when they were ISIS members waiting trial.

I asked what he thought about ISIS. 'ISIS was doing bad things,' he replied. 'They shot people for no reason. If women were not completely covered with head and gloves they punished them.'

What did he think of that?

'That was a good thing because we are Muslim.'

What did he think of women like me, wandering around alone, head uncovered?

'It's kind of disgusting,' he said. 'ISIS was doing some bad things but some good things and one of those was looking after women. Also they kept control so people weren't stealing anything.

'Why ISIS got beaten in the end was because all the commanders had Yazidi women and didn't want to fight. At the beginning they would spend one night with the Yazidi and four days with their wife but in the end they would be five days with the Yazidi.'

'Are you sure you didn't have one?' I asked again.

He didn't look at me. His eyes swivelled side to side. 'I swear to God I didn't have a Yazidi girl. Yazidis are human like us,' he insisted. 'I was trying to buy Suzanne's sisters because they were so young.'

How would you feel about your daughter being bought and sold like that?

'I wouldn't like my daughter to be treated like Yazidi girls,' he replied. 'You know they worship peacocks?' he added. 'I asked Suzanne about her religion. I told her, "I know you believe in a peacock." I asked her is your religion or Muslim religion better and she said Islam.'

I asked about conditions in jail but the general intervened. 'No questions on that,' he said.

A recent Human Rights Watch report on the boys' detention centre in Erbil had described how Asayish were using electric shocks and beatings with plastic pipes and electric cables to extract confessions. If they were doing that to the boys, what must they be doing to the men? Human Rights Watch told me they had been refused access to the adult prison.

The next prisoner to be brought in was younger and looked petrified. He was wearing a zipped sweatshirt printed with the word TEA. His name was Abdul Rahman, twenty-four, from Mosul, and said he joined ISIS when they first came into the city in 2014. 'I joined because of the money,' he shrugged. 'They were paying 120,000 dinar a month and I was married and working as a farmer growing watermelon in a village called Shora, twenty-five miles south of the city, and life was hard as diesel was so expensive for the generator.'

Like the first prisoner, Abdul Rahman said he was a security guard. The intelligence captain had that smile on his face again and I remembered how at the courts in Nineveh, the judge had told me everyone claimed to be a driver or a guard.

He worked at a town called Mushraq, which had a meteorological station that ISIS had taken over as a base. 'I was not a fighter, just a security guard working three days a week,' he said. 'I never swore the bayat and I didn't like things they did like beating people because their beard was not long enough.

'I was smoking and one day they took me and beat me but my cousin was security commander so vouched for me. Then there was an airstrike on the town so I left my post because I was afraid and ISIS took me and shaved off my hair so after that I fled.'

I asked about the Yazidi girls.

'One of my cousins was an emir, a commander of ISIS, and my elder brother was also in ISIS, in Qayyarah. He had a Yazidi girl he bought in Mosul for $2000. He used to be one month with her then one month back but then he sold her.

'My brother also bought one called Medea. She was so young, just nine or ten and living with us, but my mum and dad were not happy so they kicked my brother out. My dad told him don't bring these young girls in here, it's not good.

'He didn't sleep with her because she was so young but she used to play with his kids. He bought her to look after her.

'The whole thing was like a business. They brought thirty girls to Qayyarah – they used to cry because they were so young.'

I decided I might get further asking more generally what they thought about rape. He shrugged. 'ISIS spread propaganda that they were bringing girls to convert them and that it was our duty to take them but I wasn't sure,' he said.

How had he ended up in jail? 'When I left ISIS, I came to Shimal in northern Iraq between Kirkuk and Erbil to try and find a job but at a checkpoint in October they found my name in the system and arrested me and brought me here. I told them I didn't do any fighting, I was just a guard. I don't know what will happen to me. I hope they don't send me to Baghdad.'

The general nodded, pleased. 'They all want to stay here because here is like a five-star hotel compared to the Iraq side where they just execute people,' he said.

Kurdistan does not have the death penalty.

The third prisoner levered himself in on crutches for he was missing both of his legs. He was in a black polo shirt and brown trousers and seemed different to the others, looking directly at me, his face open and pleasant despite his appalling injuries. His name was Issa Hasim Saleh and he said he was twenty-two or twenty-three, and came from Mosul.

'We lived in the west side, close to the Old City, and my dad worked in the bazaar selling rice and dry food,' he said. 'Before ISIS came, I was a student. I worked doing carpentry and mending generators by day then college at night, trying to finish, maybe even go to university so I could get a good job such as an engineer.

'When ISIS came the first time, not just me but everyone joined them. People started clapping because they were fed up with how we were being treated by the Shia government. The situation before was so bad – there was kidnapping, killing. The Iraqi army used to come and knock on your door and ask for money and, if you didn't give it, they would shoot you or take you to jail. If you needed to get by road to another neighbourhood, the Iraqi army or police would harass you and demand money, so we were angry and had to defend ourselves.

'One day when I was sixteen or seventeen, I was arguing with a guy I didn't know. He turned out to be an army lieutenant and they took me and beat me up for no reason, not just me, there were thousands of us.'

I asked how it compared with Saddam's time.

'I don't remember really the time under Saddam as I was seven when he went, but I heard he was good for us Sunni because he was strong and controlled the Shia, and if anyone did anything bad, he would just hang them.

'When ISIS came to Mosul the first time they were not so many, maybe 200, but everyone started joining them because they were fed up, so they became thousands and the Iraqi army fled. My family was not happy – they knew something would happen but I was so angry I joined ISIS.

'I went to the mosque and swore the bayat in July 2014. Then I worked as a security guard in the emergency hospital. I was getting 200,000 dinars per month, ISIS controlled everything, but then this went down to 100,000 because they didn't have money.

'ISIS were helping people a lot – they opened the road so we could go to other neighbourhoods, put lights on bridges and did lots of things better. The only bad thing was they were not good with females and made them wear hijab. If ISIS hadn't started using a lot of religion and making people upset with them, I think they would be there forever.'

I asked about the Yazidis.

'I just saw Yazidi girls on phones – my friends at the hospital used to show pictures. My friend had a sabaya he was trying to sell for $6000, she was maybe eighteen or nineteen. We were told you can buy a Yazidi and treat her like a slave. My friend asked, "Why don't you get one?" But I grew up differently, my family taught me you should look after your neighbour. This thing was not for me, I didn't like it, we are Arabs and you can't just buy and sell women. I used to tell the girls, go back to your family but she said, "No, I want to stay."'

Which girl? I asked – he had earlier said he had only seen them on the phone. 'The ones I met,' he shrugged.

'Also I got married three months after ISIS came and have a daughter of three.'

Where are your wife and daughter? I asked.

He suddenly looked tearful. 'They are in a camp, thanks be to God,' he replied.

What happened to your legs? I asked.

'I was in the ambulance and there was an airstrike in Mosul and we tried to get the wounded out of the rubble, then while we were doing that, we heard a big noise and there was another airstrike. I came round in hospital, and my legs had been blown off, one above the knee, one below.

'After fifteen days I was trying to escape to go to Syria and Turkey in a car with my mother, father, wife and daughter but we got arrested by Americans. It was 19 November 2016. They brought my dad, driver and me here. My dad is still here but he wasn't in ISIS.'

Like the others they were still waiting for their cases to come to court.

'Now I regret joining ISIS,' he added.

Meeting ISIS face to face had not been particularly illuminating beyond making me realise how complicated it was going to be for all these communities to work together and how far we were from the Yazidis getting any form of justice.

Afterwards I discussed what I had seen with Pari Ibrahim, the young Yazidi law graduate in America, who set up the Free Yazidi Foundation to help the women in the camps.

'The problem is every perpetrator in Iraq is indicted for blanket terrorism,' she said. 'I know it's the easy way to get indictments but for a Yazidi girl it's not acceptable; they want justice for the crime that was committed against them and we have not seen that. It's very shameful. We'd like to see them indicted for war rape.'

The problem is not just in Iraq, she adds. 'Yazidi girls have been raped by many foreign fighters. I went to talk to authorities in

France, Germany, Spain and UK and they all say, "Pari, this person travelled to Syria so can be indicted for terrorism." They don't understand that if a person raped a Yazidi girl, we want them convicted and jailed for that. We need to show the world that people cannot get away with this.'

I could hear despair in her voice. 'The UK is at the forefront of pushing for ending rape in war yet cannot push for this?' she asks. 'It seems like we can't get indictments, only summits. Just talk, talk, talk and no action.'

Just as the Yazidis took rescuing their women and girls into their own hands, she believed they must do the same in the fight for justice. She and others had begun compiling a database of pictures in the hope of identifying perpetrators of rape and indicting them, and they were working with Amal Clooney and a German prosecutor. It was all being done very quietly as the women were afraid.

'We know justice won't happen within one or two years,' she shrugged. 'It's a very long road.

'Once we took some Yazidis to New York to meet the Rwandans who got the first conviction and they hugged each other and cried. For the Yazidis it was a relief to see there is one day justice.'

I did not tell her that the Rwandans had told me how for them the meeting with the Yazidis had had the opposite effect – how depressed it left them that for all their courage and efforts, rape went on.

13

Dr Miracle and the City of Joy

Bukavu, Democratic Republic of Congo

'The fighting I encountered was vicious and cruel, and on the whole, evil men prevailed,' wrote Don McCullin, the renowned war photographer, describing a visit to the Congo in 1964 amid the chaos following the CIA-backed killing of independence leader Patrice Lumumba. Powerful black-and-white images showed young soldiers pointing their guns at the heads of even younger freedom fighters they were about to execute.

The photos were in an exhibition at London's Tate Britain gallery in 2019 just before I travelled there and it did not sound as though things in the Democratic Republic of Congo had improved much.

'The rape capital of the world' was what the United Nations Special Representative on Sexual Violence had called it in 2010. Figures beyond comprehension – 1000 women a day raped, more than one in three women in eastern Congo affected, seventy in an hour … In my head I think I was putting off going there.

It took months to get the visa and when it was finally stamped in my passport it was brightly coloured and silver-embossed which was not a good thing – in my experience, the more impressive the visa, the more messed-up the country.

Within hours of booking my flight, my inbox started filling up with SOS messages from the travel office, informing me of epidemics of measles as well as monkeypox, chikungunya and other diseases I had never heard of. And of course, Ebola, the world's second-biggest outbreak. Aid agencies I contacted sent alerts about ongoing violence in the east where I was headed, which had left 6 million people displaced, the biggest number in Africa.

Crossing the border from the orderliness of Rwanda into the cacophony of Goma only added to that impression. The streets were broken and swarming, boys transporting heavy loads on homemade wooden bicycle-cum-scooters called *chukudus*. A man displayed single shoes, explaining that if he put out pairs people would steal them. Meat hanging from hooks in the sun smelled sour. Much of the city was still under a coating of what looked like molten shiny black boiled-sweets – lava from a volcanic eruption in 2002 which had covered a third of the city. Even Lake Kivu, glittering enticingly in the distance, was an 'exploding lake', full of methane and dissolved carbon dioxide, which could also erupt.

Yet, crossing that lake on the *Kivu Queen* ferry from Goma, the scenery was breathtaking. Inside the cabin a video was playing loudly in French with Chinese subtitles, but the small deck outside looked onto mirror-blue waters and rolling green hills, above which an occasional dark kestrel circled.

As the sun dipped toward the horizon, sending long rectangles of light across the water, the sky turned to blushing apricot then deep tangerine then fiery red as if painted in brushstrokes by a frenzied painter. Simple wooden fishing boats appeared silhouetted, trawling for sardines, their long delicate curved prow and bows arched like seagull wings, with the sound of men singing wafting on the breeze.

I was headed to Bukavu on the lake's southwest shore to visit a man they call Dr Miracle who had treated more rape victims than anyone on earth.

*   *   *

The road to Panzi Hospital was chock-a-block with people, goats, cars, young men selling chewing gum and airtime, women balancing pyramids of fruit on their heads, even a prayer meeting – the last two decades of war in eastern Congo had seen hundreds of thousands of people flee from the countryside into the town.

From the outside, the hospital did not look like anything special. The entrance led to two red-brick quadrangles with grass court-yards; the walkways were crowded with women in colourful block-print dresses waiting to be let through one of a series of doors into a doctor's office or lab.

Just behind, a small gate opened onto a path to a two-storey cream-painted building – the women's hospital. Inside, extending either side of the entrance hall, were large wards with row upon row of beds of women and girls.

All had either suffered pelvic prolapses or other damage giving birth, or were victims of sexual violence so extreme that their genitals had been torn apart and they had suffered fistulas – holes in the sphincter muscle through to the bladder or rectum, which led to leaking of urine or faeces or both.

In twenty years of existence, the hospital had treated more than 55,000 victims of rape.

Every day between five and seven more arrived. Dr Patrick Kubuya, the head of the women's hospital, told me he currently had 250 patients who were victims of sexual violence, and some-times as many as 300. The previous year they had treated 3093 women, of whom half had been raped.

Behind the building was a large covered terrace crowded with women sitting at tables, many with heads on their hands, looking down. From somewhere I could hear wailing.

A large placard rested upside-down against a wall, congratulat-ing its founder Dr Denis Mukwege on winning the Nobel Peace Prize a few months earlier.

I had met Dr Mukwege a couple of times in Europe, sharing an Ethiopian curry in Geneva where he was bringing survivors from different conflicts together and trying to get the international community to act. I thought this tall lumbering man with a kindly oblong face and modest manner was one of the most incredible people I had ever come across.

In his French-accented English, he had told me that when he founded the hospital back in 1999 it was to deal with Congo's appalling levels of mothers dying in childbirth, one of the highest in the world, even today seven in every 1000.

'My vision was to fight maternal mortality,' he explained. 'In France where I finished my medical studies and training as a gynaecologist, I had never seen a woman die in birth, but in Congo it was so common that women utter their last words when going into labour because they don't know if they will survive.

Dr Mukwege has treated more rape victims than anyone on earth

'It seemed terrible to me to imagine that in the same world, with all its technology and progress, that a woman can think, I am pregnant so perhaps this is the end of my life. Preventing maternal mortality is not difficult, it's a question of political will: where do you want to spend your money?'

After graduating from the University of Angers in 1983 and returning home to Bukavu, where his father was a Pentecostal pastor, he had moved to Lemera, a remote area in the south, to work as a gynaecologist in the hospital. There, he began building small centres for women to give birth, and schools for training midwives. Within a few years they had drastically reduced maternal mortality.

'I was really happy with the results,' he said. 'But in 1994 soldiers started appearing and then in 1996 the war started.'

Following the Rwandan genocide, hundreds of thousands of Hutus had fled across the western border into the forests of what was then Zaire. Among them were many of the Interahamwe or génocidaires and they took control of the vast refugee camps that had sprung up around Goma and Bukavu. The Tutsi-led Rwandan army of General Paul Kagame who had ended the genocide and taken power in Rwanda soon came in pursuit. This spill-over fighting between the Hutus and Tutsis of Rwanda sparked the First Congo War of 1996–7 and Kagame's well-trained forces supported rebel groups of Laurent-Désiré Kabila to topple long-time despot Mobutu Sese Seko, who was a byword for corruption in his leopard-skin hat.

For Kabila it was what he called 'time to harvest'. He had begun fighting Mobutu back in the 1960s, leading a Marxist revolution in eastern Congo. Che Guevara had even flown in to help, arriving with a hundred Cubans to try to kickstart the revolution. Plagued with malaria and dysentery, eventually Guevara had given up, deriding Kabila in his diary for having 'not set foot since time immemorial at the front' and preferring to spend his time 'in the best hotels issuing communiques and drinking Scotch in the company of beautiful women'.

After that collapsed, Kabila had turned to smuggling gold and timber, and ran a brothel and a bar in Tanzania. He probably would have been a footnote to history, were it not for President Kagame of Rwanda and President Yoweri Museweni of Uganda choosing him as frontman for the rebellion.

Mobutu's army rapidly disintegrated and rebel forces swept from the east across the vast country. On the night of 6 October 1996, they attacked the Lemera hospital. Dr Mukwege managed to evacuate some patients but soldiers blocked the road behind him and he could not get back for the rest. Thirty-three patients were slaughtered in their beds as well as many staff.

'It made me suffer for a long time,' he said. 'When I eventually returned to my senses, I came home to Bukavu, where I saw the same problem of women dying needlessly in childbirth.

'I thought to help women I don't really need a big infrastructure, just a few boxes of equipment, two or three small rooms and a delivery room where I can do a Caesarean if necessary and the mothers can stay for a short period after birth. I could save lives doing small things because I had knowledge.'

But then, in 1998, a second war started as Kabila's backers from Rwanda and Uganda tired of the ever more corpulent and dictatorial President. This was even bloodier, drawing in nine different countries as Kabila bribed other leaders to send him troops, which included those from Zimbabwe (in return for diamond mines which in turn helped prop up the Mugabe regime) and from Angola (for off-shore oil). It was the world's deadliest conflict since the Second World War, becoming known as 'Africa's World War', and eventually saw Rwanda, Uganda and Burundi ranged against the DRC, Zimbabwe, Angola, Namibia, Chad and Sudan. An estimated 5 million people were killed and millions more displaced from their homes. Yet I barely remember mention of it in the West.

For Dr Mukwege it was a disaster. His rooms were trashed and his equipment was looted so in June 1999 he began treating pregnant women in tents. 'That was how Panzi started,' he said.

But the first patient didn't come to give birth. 'It was a woman who had been raped 500 metres away from my place by several men and after raping her they shot through her vagina,' he recalled. 'I was so shocked I thought this must be an isolated incident carried out by someone on drugs who isn't really conscious of what he is doing.'

Over the next three months, forty-five more women turned up all with the same story. One after another told him how they had been at home with their families when men with guns came and shot dead the husbands then raped the women. 'They stuck bayonets in their genitals or sticks soaked in fuel which they set on fire,' he said. 'Some were raped by five or more men till they lost consciousness. All in front of their children. I realised then these militias were using rape as weapons of war.'

The rapes were carried out by militias allied to different ethnic groups and different sides in the war. They were also fighting over control of precious minerals such as gold, coltan and cobalt that Mukwege believes have 'cursed' Congo's women rather than making the country rich.

Each group seemed to have its own signature torture and the rapes were so violent that often a fistula or hole had been torn in the bladders or rectums.

'It's not a sexual thing, it's a way to destroy another, to take from inside the victim the sense of being a human, and show you don't exist, you are nothing,' he said. 'It's a deliberate strategy: raping a woman in front of her husband to humiliate him so he leaves and shame falls on the victim and it's impossible to live with the reality so the first reaction is to leave the area and there is total destruction of the community. I've seen entire villages deserted.

'It's about making people feel powerless and destroying the social fabric. I've seen a case where the wife of a pastor was raped in front of the whole congregation so everyone fled. Because if God does not protect the wife of a pastor how would he protect them?

'Rape as a weapon of war can displace a whole demographic and have the same effect as a conventional weapon but at much lesser cost.'

Dr Mukwege became so desperate at what he was seeing that in 2001 he contacted the organisation Human Rights Watch. They sent a team to Panzi and the following year published a shocking report which detailed the epidemic of sexual violence in eastern Congo by militias and military.*

'I thought it would be a turning point where the international community would say this can't go on, but since this time I am still waiting,' he said. 'Twenty years on I am still treating victims of sexual violence.'

President Kabila was sitting in his marble palace in Kinshasa in January 2001 when one of his teenage bodyguards walked in, pulled out his pistol and shot him dead. He was replaced by his twenty-nine-year-old son Joseph, a commander in the Congolese army, and the war officially ended in 2003. But violence and rape had continued.

'It never stops,' said Dr Mukwege. 'We have already treated 55,000 women and this is only the tip of the iceberg, because many are dying in villages, not coming to the hospital because they are ashamed, stigmatised and afraid to be excommunicated if people know. Indeed, it's my impression we are going backwards.'

* * *

* Human Rights Watch, *The War Within the War*, 2002.

Behind a door in Panzi Hospital, I soon saw what he meant. It was opened by one of Dr Mukwege's team of surgeons, Dr Desiré Alumetti, a man with a sunbeam of a smile and a red baseball cap emblazoned in white with the words DR MUKWEGE MY HERO. Inside was a children's room, cheerfully decorated with large cartoon transfers of Mickey Mouse, Pink Panther and Pluto. On an examination couch sat a small girl in a torn orange and yellow dress with short horizonal pigtails and eyes saucer-wide. Her name was Violette, she was four years old, and she had been raped.

Alongside her was her anxious mother Atosha and they had travelled all the way from Kindu in Maniema province, more than 350 miles to the west.

Speaking in a low voice, Atosha recounted what had happened. 'I went to the field in the forest to sow rice and left Violette at home playing,' she began. 'When I came home, she wasn't in the compound then I saw her crying and bleeding with her clothes in her hand. I was scared and asked what happened, "Did you fall?"'

'She said, "No, there was a man who came and took me into the latrine behind the school then put his hand over my mouth and abused me."'

'We couldn't see anyone but we went to look and there was blood in the toilet. We washed her and took her to the clinic and the doctor gave her medicine but we didn't have money to pay so took her back home. That's when we noticed the bad smell. We realised poo was leaking.

'I didn't know what to do. But in our village, there is an old mother called Kapinga, a health-worker, who heard what happened and told me to bring Violette. When she saw her, she told me to take her to Panzi immediately, we didn't even have time to go home and change clothes. We flew to Goma. It was the first time we had been on a plane. Then we took a boat.

'Since we got here last week the doctors have put her sitting in salted water to try and heal the wound and she has seen a psychologist.'

Atosha herself was clearly in shock. 'My heart is broken,' she said. 'I feel so bad. She is only four and already not a virgin. I feel guilty because I left her but I have no choice but to go to the forest and earn money to buy food.'

I nodded. In my few days in eastern Congo I had noticed it seemed to be the women who did all the work, heading off to the fields or bent almost double carrying enormous sacks of charcoal.

Why would someone do something like this? I asked.

'I don't know,' she replied. 'Maybe witchcraft, people believe raping babies gives them special powers.'

What did she think should happen to the perpetrator?

'We can't do anything because we don't know who did it,' she shrugged. 'Violette just said it's an old man. If we knew, the rest of the village would kill him. How could you do something like this to a girl of four?'

Little Violette put her head and arms on her mum's lap as if trying to shut out the world.

Dr Alumetti explained that the four-year-old had been raped through her tiny anus so brutally that the man's penis had forced a hole to the rectum, which was why she was leaking, and he was planning to operate the next day to try to repair this.

I was still trying to get my head round this when he brought in another patient. A young mother Anazo was breastfeeding her baby Chantal, just seven months old.

At first I was confused, presuming the mother was the victim. Instead, Anazo carefully detached the baby, who had a mass of curls, and laid her down to be examined. The baby immediately started crying. I had never seen such sheer fear in a baby's eyes.

'She cries whenever I put her down now,' said Anazo.

She put Chantal on her lap and lifted up the clothes and it was all I could do not to gasp at the vivid red wound around the baby's anus.

They had also come a long way, about 160 miles from Kaloli village in Shabunda, a remote part of South Kivu where gold had been found, bringing misery rather than prosperity to the villagers by attracting in militias.

'I was going to the field to work and left the baby with my younger sister when the rebels came to my village,' she explained. 'They started shooting and stealing things and my sister ran away and left the baby and came and found me in the field to tell me.'

The men were from Raia Mutomboki, one of the most feared of the region's many *mai-mai* or militias, who, according to a recent UN report, were responsible for hundreds of civilian deaths and mass rape.* The fighters would abduct women and girls who they kept in a cave as sex slaves and shout, Tchai! Tchai! – Tea Time!, before the rapes started. They would dance around their leader Masudi Kokodikoko who would choose the women he preferred, usually the youngest, and rape as many as nine of them, before passing them on to his fighters.

'Everyone fears those men,' said Anazo. 'I ran home but the house had already been attacked. They had taken the bag of rice and all my clothes and the baby's clothes. I found the baby on the bed crying so I just took her and ran away.

'But the baby wouldn't stop crying. I tried to breastfeed but she wouldn't eat. I didn't know what was wrong. Then I took off her clothes and found wounds around her anus and red all around so I took her to the medical centre. The doctor straight away saw she had been raped as the anal tissue was totally opened.

---

* Report of Group of Experts to UN Security Council, December 2018 (final report published 7 June 2019).

'When I heard that my whole body was shaking. I felt like I'd lost control, I didn't even know where I was. In our area the rebels often came and arrested people and destroyed houses and looted things but this was the first time I heard of anything like this.'

When the doctor tried to see what was going on, he saw the anal part and the vagina were touching each other – the penis had torn a hole. He said we couldn't leave the baby like that so he did what he could then sent me here. I also have a three-year-old daughter so I left her with my husband. It was a long way and cost me $200 which I had to borrow.

'When I came here, we didn't have anything to wear or for the baby because the militia had stolen all our clothes so the doctor's wife gave me some things.'

The examination over, she put Chantal back to her breast. 'Look, she can only sit on one side,' she said. 'I hope whoever did this will go to jail for years.'

I told Dr Alumetti that I couldn't imagine an adult man forcing his penis into a tiny baby.

'Sometimes they do it to push people out of the area so they can exploit the minerals,' he said. 'Sometimes they think it gives them power to make them invincible.'

I asked how he would treat baby Chantal. 'We have given her an injection against Hepatitis B and bathed her in antiseptic water against infection, then we will operate.'

He drew a diagram in my notebook of how the anal sphincter had been ruptured. Dr Mukwege grades damage in five categories, the worst being the fifth where the genital, urinary and digestive tracts would all need repair and a laparoscopy would be needed to clear the abdominal cavity.

Chantal would be the youngest baby Dr Alumetti had ever operated on. The youngest he had previously treated was seventeen months but said the hospital had one of just four months.

'It's not easy for us to see this kind of story and treat this kind of patient,' he said. 'But it's a big pleasure to work with Dr M. I've never met a man like him. Every day I say, "If I can be like this guy, what respect I will get from my family, my community, my country."'

Back through the brick quadrangles full of women, a man unlocked a barred gate and led me down a corridor into a reception crammed with files on shelves. On the wall was a whiteboard on which was written in green pen *La Pensée de la Semaine* – Thought for the Week.

> *Today, thanks to new technology and communication, nobody can say they didn't know. To close your eyes to this drama is to be complicit. It's not only the perpetrators who are responsible for these crimes but those who choose to turn the other cheek.*

Beyond was a spacious office where the man they call Dr Miracle was giving a lesson round a long table to a group of young doctors. These were part of the Panzi network he was trying to create across DRC as well as in other African countries which had a major rape crisis such as Guinea-Conakry, Burkina Faso, and the Central African Republic.

His eyes were bloodshot. It was 2 p.m. and that day he had already done four operations, two on rape victims. As usual he had started at 7 a.m., conducting prayers for his staff (like his father he is a Pentecostal pastor), and would probably work till 11 p.m. The following week he was off to Europe and the US to once more try to alert the world to the horrors going on in his country.

As he sat down next to me heavily on the sofa, he told me he was depressed. 'On Monday after examining the baby I was thinking about how medically to repair her, as a rupture of the anus is more complicated than of the vagina. And then I thought, Really, this is enough, I can't go on. Already we are treating women we previously repaired and are raped again or generations of women from the same family? Now for the last five years we are getting more and more babies. How can these things happen and we don't act? I am crying for years to stop these things but people are just denying them.'

The first time he was brought a baby who had been raped was in 2014. 'She was just eighteen months and really I didn't understand, her intestine was hanging out of her vagina, she was bleeding profusely and she was dying. We managed to save her but for me it was really shocking. The nurses were all sobbing – it was the first time I had seen them crying while treating a patient.

'We prayed in silence – my God, tell us what we are seeing isn't true, that it's a bad dream. But it wasn't, it was the new reality.

'Now, if you look at the numbers of patients coming into the hospital, they are stable, but the big problem is the number of children is increasing. Ten years ago, 3 per cent of our patients were under ten. Last year it was 6 per cent and it's going up.

'To do this with babies of seven months or four years this is not human. When we let impunity take place you authorise things even animals can't do.

'I can be operating and repairing day after day but that's not the solution. All these children and babies who are destroyed, their future is completely destroyed …'

Dr Mukwege's belief that the problem cannot be resolved at the operating table has led him to pioneer a holistic approach, widely referred to as the Panzi model.

Rape victims who arrive within seventy-two hours after the rape are given a kit to protect against pregnancy, HIV and sexually transmitted diseases. If they arrive later, they are treated for any infection, and, if they test positive for AIDS, are given drugs. Only the most severe cases are brought to the hospital so most require surgery.

As I saw him wandering around the hospital grounds over the next few days, Panzi offered far more than medical treatment.

Dr Mukwege explained: 'What we discovered was treating victims medically was not enough because of the trauma. So we established a team of psychologists to support them and began using art and music therapy. But even when they recovered mentally, we saw that to send them back to their villages was not a solution, as most were discriminated against and rejected by their family and community. To send them back was to send them onto the streets.

'So, the third pillar is socioeconomic support. If they are younger, we pay fees for them to go to school and support them. If they are pregnant, we have a refuge, Maison Dorcas, where we take care of them.

'For adult women we offer a literacy course and teach them different skills like handicrafts, tailoring and agriculture, so they can be independent. We teach them to set up mutual funds and we provide seeds and micro-loans for them to have small businesses because it's a way for them not just to earn income but to be strong and fight for their own rights.'

There was also a centre for babies born of rape as they tend to be rejected.

The fourth and final pillar was legal advice. 'We find that once we have helped the women to be self-sufficient, what happens is they come back and say, "I want justice," so we have lawyers who can help them file cases.'

This, he said, was both part of the process of healing and key to changing the situation.

'It's not something of one day – it might be six months or even five years before a woman says I am ready and want to speak up. It takes time but the only way we can change society is to end impunity. Because what is protecting perpetrators, even in Europe, is silence.

'We need to help women understand that what they went through is not normal and that if they start to speak out, it is helping not only them but the community. Even these men have families and when the women make public what they did many are afraid for their position in society and their own families.

'As long as we put the taboo on the victim rather than the perpetrator, nothing will change. But when the perpetrator starts to say, "What will be the reaction of my wife, my neighbours, my boss? This will affect my position in the community, I could lose my job and face trial," then he will think twice.'

Setting up all this system was not easy, he said. 'Many hospital staff didn't believe it was part of healthcare and were resistant.'

It was also dangerous, particularly as Dr Mukwege frequently spoke out on the complicity of the government, as much of the raping is carried out by the Congolese military. 'I've had lots of threats,' he shrugged.

In 2011 he was invited to speak at the UN General Assembly in New York by Margot Wallström, the first UN Special Representative on Sexual Violence, and the person who had described DRC as 'rape capital of the world'. But when he arrived the Congolese Minister of Health summoned him to his hotel. 'He told me you need to make a choice – either go home, or stay and give your speech, in which case you take responsibility for what happens to you and your family. My family was in Congo and I was in New York so it was a clear threat. I decided to cancel.'

The following year, in September 2012, he was invited again to address the assembly, this time by the then British foreign minister William Hague, who had become the first foreign minister of a major country to take up the issue of sexual violence. This time Dr

Mukwege agreed. He was outspoken in his criticism of the Kabila government.

When he returned home in October, five men with pistols and AK47s were waiting. 'They had taken my daughters hostage and started to shoot. I thought I was going to die. My guard Jeff of more than twenty-five years was killed in front of my daughters and I don't know how I was saved.

'They did not do anything to my daughters, rape them or anything, but of course they were waiting, thinking something might happen, which was terrifying.'

After their narrow escape, the family left the country for Belgium. But within two months women in Congo started to write to him, asking him to return. 'One day I heard they were selling bananas and tomatoes to pay for my ticket so I had to come back.'

In a sense the hospital had now become his prison, for since the attack he had lived on site with a truck of troops from MONUSCO, the UN peacekeeping force, protecting him. 'We are always in danger. I can't move without security.' Even so, he said there was often shooting. 'They come round the hospital or my house and shoot.'

One of his colleagues, Dr Gilda, was killed in 2015, shot dead while working at Kasenga Hospital. 'That was devastating to me,' he said.

His five children were grown up and though he missed them, he was glad they were out of the country, for he worried that it was slipping back into the horror of the late 1990s. 'We are in a situation now of no war but no peace,' he said.

His son was training to be a gynaecologist and though he hoped he would follow in his footsteps at Panzi, he was torn. 'How can I ask him to come back when he has young children and I am living in a prison?'

* * *

On Friday 5 October 2018, Dr Mukwege had started in surgery at 7.30 a.m. as usual. He was on his second operation when he heard patients and colleagues crying.

At first he thought something terrible had happened. But when he came out in his scrubs everyone was hugging him. He had been awarded the Nobel Peace Prize, jointly with Nadia Murad, the young Yazidi activist, for their work highlighting the use of sexual violence as a weapon of war.

Surely this meant the international community was now taking this issue seriously?

He shrugged. 'Maybe the Nobel is an honour but our fight is not for an honour, it's to stop what is happening to girls and babies in Congo.'

I asked him why Congo was so bad for women. 'It's a good question,' he replied. In Goma I had been baffled about why it was the women who went to the fields day after day or to collect firewood and water, even though there was a huge risk of them being kidnapped and raped. A Belgian man I had spoken to who had lived there more than twenty years told me he thought the real problem was the patriarchal culture, pointing out its high levels of domestic abuse.

For Dr Mukwege, the violence was too extreme and methodical for this to be the explanation. 'Typically, the women we see have been raped not by one man but three or four, usually in front of the husband and children and involving torture like a piece of wood inserted in their genitals so their genital apparatus is totally destroyed. It's systematically done and has nothing to do with sex.'

He traced the violence back to the influx of génocidaires from Rwanda and subsequent wars but believes mostly it is about control over resources.

In his acceptance speech in Oslo in December, he began, 'My name is Dr Mukwege. I come from one of the richest countries on the planet. Yet the people of my country are among the poorest of the world.

'My country is being systematically looted with the complicity of people claiming to be our leaders. The Congolese people have been humiliated, abused and massacred for more than two decades in plain sight of the international community.'

The country created by Belgium's King Leopold II in 1885 as his personal fiefdom has been endlessly plundered by its leaders for its gold, diamonds, copper and tin, often with the connivance of multinational mining companies. But in recent years other minerals had become important, those key to the technological revolution. The DRC supplies two thirds of the cobalt needed for the batteries of electric cars, mobiles and laptops as well as coltan – columbo tantalite, from which comes tantalum necessary for their capacitors. Household names like Microsoft, Apple and IBM all relied on minerals from there and probably every household in the West had at least one of their products.

This infuriated Dr Mukwege. 'My feeling is that C ongo is part of the human community and Congolese babies are human too so I am surprised that everyone is using the natural resources of Congo yet few are thinking it's a stain on humanity to treat women and children the way they do.

'In the West they need these minerals for their phones, laptops and electric cars. I myself have a mobile phone. But buying conflict minerals is not acceptable. It should be done in another clean way. And to let this go on for twenty years … The world can't say it didn't have the possibility to stop it.'

The problem, he said, went right to the top. 'What I know is that rape can't just be used as a weapon of war without responsibility. We must not just blame the perpetrators but ask who told them to rape?

'In this region we've had twenty years of people killing, raping, destroying, and they are still the ones who are leading the country and military and police and intelligence. When you accept this, you accept people who completely lost their minds – and I think most of them are sick.'

In his Nobel speech he had talked of a report which he said was 'gathering mould in an office drawer in New York' called the Mapping Report, a UN investigation into war crimes in Congo. This, he said, described no fewer than 617 war crimes with names of victims, dates and places but left the perpetrators nameless.

'The Mapping Report is a UN report so why keep it in a cupboard?' he told me. 'We know the people who committed these crimes are still leading the country.'

I told him his Nobel address was one of the most powerful speeches I had ever heard.

'Everyone applauded but nothing happened,' he said, sadly. 'We need the UN Security Council to say no, the war in Congo is not acceptable, and action must be taken.

'We need an international mechanism to bring all these perpetrators to court to start an investigation. We know the ones who are leading the country are the ones who are perpetrating the crimes so we can't ask them to do the investigation.'

On 30 December 2018, a few weeks after the Nobel speech and a few months before my trip, presidential elections finally took place after two years of delays. When we'd met before, Dr Mukwege had worried they wouldn't happen, as he was convinced that Joseph Kabila had no intention of relinquishing power.

He laughed wryly when I asked him about them. 'I went to vote at the polling station in the local school. It opened at 7 a.m. but the machine didn't arrive till 5 p.m. for more than 30,000 people to vote so most of us did not get the chance.'

Initially, there was surprise when an opposition candidate Félix Tshisekedi was declared victor. Later it emerged that he and Kabila had done a deal before the elections. The real winner according to monitors of the election for the Catholic Church was another opposition leader, Martin Fayulu.*

There was little reaction from the West, governments apparently believing that some change was better than none, even as Kabila remained in the presidential house and his Common Front for Congo won a landslide in Parliament.

'Kabila is now even stronger than he was before,' said Dr Mukwege, shaking his head. 'Now he has control of not just the military, intelligence and police but the senate, parliament, local government and governors, so all the power is in his hands.'

After DRC was labelled the rape capital of the world in 2010, President Kabila had appointed a special advisor on sexual violence, Jeanne Mabunda, and promised zero tolerance. Since then he had claimed his country was being 'held up as an example' of how to fight sexual violence. In 2016 Mabunda flew to Bukavu and claimed that the number of rapes had fallen by 50 per cent in the two years since she was appointed.

'This is all just PR,' said Dr Mukwege. 'On the ground nothing has changed. If I'm still getting babies, how can I say there has been a change?'

There was little love lost between the Kabila government and Dr Mukwege. In 2015, the government suddenly presented Panzi with a $600,000 bill for years of back taxes despite the fact that hospitals in DRC are supposed to be tax exempt. Eventually this was withdrawn after an outcry.

When I first applied for my visa with an invitation letter from Panzi Hospital, I was told to get a letter from somewhere else if I wanted it to be approved.

---

* Tom Wilson, David Blood, David Pilling, 'Congo Voting Data Reveal Huge Fraud in Poll to Replace Kabila', *Financial Times*, 15 January 2019.

They had even accused him of spreading red mercury chrome ointment on children to fake injuries for journalists.

Though some commanders had been brought to justice, Dr Mukwege's pessimism was shared by Daniele Perissi, an Italian jurist I later spoke to who had been in Bukavu for four years heading the Congo office of TRIAL International, a Geneva-based NGO founded by a group of lawyers and victims to fight impunity round the world.

'I don't want to sound overly pessimistic but while the state has done some things like stopping recruitment of child soldiers into the armed forces, unfortunately for rape it's not the same story. It continues to be committed by everyone.'

He told me that even judges and magistrates they were working with on cases were involved. 'The fact we are now seeing teachers, lawyers and judges carrying out these crimes shows that the culture of impunity is so entrenched in society that it not only trivialises these crimes but also sends the message that it's normal for people in positions of power to do this.

'We had one case of a judge who was by day presiding over a mobile tribunal judging sexual violence crimes and at night abusing the 16-year-old daughter of his hosts.'

The sense of moving one step forward, two back, was compounded by a case in the International Criminal Court of Jean-Pierre Bemba, a Congolese warlord and former Vice-President to Kabila, before he ran against him in the 2006 elections.

In 2008 Bemba was arrested in Brussels under an ICC warrant and charged with eight counts of war crimes and crimes against humanity committed by fighters under his command during the 2002–03 conflict in the Central African Republic, when he had sent 1000 troops to prop up its then president.

In March 2016 the ICC found Bemba guilty of murder, rape a nd pillage of civilians by his men. It was a historic decision – the first conviction by the ICC on sexual violence and the first time it had found a commander guilty for actions committed by his troops.

But two years later, in June 2018, they reversed the decision and acquitted Bemba, leaving him free to return to the DRC and participate in elections.

'This is the exact opposite of the message we need to send,' said Perissi. 'People in DRC feel that if even the ICC does that, what kind of hope can we have?'

Mukwege was horrified. 'Someone did these things. Women of the Central African Republic fought ten years for this. If you acquit him then you should prosecute someone else for what happened. If you don't, it means for the victims there will never be justice or reparations. How can victims rebuild their lives if they feel our suffering was accepted by the community?

'Women have the impression that not only are they being accused in their own communities for being raped, but the international community is accusing them of lying, so they are accused a second time.'

I mentioned attending the ISIS trials and hearing the frustration of the Yazidi women that what happened to them was not included in the charges.

He nodded. 'I have spoken to women in Korea, Colombia, Bosnia, Iraq … and they all say when they raped me, they killed me. You are just convicting people because they killed but what happened to us is worse because you left someone alive but with the feeling they don't exist at all, they are already dead inside.

'This makes me feel we need another word for rape because I think, in the minds of men, rape is only a sexual relation not accepted by victim, almost as if it's normal.'

I wondered how he coped being confronted day after day, year after year with the worst evils of man.

'The women are my therapists,' he replied. He went on to explain: 'The first time I was seeing ten cases, then forty, then a hundred, a thousand, ten thousand women ... do you think that was easy? I said to myself it's not possible. I couldn't sleep, I started having nightmares. I'd say where are my daughters and start trembling, wondering what would happen to them. I even thought about moving abroad.

'But throughout my entire life, whenever I have felt lost, God has opened a narrow door for me to pass through.'

The doorway on that occasion was a visit from Eve Ensler, the American author, actress and activist best known for her ground-breaking play *The Vagina Monologues*, which opened in New York in 1996 and went on to be performed all over the world. She used the proceeds and publicity to create her V-Day movement to raise money to end violence against women and girls.

They had met at a UN event in New York and he invited her to come to DRC to visit the hospital. 'I remember that day well. It was a Saturday in 2007. Eve had arrived at the hospital and asked the women about their lives and they started dancing, each woman in the style of her village. It was incredible. I saw then that all was not lost and I should not give up because if these women could express the strength within them despite all they had gone through, then I should fight alongside them. For the first time after the dancing I went back to my house and slept like a baby.

'So now, every time I think, Aagh, this is enough, I remember those women dancing. I am suffering but they are suffering more than me yet still loving, still transforming hate into love and that really helps me.'

The same thing had just happened that week, he said. 'Just as I was despairing about the babies, a woman came who we treated long ago and helped, and brought her daughter who had just grad-uated, and said all these terrible things happened to me but I have a daughter who graduated. She was so happy and proud, with so much dignity that it infected me and I felt all is not lost, we still have hope and we will overcome these evil things.'

Ensler was equally moved. 'I was utterly blown away by Dr Mukwege,' she told me. 'I couldn't believe there was such a man on the planet devoting his life to ending sexual violence or such a place.'

I couldn't get the children out of my head. Next morning, I stopped by the hospital. Violette, the four-year-old girl, was sitting and waiting for surgery, eyes bigger than ever.

A little further on from the hospital, past a dusty field where some men were kicking around a football, we turned off onto a muddy track along which women were selling charcoal from sacks, and a makeshift camp of ragged red-eyed boys, who turned out to be former child soldiers. At the end we came to two large black gates painted with unlikely words, *City of Joy*.

Two female guards took my bag, allowing me to keep only my phone and notebook, before they let me through.

Inside the walls were lush green gardens full of flowers, trees and birds singing. A smiling young woman, pleasantly plump in lime green, showed me into an office. The door opened to an explosion of colour, flowers, rainbows, photos, hearts, bowls of sweets and inspirational sayings. My eyes were drawn in all directions. *If Congo Is the Worst Place to Be a Woman, City of Joy Is the Best*, read one.

Presiding over it all, like some fabulous bird of paradise, was a tall striking figure with a long multicoloured Missoni-style cardigan in blue, red and gold over black pants and high black strappy sandals, dangly red-beaded earrings from gold discs, flashing eyes and a mass of tiny copper ringlets.

This was Christine Schuler Deschryver, mother, grandmother, director and founder of City of Joy, Vice-President of the Panzi Foundation, and best friend of Dr Mukwege. She laughed at my popping eyes. 'I like colour, life is not just black and white,' she said. 'Dr M. says my office is exactly like me!'

Next to her desk was a sign proclaiming, *V is for Victory, Vagina, Valentine's Day.*

'Here at City of Joy we talk all day long about vaginas,' she explained. 'I arrive and the girls ask, "Christine, how is your vagina today?" I say, "OMG, it's in a bad mood!"'

It was also the slogan for Eve Ensler's organisation V-Day. The centre owed its beginnings – and its $600,000 a year running costs – to the same visit to Panzi from Ensler in 2007 of which Dr Mukwege had spoken. 'You know, usually when famous people come like the Clintons they promise a lot and nothing happens,' said Christine. 'I told Angelina Jolie, you celebs all come here then do nothing. But Eve was different. When she came here, she had cancer and was maybe 60lb, just bones. She asked Congolese women what they wanted. They said we want power, we want to be leaders. At the time we were starting to build the centre and women survivors came and started dancing and dancing. Many had come from the hospital and afterwards there was blood on the floor. I showed Eve and she said, "That gives me an idea. Those women were sick but were still dancing. Why don't we get a billion women dancing?"

'The women had asked for a house for them to be independent so we built a centre and the women chose the name.'

I asked her to tell me about City of Joy. She laughed again. 'I don't know how to describe it: it's more than a place,' she replied. 'Let's go and see.'

We walked through the gardens, passing a heavily armed guard in black, incongruous in the peaceful setting, and a grove of orange trees which were planted by her and Dr Mukwege six years earlier. Beyond these were mango and avocado trees and a herb garden. It was an astonishing haven from the chaos outside; there was even a meditation hut. We also passed cages of rabbits and a hen coop from which a girl was bringing a basket of fresh eggs.

A line of solar panels provided electricity. 'We get nothing from the government,' shrugged Christine, 'no power or water so we have these and a generator.'

'Building it was a complete nightmare,' Ensler had told me. "Not only were there no roads, no electricity and no water but I had stage 3–4 cancer and almost died. I attribute my life to the women of Congo as I knew I couldn't die as I'd made a promise to open this.'

We arrived at a terrace where a group of girls were knitting and sewing. The moment they saw Christine they leapt up and started dancing and singing. 'Mama is around, let us greet her and dance to her,' they crooned, waving their embroidery and laughing. It was so infectious I jumped on the step to join in.

I could see why it was called City of Joy. Yet all of these women were survivors of rape aged eighteen to thirty and had been there less than two months. Christine explained that she adapted the intensive six-month programme to individual needs but around

half the time was spent in therapy, using art, music, meditation and yoga. There were also self-defence and fitness classes, and they were shown how to take care of themselves as well as their hair and make-up.

Hygiene was also important. Behind a locked gate we saw the accommodation, nine houses each with three rooms and ten beds with mosquito net, as well as a bathroom. Each has to choose someone to be their mayor and keep their house clean and tidy.

'These girls have never had showers or electricity or brushed their teeth with a toothbrush or slept on a mattress,' said Christine. 'One girl refused to stay because of the shower: she said water is coming from the roof not the river so she thought it was spirits.'

A key element of their time at City of Joy is learning to tell their stories. This intrigued me as I endlessly worried about re-traumatising survivors by asking them to recount such terrible events.

'It's all about giving respect and them owning their stories,' explained Christine. 'After a month when they start to tell their stories, sometimes OMG ... and the transformation after six is huge. We turn pain into power and give victims strength to be leaders in their communities.'

As the daughter of an affluent white Belgian man and a poor black Congolese woman, Christine knew about prejudice. 'My parents were from completely different worlds – my father from a rich family, my mum an illiterate tea cutter on his parents' estate, so it was forbidden love. My father's family cut them off and I suffered to see my mother suffering.

'I think I was born an activist. All my life I spent helping others. I was at a Belgian school which had only a few black students and I fought like a boy to protect them.'

Her father Adrien was a conservationist. He founded a national park called Kahuzi Biega near the western bank of Lake Kivu, not far from Bukavu, as one of the last refuges for rare lowland goril-

las. I got the impression there was not much love lost. 'Of course
gorillas are more important than people,' she shrugged.

She first came across victims of sexual violence when she
worked as coordinator for eastern Congo for the German development agency, GTZ. 'One of the organisations we funded was
UNFPA [the UN Population Fund] and the money was used to
count broken vaginas,' she said.

She met Dr Mukwege in 1994, before he started Panzi and
began helping him. 'The need was so huge and nobody was interested. I will never forget the smell of rotting bodies, women walking like ghosts … It was me who buried the babies and listened to
the stories so I absorbed all the bad.'

Mukwege was a regular visitor to City of Joy, where he schooled
the girls on some unexpected subjects. Christine explained: 'When
I talk to the girls, most haven't had an orgasm, they don't know
what it is. For them sex is all about satisfying the men. But the
Congolese girls see me as white as I am the first coloured they've
met, so I can't talk to them about deep cultural things. I told Dr
M. this and he came here. We've been close friends for twenty-five
years but I didn't recognise my friend. He told them, even we men
in the night we have accidents … he was talking about masturbation! He asked the girls what do you feel in the night and one said
we are like a chicken that poops and we don't know what to do, it's
spirits taking hold of us. He says no, it's normal, it's like an orgasm.
I couldn't believe it. He's a pastor, a conservative man and there he
is talking about masturbation and orgasms.'

One thousand, two hundred and ninety-four women had done the
course in the eight years since City of Joy opened in 2011. On
leaving, each was given a phone programmed with a contact
number to keep in touch. Thirteen had died and they had lost
contact with twelve. Only one girl they know of was raped again.

'When they graduate they are so proud,' said Christine. 'They go back to the community and share what they've learnt with others, work with local NGOs or create their own. One is a director of a school; another, Evelyn, is chief of a whole village; one in North Kivu is making compost and teaching how to protect the environment. We cannot protect women without protecting Mother Nature.'

She recently bought a 300-acre farm where they keep pigs, sheep and rabbits, have fish ponds and produce soya, rice and vegetables. 'We have no machines and already in three years with 200 workers we produced more than 70 tonnes of rice. We used to say we transform pain to power – now it's pain to planting – the healing process of nature. When I go to the farm and explain why bees are important, the girls think I'm mad, then when I explain they are like, OMG, the magic of nature!'

The farm also helped provide food for the centre, where Christine's eventual aim was to be self-sufficient. She took me to a large hall where women were sitting at long tables, tucking into bowls of yam and beans, and chatting away. Seeing them, you would never imagine what they had been through.

Behind a wooden partition at one end was a room in which two young girls were watching a baby girl sleeping. The mother Naomi was just fourteen. 'She had her first baby at eleven after she was raped but her family killed it,' explained Christine. 'She ended up in Maison Dorcas but she took her pillow and was holding it like a baby and when they sent her to school other kids used to insult her, calling her words that meant she was "empty", so she asked a boy to sleep with her and got pregnant again. Maison Dorcas wanted to kick her out so I took her in and soon she will go back to school.'

Naomi had named the baby Christine. 'I love children!' said Christine. At fifty-five, she was a grandmother of two, but her grandchildren and her own children were living in Belgium. Her husband Carlos Schuler runs a guesthouse and tourism business and much of their income goes to help children of rape.

The other young girl in the room was a nine-year-old. 'She was the product of rape and her mother didn't want her,' said Christine. 'She needs love. They all do. I'm convinced you can change the world only by love.

'In the kitchen we have a worker who was raped so many times and got pregnant, rejected her baby and tried to kill him. She was sent back to Panzi for psychological help. We saw her naked in the street throwing stones, then she came here and said, "I want to see Mama Christine." The staff told me not to meet her, she was dangerous. But I took her in. She came on the six-month course and after five she turned crazy again because she didn't want to leave. So I said, "Give her a job." Now she's been working here four years, she has bought a house and is looking after her child and she's totally fine.

'It's about giving a woman value. I hug them then they are healed and people say I have magic hands, but it's just love. I ask who remembers being hugged by their mum and none of them do.'

All this loving had taken its toll on Christine. 'After ten years it was too much,' she said. 'I felt so guilty. I lived in this beautiful house when all this horror was going on. I stopped eating, just vitamins and coffee, and became anorexic. I was like a zombie with dark circles, and so weak, I couldn't stand. It was like my body didn't belong to me anymore. I had anxiety and panic attacks. I felt suffocated, seeing all the soldiers then the children.

'I said, "Christine stop, it's too much." In autumn 2015 I told the staff I was going for training and went to Belgium for two months. But after three days again I started having flashbacks. Every time I closed my eyes, I could see little Christine, naked in the street screaming for help and no one coming. Eventually someone sent me to an old professor in Brussels who helped me. Now I use some of what helped me, here.'

She was worried about her friend Dr Mukwege. 'He's someone who could work anywhere, but, because he loves his country, he has risked his life and is a prisoner, living at the hospital. But he is sixty-four and I think it's time for him to take care of himself.'

She too had received many threats, hence the security around the centre, particularly after she made a documentary in 2010 called *Blood in the Mobile* with Danish director Frank Poulsen. 'We wanted to prove the way minerals were plundered, and show it is an international issue with lots of countries involved,' she said. 'If you made a map of all the rapes you would see it's mostly round mines. It's an economic war to terrorise the population.

'My brothers are pilots so I asked them to take me into the bush to places where coltan is mined for phones. I will never forget an old woman of eighty-six who asked me, "What were they looking for raping me, in my long dry breast, my dry skinny body?"

'Tell me is that sexual? If you have a sexual need, why don't you just go and rape an adult, you wouldn't rape the dry body of an eighty-six-year-old woman or a tiny baby? Or why make it public, open the vagina and put fuel and set fire in front of all the village so people leave the village? I even met a young girl who had been forced to eat her own child. She had nowhere to go. It's a massive destructive weapon.

'With a little bit of will the international community could end this war. But there is no will because they all have an interest in DRC being a mess so multinationals can continue to plunder coltan, gold, etcetera. Unfortunately, we also have most of the cobalt needed for the batteries of electric cars – when I heard that I said, "Oh my God, no!"*

'At the end the Congolese people are getting no benefit. This country never belonged to them, they are just used. Much of our

---

* More than 60 per cent of the world's cobalt is mined in DRC according to US Geological Survey 2018.

gold is sold by Uganda. Even our coffee from North Kivu is being sold as Rwandan with this beautiful packaging.

'The Congolese women suffer so much. They tell me, okay, if we are raped, fine, we go to the river and wash, *C'est fini*, we don't talk about it. But when they put fire inside and destroy genitals ... And, now they are not just raping women but cutting vaginas.'

She gestured toward her assistant. 'Look at Jane – Dr M. operated twelve times but can't repair her, she's in deep pain. Outside is a beautiful house but inside is totally broken. When I think I have a problem I think of Jane and I will never complain.'

In a neon lime dress with embroidered cuffs and shoulder panels and red and yellow beaded earrings, Jane Mukunizwa is almost as colourful as her boss, but she is short where Christine is tall, and walks slowly, holding herself carefully.

'I was fourteen the first time I was raped by the Interahamwe,' she begins. 'It was 2004 and I was at my uncle's place in Shabunda with my family when around midnight someone came knocking at the door. But it wasn't normal knocking. The rebels forced the door and tied our hands together with twine. They took us, all the family, into the forest and stole everything from the house then told us to carry it all on our heads. After a while they released my grandmother but kept my uncle and us teenagers. They made us walk all day. If you said you were tired they would kill you.'

She started speaking quieter and slower. 'One day they killed my uncle in front of me. They cut his head and genitals off and left the body.

'We were tied to the trees with our arms out as if we were being crucified. It was as if we had already died and in pain as we were given nothing to eat. Sometimes they cooked food and wouldn't give us any. They would eat bananas and just give us the skins.

'If someone wanted to rape you, they could just come and take you as they wanted. I have no idea how many times I was raped, they just came again and again, more than three times a day and not just one, sometimes this one then that one.'

She closed her eyes for a moment then continued. 'We were there two weeks until the army came and rescued us in a gun battle. They brought us to Panzi and I couldn't even recognise where I was, I was in such a bad state. All my internal organs were damaged. After that first operation I went back to my village but then I was raped again, so Dr Mukwege decided I couldn't go back. He was right because if you know there's a snake in the forest you won't step in it again.'

Outside, in the garden, a tropical downpour started and the birds were making a racket, as if trying to make themselves heard.

'I had twelve operations so far, the last time last year. I'm living in pain all the time but I try to adjust myself and carry on. Dr Mukwege did what he could. If I'm here now, speaking to you, it's because he did his best.

'When he saw how hard my case was, he introduced me to Christine and she brought me to City of Joy. Coming here changed my life. It made me feel independent. I had never been to school but here I learnt to read and write and learnt to do technical jobs so I could earn a living. But more than anything, City of Joy taught me how to be loved and love each other. Christine is such a lovely mother. Her courage and the way she tries to transmit her empathy to all, that gave me such encouragement. Never in my life have I experienced the love I do here.

'I've been here seven years and became a teacher myself and share my story with others to help them open up. With my salary I bought a compound just behind the centre and have also adopted four children born from rape.'

'Do you think women who have gone through such terrible things can ever really recover?' I asked.

'I think you can rebuild but only *pole pole*,' she replied, using the Swahili expression for step by step. We hugged then she said, 'I want to ask you something.

'When you go back,' she said, her eyes boring into mine, 'I want you to tell people what you have seen. Some of our politicians say we don't have sexual violence but it's not true, there are still now girls being raped every day, girls from all different areas, and all have the same story. Please be our voice because we can't reach your country.

'When I hear our government saying there is no sexual violence here, it's like they are stamping their foot on a wound. It's not just the rape, it's what it leaves behind – infection, damage of organs, trauma … Look at me: I can't give birth and if I want to get married, it's not any man who can take me as his wife as I am so damaged.

'I learnt a lot because of what I went through and am now trying to learn French so one day I can try to tell the whole world about this.

'Women are being killed and treated like animals in this country. It's thanks to Dr M. and Christine if today we're not ashamed and can walk in the community. Before everyone would point their finger and say those are abused women. Now I can walk anywhere and even if people say she was abused I don't care because I understand it wasn't my fault.'

14

Mummy Didn't Close
the Door Properly …

Kavumu, Democratic Republic of Congo

The people of Kavumu were angry. They were angry because we had kept them waiting under a hot sun in a small yard by a coop of squawking chickens as we didn't realise quite how long it would take to drive the twenty miles from Bukavu on the broken road (apart from one random speedy stretch of Chinese-built highway). They were angry because they lived in mud-floored tin-roofed shacks made from bits of wood nailed together, had no water or electricity, and on a good day might earn one or two dollars while their rulers lived in luxury. (President Kabila had an estate just down the road.) Most of all they were angry because of what happened to their daughters.

I walked into the yard where dozens of parents were crammed on benches and everyone started to speak at once. A couple of women had babies suckling from their breasts and three men were squeezed together under a blue umbrella. The light from the sun was blinding. Eventually a woman in a bustling banana-yellow dress pushed forward, introduced herself as Nsimiri Kachura Aimerante, village president, and yelled at everyone to be quiet and put up their hands.

The first to tell his story was Amani Tchinegeremig, a subsistence farmer and widower with a nine-year-old daughter. 'We don't have beautiful houses,' he said. 'We live in simple shacks like this divided into two for parents and children, but sometimes when we woke up, we found one of our daughters missing. I was the first one it happened to.

'I started looking for her everywhere. I was knocking on the door of a neighbour's house when I saw a body in the bush, lying down, covered in blood. The attacker had tried to force clothes in her mouth so she couldn't cry and she was absolutely destroyed. She was just three.

'I took her to the clinic and they transferred her to Panzi hospital where she was operated on. She's fine now physically, apart from pain in her womb, but she is always disturbed, she is scared of people and doesn't like to be in public. She can't even go outside on her own especially in the dark.

'We thought it was a one-off but after that other children started disappearing. Soon there were ten, twenty cases.

'The men were entering our houses in the night and snatching children. At the beginning it was hard to know it was rape as many of the children were babies or toddlers who couldn't speak. We found bodies of babies who had been raped and their genitals destroyed.'

People started murmuring in agreement. A white chicken wandered around, pecking near my feet. Sweat was dripping down my face. I wanted to hear from the mothers but a man in a pink shirt under the blue umbrella intervened. His name was Eric Safari Zamu Heri and he wanted to tell me who was behind this.

'There is a group of people called Jeshi ya Yesu [Army of Jesus], like a cult but with weapons, used by a local politician called Frederic Batumike, they do anything they want. In 2012 they assassinated our village chief.'

Batumike, I later learnt, was a provincial MP and father of nine who was known as Ten Litres for his small stature – this being the size of the plastic jerry cans used to collect water. He was also a pastor who held services at his home and at a network of churches he had set up. He had recruited a witchdoctor who told his militia that if they raped babies and small children, they would get supernatural protection so bullets could not wound them, and, if they mixed virgin blood with herbs, they would be rendered invisible.

'He was sending his people to go in different houses, picking little daughters to abuse,' continued Eric.

One of those houses was that of Consolata Shitwanguli, a middle-aged lady who made me think of a sunburst with her orange scarf wrapped around her yellow T-shirt, but her eyes were liquid sadness. Her daughter Neema was just six when she was taken.

'It was a Sunday night,' she said. 'Neema went to sleep with her brothers and sisters about 9 p.m. then I heard people passing by and my daughter crying, and then saw the front door opened. I was afraid so I told the other children to look for their younger sister. We got the neighbours and went into the fields. We found her standing up and shaking and her hair all dusty and asked her what's going on. She said down here it hurts. I saw they had damaged her vagina. I woke up my neighbours and they took her to the medical centre. The doctor said it wasn't possible for him to treat her and sent her to Panzi where Dr Mukwege operated on her. She was there three months. My heart was broken but I couldn't do anything.'

After that the women of Kavumu stopped sleeping and stayed awake watching their doors as they were so poor they could not afford padlocks. Some fixed wooden brackets through which they slotted a bar across at night but would wake to find it on the ground.

I wondered where their husbands were. Some had gone to Shabunda to look for gold, said Nsimiri, the village president in the yellow dress. 'But if you listen, you will see the women say men entered by witchcraft.'

One of the youngest victims was the baby daughter of Furata Rugenge, a young woman with a new baby tied papoose-like onto her back.

'I was in the house, my husband was away, and it started raining and a man came in and asked for shelter. He had a black bag with a kilo of rice which he asked me to buy but I told him I didn't have money. I have four children and he asked, "Are all those children yours?" then he picked up my baby Alliance who was sleeping and said, "She's beautiful."

'I told him, "It's already night, can't you go back to your home?" But he gave me the rice and asked me to cook it. We didn't have food so I made a fire and started cooking then I noticed the man had left. In the middle of the night I was breastfeeding the baby, put her on the floor and she started crying and I realised something bad had happened. When I picked up the baby, I saw she was full of blood and dust. I started crying and shouting and neighbours came. They went to the man's house and saw him just opening the door, all muddy. They made him remove his clothes and found his penis covered in blood. They asked him, "Where has this come from?" and he said, "My wife has her period," but she said, "That's not true."'

Alliance was the first baby Dr Mukwege had ever treated, the one he had told me about. 'I got the call as I often do to send an ambulance fast,' he said. 'It came back two hours later with an eighteen-month-old baby girl bleeding profusely. When I got to the operating room all the nurses were sobbing. The baby's bladder, genitals and rectum had all been severely injured by the penetration of an adult.

'Then another baby came, then more. There were literally dozens of raped children.'

Among them was seven-year-old Ushindi. Her mother Nyata Mwakavuha, in a white-and-blue dress with orange headscarf, explained. 'It was the middle of the night and we were sleeping,' she said. 'Ushindi was in bed with her brothers and sisters. Strange people forced the door and took her and raped her outside then brought her back and left her in the sitting room. After they'd gone, she cried out and told me she wanted the toilet. I went in and saw she was shaking and full of blood. When I saw that I also cried out and neighbours heard. We took her to the medical centre and they said we had to go to Panzi. I felt like they had poured something evil into the house that I could taste in my mouth.'

Monitoring all these children who came into Panzi was Georges Kuzma, a French police investigator with twenty years' experience of working on terrorism, who was working at the hospital for Physicians for Human Rights, training doctors in gathering forensic evidence.

'I made a map of criminality so saw the prevalence of cases in Kavumu and went with Dr Alumetti to find out what was happening, and collected lots of data, but the government did nothing.'

Eventually, Dr Mukwege decided to travel to the village. 'I wanted to ask the men, "Why don't you protect your babies, daughters, wives?" To my surprise, the villagers knew the suspect. Everyone was afraid of him as he was a member of the provincial parliament. His militia had been terrorising the village.'

In the end forty-eight children were raped between June 2013 and 2016 – the youngest eighteen months and the oldest eleven. After raping them, the men would take the blood from the ripped hymens, believing it would protect them in battle. Two were so badly hurt they died before arriving at Panzi.

The local prosecutor refused to start a serious investigation. He became known as Monsieur Cent Dollars because, when anyone came to lodge a complaint, he would demand $100. In some cases when parents went to police, they themselves were arrested and $100 demanded to release them.

Kavumu seemed a vivid example of how President Kabila, like previous leaders before him, had run down the state, lining their own pockets while providing nothing. Far from protecting them, the state's only interaction with the community was to prey on people like parasites. That very morning on the way there, traffic police in orange jackets had stopped our car on the pretext of nothing, demanding non-existent papers from my taxi driver for which absence we must pay 'fines'. He was used to it. 'They have a daily target,' he said.

A dossier was compiled by Kuzma and Panzi Hospital and presented to the UN peacekeeping force and government. 'It was met by deafening silence,' said Dr Mukwege.

'I tried to engage Madame Kabunda, who Kabila had appointed as special envoy on sexual violence, but to no avail,' said Kuzma, himself a father of three daughters. 'For three years we were quite alone – many times I asked the UN to support us but they said there is no crime against humanity. The ICC laughed at us. It was very frustrating.

'It was the hardest case I ever worked on in Africa – more than forty young girls raped without any response from the government. Then the fear and the magic, it made me think of *The Sorcerer's Apprentice*.

'We don't know how they got into houses to get the babies – there was talk of the mothers being drugged, though there was no biological evidence, and also some talk that parents had provided their children for money.'

The parents were desperately poor and could not afford lawyers. But Panzi Foundation provided help and encouraged them to file a case along with the international organisations Physicians for Human Rights and TRIAL International.

'Of the thirty or forty mass crimes I've worked on in four years in DRC, it was the most shocking and emblematic case,' said Daniele Perissi, the young Italian jurist who had arrived in

Bukavu to head the TRIAL office in 2014 as the first cases came in.

'It captures so many of the problems DRC faces but also from the human perspective, the fact that the victims were so young and will be facing consequences all of their life – some won't be able to give birth, and, in a culture where that's what women are seen as for, this means they will be ostracised.'

The first thing he did was to try to coordinate all the lawyers working on behalf of different victims to form a collective of eight who were all sharing what they knew.

A rift developed in the village between the families of those who had been taken and the rest who did not want to be involved and feared reprisals. Even within the affected families there was division.

Perissi was not surprised. 'In general it's difficult to get families of victims of sexual violence in DRC to go through justice because of the cultural and social stigma and the general belief the justice system doesn't work, which generally speaking is true. But here it was particularly tough because you had so many levels – not just the cultural stigma but the vulnerability they felt. Batumike was a Parliamentarian but it was more accurate to think of him as the warlord of the village, as he was from there, the police were in his pocket and he was doing whatever he wanted.'

That fear intensified after a local human rights campaigner Evariste Kasali was shot dead at his home in Kavumu. He had been investigating the rapes for an NGO called Organisation Populaire pour la Paix.

The biggest obstacle, however, was the prosecutor. 'He had no interest in trying to solve this or bring forward the cases, partly because of endemic corruption and also he was scared of Batumike,' said Perissi. 'The bottom line was he wouldn't do anything.'

The lawyers decided the best option was to get the case switched to a military prosecutor as these were generally regarded as less corrupt, and also were based in Bukavu so out of Batumike's sphere of influence.

'The only way to bypass him was to say we had prima facie evidence suggesting this might be a crime against humanity, and for that the only competent authority was a military court.'

So by the start of 2016, a military prosecutor took over, and police then got more resources to visit churches of the cult and investigate.

Meanwhile some desperate parents scraped together and borrowed money to send someone to a witchdoctor in Goma with discarded items they had found on the ground near the raped children including a syringe and a handkerchief. They believe this was the turning point. 'He neutralised the magic power so one of them betrayed the others and led to their arrest,' said one.

Whether it was black magic or policing, in June 2016 Batumike was arrested along with seventy members of his militia. But still nothing happened. Villagers became so fed up they set fire to the local police post.

One difficulty was gathering evidence – parents did not know much and the victims were either too young or too traumatised to provide good information. The team was also concerned about re-traumatising them.

Kuzma organised video interviews of the children in December 2016 and worked with Dr Muriel Volpellier, a French clinician who was the lead doctor at the Haven sexual assault referral centre in St Mary's Hospital, London. She had advised on forensic collection of evidence in various conflict zones and spent six months at Panzi in 2014.

Improving their forensic capacity was a challenge, she said. 'At the Haven where I work, we get maybe one or two victims a day, and a forensic examination of one victim takes four or five hours – but if you have thirty or forty a day coming in with just two doctors, it's very different.

'There is often no power to keep swabs frozen, or light, so the doctors have to use headtorches for the examinations and some-times no water. The more we know about DNA the more we know about the possibility of cross contamination so everything needs to be very clean.'

If she called in police, they would often say they could not come because they had no petrol.

The group also brought in Jacqueline Fall, a Senegalese child psychologist working in Paris, to carry out the interviews. These were videoed so the police could watch the discussions from an adjoining room without being seen, and ask for any clarification through earpieces, so they would not be intrusive and minimise the trauma.

The children and parents were taken in a minibus to a house where snacks and flowers had been laid out to make it cheerful. First Dr Volpellier carried out the physical examinations with Dr Alumetti who had operated on many of them. They saw thirty-six of the forty-two children and all but two consented to the exam.

'Many said they've stolen my womb, so we were able to reas-sure them,' said Volpellier. 'They were very stoical and didn't let out much,' she said, though at times 'their look got lost in the distance'. 'They had lost faith in adults' ability to protect them. One victim who was five years old at the time of the assault kept saying, "I was taken because mummy did not close the door properly."'

How the men had got into the small houses and taken the chil-dren remained a mystery. Volpellier heard stories of a powder from a local flower called angel trumpet, said to contain scopolamine which can 'zombify' victims. It was not the first time she had heard of this. 'In the Middle Ages in France people were throwing this powder on people in the streets and they became so out of it, they were robbed.' She contacted colleagues to try and find a way to test biologically but to no avail.

One problem was that, because of their young age, the brutality of the crime and the fact it took place in the dark, only one of the children could identify her perpetrator. No evidence had been taken at the time and in some cases three years had passed.

However, through small details – such as the size, language and clothing of perpetrators – they were able to establish some important connections. Several of the children mentioned their rapists wearing red T-shirts – Batumike's group called themselves the Red Army.

Finally, in September 2017, partly on the basis of the videos, the military prosecutor indicted eighteen defendants for 'acts of rape constituting crimes against humanity'.

The videos were later used in closed-door hearings of the court so the victims did not need to testify.

Perissi from TRIAL did not even think the parents should testify. One of the first mothers called to the stand collapsed and had to be taken to hospital so the judges realised that even for them it was too traumatic.

In the end eighteen parents testified in court in Bukavu as well as six or seven witnesses, their faces covered and identities protected by voice distortion, except for the village chief. 'I refused to because I said it's like we are ashamed,' she explained.

Nyata was one of those who testified. 'I decided I would speak out so they could send these people to jail and not hurt any more children,' she said.

Finally, on 13 December 2017, came the verdict. Batumike, and ten of his militia, were convicted for murder and rape as crimes against humanity, and sentenced to life imprisonment. In the village there was singing and dancing, even among those who had been against pursuing the case.

It seemed a historic victory not just for the villagers but for all those fighting against sexual violence in the DRC. 'It sent the message that even in DRC with someone in power, it's possible to have justice,' said Perissi.

The men appealed but on 26 July 2018 their convictions were upheld. Dr Mukwege was relieved – when Jean-Pierre Bemba was acquitted by the International Criminal Court in June, he panicked, thinking this would be seen as a signal by the Congolese courts to also overturn the Kavumu verdict.

However, the case had gone back to court again, this time to the Supreme Court in Kinshasa, on a technical issue.

Moreover, the court had not attributed government responsibility, despite lawyers' arguments that the state had failed to protect the children for three years, so there were no state reparations.

The villagers were baffled. 'The community decided to work with government justice but even when we pointed to the culprits and they were convicted, till now we don't know what happened to them,' said Amani, the man who had spoken first. 'Are they in jail? We don't know. We don't even know what the Congolese government thinks, they said nothing. These were tiny children raped, is that okay?'

'We are still insecure,' complained Nsimiri, the president. 'Since the Army of Jesus were arrested in 2016 the rapes have stopped but we parents have become their enemies so are targets and we are getting threats, maybe from the sons of these people. We want the government to protect all the families – and also to compensate us.'

Although the convicted men were ordered to pay reparations of $5000 per family – and $15,000 for those whose daughters died – this had been put on hold while the case was still under review.

Even then 'it will be an uphill battle,' warned Perissi. 'For victims to identify the property of Batumike, then ask the court to seize it, then get the money will be a real challenge.'

When I discussed the case with Christine Schuler from the City of Joy, she said compensation was key. 'Without reparations we can't have peace,' she said. 'It's not necessarily money – it could be building them a school, a hospital or a place for women to learn.'

But when an NGO provided some money to the village to build houses, it disappeared.

Five of the affected families had fled the village, not only because of fear of reprisals. Every parent I spoke to said they believed their girls were ruined. Dr Mukwege told me the long-term effects on the girls' sexuality and fertility will not be known till they reach puberty, but the villagers refer to them as 'our destroyed daughters'.

At City of Joy Christine Schuler had told me a chilling story. One day Dr Mukwege had brought ten of the children of Kavumu to her office which, as I had seen, was so full of butterflies and colourful knick-knacks that he refers to it as Ali Baba. 'One of the kids took a plastic doll off the shelf and asked if she could have it. I told her it had been given to me by a child in America who said it would protect me so I gave her something else and put the doll back. Then she said to the doll, Don't sit like that or they will rape you. The child was four years old. Dr Mukwege and I looked at each other.'

Consolata, the sunburst lady, told me: 'I was very happy when those people were convicted and I hope they stay forever in jail, but since that day my daughter is always sick, complaining about womb pain. I don't think she will have a good future as everyone knows what happened to her.'

Nyata agreed. 'My daughter is always complaining about head-ache and backpain. One day she was taunted by a classmate who said "you were raped" and she fainted. I'm afraid she will have problems in the future. I would like to move somewhere where no one knows so she could have a good life but I am just a poor mother.'

As the villagers recounted the attacks on their babies, and their frustration at the lack of state action or compensation, their anger grew all over again. The squawking of the chickens got louder and in the sweltering yard I could feel rage solidifying around me, like a storm building.

Felix, the local activist who had taken me to the village, told me he thought we should go. 'These people don't believe in the justice system,' he whispered urgently. 'Last week they burnt someone alive. He was a thief and they beat him and he was taken to the medical centre, but people refused to let him be treated and dragged him into the main street and set fire to him.'

It was time to leave. I edged my way to the exit of the yard, thanked them and walked quickly along the dirt track, dodging the trickle of sewage, as I went up to the main road and into the car.

We were headed to the next village Katana, where we had heard from a local woman working at the City of Joy that more children were being abducted in the night and raped. This time, she said, they were also slitting their vaginas with knives.

Just the previous week, an eighteen-month-old baby girl and a four-year-old had both been snatched in the night. Panzi had treated four girls abused and one had been killed.

'I have never seen such horror since my birth,' said Felix. 'The children flock to a village in an extremely critical state. Like thousands of civilians, we are abandoned in our territory at the mercy of militia men who kill, violate and plunder for reasons obscure. Our government does not care.'

It was not the first time such things were happening in Katana, according to Daniele Perissi from TRIAL. He had been lobbying the UN mission and local authorities to get patrols into the area. 'We want to make sure the state don't make the same mistakes as in Kavumu.'

This time the villagers had decided to take matters into their own hands. Felix showed me a series of photographs on his phone.

In them were crowds of angry people holding two sticks with something on. Then he zoomed in. They were heads. Heads of young men.

'They are two brothers they believe behind the rapes. They beheaded them.'

My translator Sylvain was looking nervous, as was Rodha, the psychologist who had been helping me with the interviews. Ahead of us the broken road had collapsed altogether. 'The driver says if we go further we may not come back,' said Sylvain.

We turned round. On the way back, I kept thinking of the words of Nyata, the Kavumu mother who had bravely testified. 'I'm shocked all these rapes of children are still going on,' she told me. 'We thought we had made a difference.'

15

The Lolas –
Till the Last Breath

Manila

Heavy storm clouds rumbled overhead as I pushed open the black metal gate in a suburban street of northern Manila and entered a small house. Inside, a stray marmalade cat wandered through, arching its tail into a question mark, and two little old ladies met and embraced.

Lolas Narcisa and Estelita still fighting for justice in their late eighties

They discussed their health, their grandchildren and great grandchildren, the journey there to Quezon City in the capital's notorious traffic: nothing out of the ordinary.

They were there, however, because they shared a most terrible bond. When they were girls so young that they had not even started their periods, they were raped over and over by Japanese soldiers who had occupied their country.

On the wall behind them, row upon row of faces of old women looked out from a photo montage, some stern, some kindly, some gazing directly, some looking away with haunted eyes.

All of them were 'comfort women' kept as sex slaves by the Imperial Japanese Army during World War Two in one of the biggest officially sanctioned systems of sexual violence and trafficking in history.

It's a term they don't like, preferring Lolas, an affectionate name for grandmother in the local Tagalog language.

174 surviving comfort women came forward but most have since died

Those on the wall are 'the departed'. They died without receiving justice, no apology, no compensation, not even an acknowledgement of the terrible wrong that was done to them. Their own country's history books carry no mention of them.

Among them was Lola Prescilla who, after her captivity, could never again sleep a full night, so embroidered murals of flowers and houses while her children were sleeping. And Antonita who used to loiter round the crumbling Spanish fort in the remains of the old Walled City so she could point tourists to the dungeon where the Japanese executed her husband before she was enslaved.

Of those who came forward, only nine were known to be left, most of these bedridden, hard of hearing or suffering dementia. Lola Narcisa and Lola Estelita are among the last survivors still standing, both knowing they will almost certainly die without justice.

Lola Narcisa Claveria, who everyone calls Lola Isang, was just twelve when the Japanese soldiers came for her in 1942.

Everything about her was neat, from her black dress sprigged with white leaves and matching black-and-white slip-on sandals to her short white hair tucked behind her ears, small gold rings in her ears and the single gold band on her wedding finger.

When she cried, the tears fell neatly and silently and she dabbed at her eyes with a perfect white flannel square taken from her flower-embroidered bag.

The ordeal she was describing happened more than seventy-five years ago. Yet to this day if she hears screaming, she freezes, thinking Japanese soldiers are coming.

'It is an everlasting nightmare,' she said.

The events leading up to her nightmare started the other side of the Pacific on 7 December 1941 with Japan's surprise attack on the US Naval Base at Pearl Harbor, one of history's most shocking intelligence failures. A day later, Japan launched its invasion of the Philippines. The archipelago of 7000 islands had been America's first colony, captured from Spain in 1898 and made a US territory along with Guam and Puerto Rico in exchange for $20 million compensation. Manila had become a basketball-crazed slice of Little America.

General Douglas MacArthur, the US military commander, living in his penthouse in Manila Hotel overlooking the bay, was caught woefully unprepared. When Japanese bombers struck, they found the small number of American warplanes under his command neatly lined up on the ground, and destroyed them. MacArthur was forced to flee with his forces to the Bataan peninsula and the small island of Corregidor from where in March 1942 he escaped in a torpedo boat to Australia with his family, following one of America's worst ever defeats, though it would be portrayed by the Pentagon as a heroic escape.

Japanese soldiers arrived in Narcisa's birthplace of Balintog, north of Manila, the following year. It was, she told me, a peaceful farming village where people grew rice, corn and vegetables and fished in the river. Her father was *teniente del barrio* – village head.

'The Japanese came through the village and found one house empty so were suspicious it was being used by guerrillas and demanded to know where the residents were. When they asked the neighbours, they said they did not know and directed them to my father.

'That's when the soldiers came to our house. They were wearing camouflage uniforms and these caps with fitted cloths at the back. They had rifle bayonets and ropes and Filipino porters and they were angry. They told my father, "You are village head, you must know where these people are."

'He said maybe they went to fish in the river or to farm. The Japanese gave him one hour to find them. After an hour the soldiers came back and my father told them he could not find the people. They asked him how many children he had. He said eight – five girls and three boys. They made us all line up. But when they counted, we were only seven as one of my sisters was working in Manila, staying with our aunt.'

Narcisa began twisting her ring over and over as she spoke.

'The Japanese got more and more angry,' she continued. 'They said, "You're lying, there are only seven! Maybe one of your children and the owner of that house are not here because they are guerrillas."'

She took the white flannel out and started dabbing her eyes.

'They kept insisting and my father kept denying he knew anything. Then they tied his hands behind him and took him downstairs (we were on the second floor) and tied him to a post then they started torturing him by peeling off his skin with bayonets like they were skinning a carabao – a water buffalo. He was pleading for mercy. We begged them to stop.

'Suddenly they picked me up and threw me so hard my left arm broke and it was numb. Then I heard my mother on the second floor begging them to stop so I ran upstairs and saw one of the Japanese soldiers raping my mother.

'She was beautiful, wearing a kimono and long skirt and her skirt was pulled up and he was thrusting himself into her and I couldn't do anything. My brother and sister were also trying to pull him off but the soldiers threw them into the kitchen and stabbed them with bayonets.

'My father was still pleading with the Japanese to stop so I ran back down with my two elder sisters and the soldiers ordered us to walk to their garrison in the Municipality Building which was about a kilometre away. The last thing I heard was my father screaming. We walked up a hill and when I looked back at our house it was already on fire.'

She shook her head and more tears slowly fell down her cheeks.

'When we got to the garrison, they took my sisters Emeteria and Osmena directly inside but I was taken to another house as my arm was swollen and painful and I was shaking with fever. There was a Filipino collaborator and he gathered herbal medicines and leaves to make a poultice to put on my arm.

'I was there a couple of weeks. When I was brought into the garrison a Japanese soldier called Tarasaki told me to take a bath. I told him I don't have anything clean to change into but he got angry, shouting at me, "You smell!" He gave me drawstring pants and uniform. After I washed, he pulled me into a room and that's where he raped me.

'Then he brought me to the garrison where they had taken my sisters. Emeteria was just staring out and I could see something was very wrong but we weren't allowed to speak. Another woman had escaped so, if we talked, they hit us with horsewhips. Osmena had disappeared and we never saw her again.

'We slept on a cement floor with blankets. Almost every night we were being raped, sometimes by two or three soldiers, and in front of the others.

'In between they made us cook and do their laundry and fetch water. But also, because there was a shortage of food, the Japanese asked the collaborators to look for places where it was available and then we would move. We had to walk barefoot and the ground was so hot and hard we had painful blisters and would end up crawling on our knees.

'On one of those walks I managed to talk to Emeteria and asked what had happened. She said, "Thank God you weren't brought here directly because they raped me over and over and burnt us with cigarettes and with the red-hot skins of grilled sweet potato." Till now no one knows what happened to my other sister.'

Her voice became hard to hear as rain started pummelling on the roof, a tropical rainstorm that went away as quickly as it had come.

'If I'd had any chance of escape, even the smallest, I would have done it because it was so hard. Every day I would pray that night would not come and the sun would not go down because then the Japanese would rape us.

'Then one day the Americans started bombing the garrison. I ran with my sister, literally running for our lives. We only stopped running when we were two or three miles away. We could hardly walk and fell to our knees.

'An old man and his child passed with their carabao cart and gave us a lift. When we arrived in the barrio we saw all the houses burnt down and learnt that my parents, brother and sister had been burnt to death.'

Eventually the two girls found two of their brothers who survived the war. But it was not the end of their ordeal.

'After the war my sister and I were traumatised. We almost lost our minds. We were afraid of men, we would always think they were Japanese soldiers. My sister was worse. And we asked ourselves who would marry women who had been raped by hundreds of Japanese? Some people called us names like *tira ng hapones* or Japanese hand-me-downs.

'I met my husband Anazito through my brother. He also had sisters who were taken by the Japanese and never came back so he knew and was very supportive. He told me, "I'm not judging you because I know what happened." It was hard for me to have intimate relations. He did not force me.'

In the end she had six children but no peace. 'I knew if I kept hiding this there would always be a knot in my chest,' she said.

Around 200,000 girls and women in Asia are believed to have been forced into sexual slavery by Japanese soldiers during the Second World War. The majority were from South Korea but also from other countries occupied by Japan, including China, Malaya, Burma, what is now Indonesia, and the Philippines, as well as a smaller number of European origin.

It was an official system, ironically created to assuage international outrage at the mass rapes of Chinese women and girls in 1937 by the Imperial Japanese Army during their onslaught on Nanjing in the Second Sino-Japanese War.

Emperor Hirohito and his Department of War responded by setting up a series of what they called 'comfort stations' to regulate sex. Young women who thought they were being recruited as nurses, laundry workers or restaurant staff, found themselves interned in military brothels in occupied territories and kept as sex slaves. Others like Narcisa were simply snatched off the streets.

Yet after the war there was silence in Japan as officials insisted the comfort stations never existed or that the women were paid prostitutes.

It couldn't stay hidden forever, as gradually more and more brave survivors came forward. But, although what had happened in South Korea became well known, in the Philippines it remained hidden even though almost every major city and garrison had a 'comfort station'. For decades no one talked about it.

Then one day, in 1992, Narcisa was listening to the radio while cooking, when a woman called Rosa Henson came on air. She told of how she had been fifteen when abducted by Japanese soldiers and kept for nine months being raped, sometimes by as many as thirty men in a night. 'I lay with my knees up and feet on the mat as if giving birth,' she said. 'I felt like a pig. Now I am telling my story so they will feel humiliated.'

Rosa was the first survivor to go public and Narcisa couldn't believe what she was hearing. 'I had been praying and thinking, How can I tell my story? So when I heard Rosa call on women who had been violated to come forward, it took me a while but finally I realised this is the way.'

There was however a major problem. Narcisa had never told her children what had happened to her.

'Me and my husband had decided not to tell the kids when they were at school so all we told them was we were imprisoned in the war. We said, "When you have problems with us you should be thankful you have parents because ours were killed."

'The children found out when they saw me on TV doing an interview. When I went home one of my daughters told me, "I'm ashamed of what you're saying – you didn't tell us you were raped. How can I see my friends anymore after what you said? You have brought shame on us." They stopped talking to me for a long time.

'It was so painful because I was already a victim of the Japanese soldiers. I didn't expect my children to do that. So I was victim twice – of the Japanese and my family.'

Eventually her husband explained to them what had happened, telling them 'don't blame your mother, she had no choice' and that they hadn't told them because they were too young.

'It took a while for them to understand and accept,' she said. 'Now they support me in the call for justice and are very active. They promised me, "If we don't get justice while you are still alive, we will continue the fight."

'I go on protests whenever I can as till now I feel so angry at what those Japanese did to me and my family, that if I saw them today I would kill them. At the time I could not do anything, I felt so helpless.'

Over time around 200 women came forward. An organisation called Lila Pilipina was formed in 1994 to help them, and opened a refuge for the Lolas to meet. Some lived there though they have since died.

It was there that we met. On a poster on the back wall were two lists of five demands to the Japanese and Philippine governments. Narcisa and I read them together. From the Japanese they wanted release of the information about comfort stations in its war archives, acknowledgement of what happened to them including in school textbooks, compensation and a formal apology to be issued to the women. From their own government they wanted what had happened to be officially declared as a war crime; an official investigation; inclusion in history books; historical markers to be erected round the country so the new generation would know how the women had suffered; and material support. Not one demand had been met, she said.

'What's even more painful than the Japanese silence is that none of our presidents, no one from the government, has listened to us, from the time of President Ramos [in power 1992–8 when women started coming forward] to now, not one, though we've been begging them and begging them.

'Every time a new president is elected, the first thing we Lolas do is go to Malacanang Palace and submit a petition to make it a priority. If only one president had listened to us and told the Japanese government they had an obligation to us and to recognise what was done, it would have felt like some justice for us. But they have ignored us, not even showing us pity.'

She drew a comparison with South Korea where the government had supported its women, helping secure an apology and compensation.

Even there it took almost fifty years, until 1993, for Japan to officially acknowledge what had happened with an apology from Prime Minister Morihiro Hosokawa. One of his successors Shinzō Abe then criticised him and only in 2015 was an agreement reached with South Korea to finally pay one billion yen (about $8.3 million) in reparations to the surviving women, by then numbering less than fifty.

There too it had taken a long time to break the silence. Before my trip to Manila, the Korean Council for the Women Drafted for Military Sexual Slavery by Japan had sent me video testimonies of some of the last surviving comfort women. One of them was Kim Bok-dong, who was by then ninety-two and suffering from cancer. A little woman with her grey hair in a neat bun, she told how she came from a poor family and when she was fourteen, and should have been at school, two Japanese soldiers had come to their house and ordered her to go to Japan to work in a factory making soldiers' uniforms. 'My mother said I was too young,' she said, 'but they said if I refused, they would treat me as a traitor. So I went, but the place was not a factory.'

Instead, when she got off the ship, she found herself in the Chinese province of Guangdong where she was kept in a building with around thirty girls and forced into sexual slavery. The first time was with such force that the bedsheet was covered in blood. 'A young girl cannot fight adult men,' she said. She and the other comfort women would be raped for hours day after day, so many times that they lost count. Worst of all were Sundays when it went on from 9 a.m. to 5 p.m. The soldiers lined up, one after the other, and if one took too long, they would bang on the door. By 5 p.m. the girls wouldn't be able to stand and doctors would come and give them injections to keep them going.

Kim said she and two other girls eventually decided 'we're better off dead' and tried to commit suicide by drinking strong alcohol, using money her mother had given her for food. They ended up in hospital, their stomachs pumped, then taken back to the 'comfort houses'.

She was moved from Guangdong to Hong Kong to Singapore, where the Japanese dressed her and others as military nurses to conceal what they had done. Finally, at the age of twenty-one, a year after the war was over and with Korea independent, she was shipped back to her family. They had no idea what she had endured in those eight years and she never told them until finally she explained to her mother why she was refusing her entreaties to get married. 'I didn't want to screw up an innocent man's life,' she said. Her distressed mother had a heart attack and died.

Kim went on to run a successful restaurant and eventually did marry. But she never told her husband what she had been through and they never had children, she believed because her ordeal had left her so damaged. It was only after he died that she began to speak out, in 1992 when she was in her sixties.

Lonely, Kim moved into a home known as the House of Sharing with other former comfort women and found some solace in painting. One of her first artworks was entitled 'The Day a 14 year old Girl is Stolen Away'. She started participating in the weekly Wednesday demonstrations in front of the Japanese embassy in Seoul, braving the insults they often received, and established the Butterfly Fund to help victims around the world with the proceeds from her paintings and reparations that they eventually received.

But Kim was still waiting for a formal apology from Japan. Sometimes, she regretted coming forward. 'If no one knew, I could live quietly,' she said. 'But I won't pass away until we get Japan to repent its past and restore our dignity.'

There had been no apology at all in the Philippines. The two countries had become close allies and Japan was their biggest source of investment and foreign aid. Japan was important too for military help to counter Chinese expansion in the South China Sea, a strategic waterway through which trillions of dollars in trade pass each year, and has rich fishing waters, in particular the disputed Spratly Islands which are believed to hold vast reserves of oil and natural gas.

During my stay in Manila there were protests after the national-security advisor revealed that 113 Chinese fishing vessels had been spotted 'swarming' on Pag-asa, the second largest island. He accused Beijing of bullying, repeatedly sending its warships and research vessels into the area.

'I know the Japanese government is putting money in the pocket of our government but can't they even show us mercy?' asked Narcisa.

They had even less hope from President Rodrigo Duterte who since taking office in 2016 had become known as the 'misogy-

nist-in-chief'. This was a man who wolf-whistled at a female journalist in a nationally televised press conference, called women
'putas' or whores at an event recognising outstanding female
police and army officers, boasted about sexually assaulting a maid
when he was a student, and joked about rape.

That was not all. In December 2017 a two-metre-high bronze
of a blindfolded young girl with a lapful of flowers was erected on
the seafront Roxas Boulevard to honour the comfort women. But,
just four months later, it disappeared one Friday night after the
Japanese Minister for Internal Affairs Seiko Noda visited President
Duterte and told him, 'It's regrettable for this kind of statue to
suddenly appear.'*

A statement from the Department of Public Works and
Highways on 29 April 2018 announced that the statue had been
removed 'to give way for the improvement of Roxas Baywalk
Area', adding that it was installing pipes and constructing 'lateral
drainage' in the area.

Questioned about the disappearance, President Duterte told
journalists he was not involved. 'Whose initiative was it?' he asked.
'I really don't know. I didn't even know that it exists. But it has
somehow created a bad, you know … it is not the policy of government to antagonise other nations.'†

The sculptor was so scared that he had gone into hiding.

'If I saw the person who removed the statue, I would hit them,'
said Lola Narcisa. 'I know they don't want people to see what
happened to us, they want to sweep it under the carpet.'

That was not all. At the start of the year another statue had
been removed, this time from private property. A bronze of a
young woman with fists resting in her lap was taken from a

---

* ABS-CBN News, 10 January 2018.

† *The Inquirer*, 29 April 2018.

Catholic Mother of Mary shelter for the elderly and homeless in San Pedro, Laguna.

The only tangible acknowledgement I could find of what happened to the women was a small plaque in the undergrowth of a park by the bridge from the Old Walled City to Chinatown. On it were engraved the words: IN MEMORY OF THE VICTIMS OF MILITARY SEXUAL SLAVERY DURING THE SECOND WORLD WAR.

Lola Narcisa said she would not give up. 'Until my last breath, I will shout to the whole world what they did to us,' she said. 'I still feel the pain. If only the Japanese government could just recognise and admit what they did to us. It won't go away but it will help ease the pain. I pray every day I will see justice before I die, that's all I pray.'

She shook her head. She knew that the Japanese reaction to the statues suggested they were hardening in attitude. Japan still had century-old rape laws which require prosecutors to prove violence or intimidation, making it hard to secure convictions if victims did not 'fight back'.

In 2017 Japan also managed to block an international petition to UNESCO to include artefacts and documents relating to comfort women on its 'Memory of the World Register', pointing out that it is the single largest contributor to the organisation.

What had happened was so long ago that I wondered if, at eighty-seven, Narcisa ever felt she should just move on and try to live her remaining days in peace rather than going to schools and protests and talking about her suffering?

'Sometimes I also think, Why do I have to tell my story over and over?' she replied. 'Because when I do, I remember the pain, what happened to my parents and my siblings, and whenever I hear on the news about women being raped, I get very angry. Why are these things still happening to the Yazidis and others?

'Until we get justice, it will keep happening. In my view these people doing these things should not be put in prison, they should be killed. And it's not just the perpetrators who must be brought to accounts but the governments who turn a blind eye.

'It's impossible to forget what we went through. How can we forget? That's why I don't stop. My voice is all I have and I will use it till I die.'

Lola Estelita Dy spoke with her emotion much more contained but no less powerful. She struggled to hear, not just from old age, but because her head was smashed against a table while she was in Japanese captivity.

In a shirt buttoned to the neck, fitted trousers and wire-framed glasses, she had a mannish air, like the tomboy she says she once was, though her trousers were purple and there were sequins on the green waves patterning her shirt.

To my surprise, she greeted me in English – she had learnt a little, she said, when she travelled to the UN in New York to press their case, something she had never imagined.

Like Narcisa she grew up in a rural area, a town called Talisay on Negros Island with her parents, two sisters and two brothers.

'Life was good,' she said. 'My father and brothers were farm-hands on the local sugar plantation. We also had a cow and water buffalo. My mum had a mom-and-pop grocery inside the planta-tion. I was at school.'

When the Japanese came in 1942 things changed drastically. They took over the sugar mill and used it as their barracks and everyone lost their jobs and the school was closed. She was twelve at the time.

'People were afraid of the Japanese so ran away,' she said. 'I took care of seventeen hens and every day they laid many eggs, maybe seven or ten which I traded with the Japanese.'

For the next two years she worked as a labourer in a stone quarry on a nearby Japanese airbase. 'My job was to gather stones from a dry riverbed and pile them up so they could be used to pave roads. We worked eight hours a day and were paid two cans of rice. Every day we were picked up in a truck and taken to work then back. We weren't held at gunpoint but we had no choice if we were to live.

'One day in 1944 we heard the drone of a plane but could only see smoke. Then on the second day we saw it and the star on the wing and knew that the Americans were coming. They were dropping leaflets telling us to stop work as they would start bombing. My father told me to leave work so I went back to raising the hens and vegetables and rice-cakes to sell in the market.

'The market was in the plaza by the church and one day the Japanese came with a truck full of people and said they were rounding up suspected guerrillas and spies. I tried to run away and find a hiding place but I tripped and they saw me. A Japanese soldier grabbed me by the hair, crossed my arms and dragged me to the truck. There were other women on the truck but we were guarded by a soldier with a rifle bayonet so couldn't speak to each other.

'From the top I saw they were making the men they had captured line up by the well in the square and beheading them with a bayonet one by one then throwing them in. Anyone who tried to run away was shot.

'Once they had killed them all, onlookers were told to go home but we women were taken to the garrison in the sugar mill about a kilometre away. When we got there they made us lie down. I was taken into a building with a series of rooms and a Japanese soldier came and started kissing me then raped me. The first time, I froze with fear, then another soldier came and I realised I had to fight back. So I did but he was angry and slammed my head on the table and I lost consciousness.

'That night a Filipina woman who worked with the Japanese came to me and said if you want to live, you better let them do what they want. She was a collaborator but she was nice to me.

'The plantation was very large and there were several houses where they kept women but I didn't see the others.

'There were two or three soldiers coming every day raping me. I would close my eyes and pray it would be over soon. I don't remember how long it went on for, maybe three months.

'Eventually the Japanese began getting uneasy and most of them retreated to the mountains. One morning I woke to lots of commotion, people screaming the Americans had come. As soon as I could I sneaked out and ran to my parents' home.

'I told my mum what had happened to me but not my father and our neighbours did not know. I went back to school for a year. But I could see in people's eyes what they felt about me and knew there would always be talk that I was raped by the Japanese, so in 1945 I decided to move to Manila where no one knew me.

'It was hard to start with but I got a job as nanny to three children for a woman who was manager for Palmolive soap. Later I became a sales lady in a shoe shop. I met my husband while working there and we had five children but it was hard for me having sex and in the end we separated. I never told my husband what had happened to me – he died not knowing.'

In 1992 she was doing her laundry with the radio on when she happened to hear Rosa Henson telling her story and calling on others to come out and report to a documentation centre.

'I also saw her on TV. To start with I thought it was shameful to come out and she should have stayed quiet. But I kept thinking about it and eventually I decided Rosa was right so I went to the office for Taskforce on Filipino Comfort Women which had been set up by women's organisations to campaign for justice and later became Lila Pilipina.

'I went alone and told my story and met other Lolas but decided not to face the public. They offered me counselling, which helped. But every day of my life if I am not busy doing something, I remember what happened. That's why I have a compulsion to keep doing things until I am so tired that I sleep. If I see a movie with a scene about rape I can't watch.

'I didn't dare tell my children. I felt shame. Other women who had spoken out before me had been rejected by their children and I couldn't bear that to happen. Eventually I thought there was safety in numbers, so I started to join the weekly rallies outside the Japanese embassy when there were lots of Lolas, and one day my daughter saw my face in a newspaper photograph.

'I explained that the Japanese were masters at that time and I couldn't do anything. The children were shocked but accepted. Now they have joined the fight and I'm confident they will continue after I'm gone. And my grandchildren.

'It's important to get an apology to establish the principle that the Japanese did it. Why should they keep denying it? As long as Japan don't publicly admit it's a crime and define what they did as a war crime, there will be no settlement for me. The crime should be recognised historically.

'There has to be an end to wars because I'm afraid what happened to me could happen to my daughters and granddaughters.

'I still have hope whatever little justice there is can be obtained. But I am very discouraged by Duterte because he is a puppet of Shinzō Abe, who I am very angry with, because he is a thief in the night.'

She was referring to the removal of the statue. 'I was on the committee for the statue,' she said. 'It was because of me the girl had a garland of flowers on her skirt. In South Korea I saw people put flowers on the statue outside the Japanese embassy when they protested every Wednesday – what we call *cadena de amor* or chain of love, pink flowers.

'We are small people but as long as no state actors are taking the lead and governments do nothing, it's very difficult to get justice.'

Yet she said, individual Japanese often approached her wanting to apologise on behalf of their government. In late July 2019, a few days before we met, there had been a convention in Manila. 'There were some Japanese private citizens attending and they kept coming up to me and even offered to bow down before me in ceremonial cleansing but I said it has no meaning because it should be your prime minister who is doing that.'

In the rape camps the girls had been made to bow in the direction of the Emperor every morning.

For the same reason she had not wanted to accept money offered from the Asian Women's Fund in 2000. 'That's private, not government, so not reparations and I didn't want it,' she said. 'It wasn't much,' she added, '20,000 yen [about £115].'

Before I left, she had one more thing she wanted to say. 'I feel sad when people refer to me as a comfort woman. I want to be known by my name. The meaning attached to it is you're a bad woman. That's why we call ourselves Lolas.'

We all had lunch together, boiled rice and whole fish, and were joined by a younger woman, perhaps in her sixties, who had come to the house to help prepare the meal. Her name was Nenita, known as Nitz, and she told me how she had grown up knowing there was something not right about her mother Crisanto Estalonio.

'Sometimes she was very kind. Other times she was very strict and she didn't want us to go out with other girls,' she said. 'If she saw an airplane or heard footsteps or a commotion she would hide under a table or bed. Sometimes she fainted and we wondered why.'

They found out when she joined Lila Pilipina. 'She was nineteen when the Japanese came and already married but her husband was beheaded by the Japanese and they took the blood and drank it.

She fainted and when she came round she was in the garrison. She was kept there three months being raped by so many men.'

She died in 2000. Solidarity from the other women had lessened her feelings of shame, said Nitz, but she never knew peace. 'I want justice for my mother because as a family we were also victims,' she said. 'Her fight is our fight too.'

'The call of the Lolas has passed to the next generation,' said Joan May Salvador, who runs Gabriela, the alliance of women's organisations in the Philippines, and who had translated for me. 'The Lolas were the first to say rape is being used as a systematic way to subjugate women and show the power of men.

'Most of the places where it happened have been destroyed and there are no memorials so we have only the Lolas. We are still trying to find more so we can learn from them while they still live.'

That struggle was more important than ever, with sexual violence so much on the rise under Duterte that one woman was being raped every hour. 'If the most powerful person in the country is joking about violence against women, people think it's okay,' she said.

She told me how the previous year when addressing a group of former rebels from the New People's Army, a long-running communist insurgency in rural areas, Duterte had publicly told soldiers to shoot female rebels in their genitals. 'If there is no vagina, they would be useless,' he said.

Not surprisingly in such a climate, women felt it was pointless to try and get justice. 'We have a helpline for victims of sexual violence and every day get between nine and twelve calls from women,' said Joan. 'But when we ask if they want to file cases, they say they would rather move on.

'Even reporting to the police is difficult – you know you will be ignored and there will be victim-blaming. The first thing they will ask is what were you doing out at that time, what were you wearing?

'And if she was raped by state military or police, forget it. At Gabriela we've had cases of women, mostly minors, raped by state military forces but when they file cases, they don't come to court for years. Military chiefs say we are going to relieve the person responsible but then we find they have just transferred them.

'Someone needs to stand up and say this is not right or it will go on and on.'

Lolas Narcisa and Estelita nodded.

Afterwards I watched these dignified old women standing arm in arm to bid me farewell and wondered what it must be like to live your whole life burdened with something like this. This, the last stop on my journey, was where the fight for justice first started. And though it is so sad that these last surviving Lolas would almost certainly die without justice, their strength and determination are an inspiration for all of us.

Postscript

Giving the Nightingale her Song

On a brilliant blue-skied July afternoon in Stratford-upon-Avon, swans were gliding serenely on the river, while I sat in the dim auditorium of the Royal Shakespeare Company and watched *Titus Andronicus*, the Bard's most brutal play. This production, directed by a woman, Blanche McIntyre, spared the audience nothing. Murders, beheadings and cannibalism came at us in full technicolour gore. In Act One, the Roman general of the title slaughters his own son. By far the most disturbing scene, however, was the rape of his beloved only daughter Lavinia by Chiron and Demetrios, sons of the Goth queen Tamora whose forces the Romans have just defeated. Tamora has been captured among the 'spoils of war', and, in revenge, her sons not only rape Lavinia but slice out her tongue and cut off her hands to leave bloody stumps.

Once I would have admired the acting, the edgy staging and the poetry of the dialogue but thought it far-fetched. Now my head filled with the faces of all the violated women I had met. Their tongues may have remained intact but too often they too had no voices, their words falling like leaves in a forest with no one there to hear them.

Lavinia's uncle Marcus comes up with the idea of spreading salt across the table and, with a stick in her teeth, she traces out the word *Stuprum* – rape in Latin – followed by the names of her perpetrators.

Shakespeare is thought to have been inspired by the story of Philomela from the Roman poet Ovid. Philomela was an Athenian princess who was raped by her brother-in-law Tereus, the king of Thrace, who then cuts out her tongue to stop her telling the world. Philomela weaves the story in a tapestry which she sends to her sister Procne, prompting her to kill her own son by Tereus and feed him to the king in a pie. The sisters flee and are turned into birds by the Gods, Procne a swallow and Philomela a nightingale – a bird which in female form has no song.

'These miseries are more than can be borne,' laments Marcus to his brother Titus Andronicus.

This has been in many ways a journey through the worst depravities of man and I thank you for bearing with me, for I know it has not been an easy read. But I hope it has also revealed unexpected heroes – as well as bringing home to you why so much more needs to be done to end this scourge of man.

My book is far from exhaustive. Sadly, there is war rape in so many countries – from Central African Republic to Colombia and from Guatemala to South Sudan – that if I had covered them all, my own tapestry would have been never ending.

The United Nations Office for the Special Representative on Sexual Violence in Conflict lists nineteen countries in its 2019 report and named twelve national military and police forces and forty-one non-state actors. This was not meant to be a comprehensive list, it noted, but one compiled from where credible information was available.

For my part, I focused on places I had reported from as a journalist, and in particular where sexual violence was used as a weapon of war, aimed at a specific community and directed from the top. Though of course no official strategy is needed for rape to be rampant in wars where impunity reigns. And aside from rape, we have seen how militaries and militias have used sexual slavery, forced marriage and pregnancy as well as stealing babies of opponents and forced sterilisation of communities they wish to wipe out for religious, ethnic or political reasons. The resulting children of rape often find themselves outcast from their communities – or in the case of the Yazidis, separated from their mothers – for something that happened before they were born.

The last few years have also seen shocking revelations about sexual abuse by peacekeepers and aid workers, the very people tasked with protecting the most vulnerable.

Nor is rape only carried out on women or girls. Male rape is rarely discussed for it is even more of a dark secret, particularly in the Middle East and Africa where there is a common myth that survivors must be homosexual or will become so.

Yet one study in 2010 in eastern DRC found that almost one quarter (23.6 per cent) of men in conflict-affected territories had experienced sexual violence – an estimated 760,000 men.* Aside from the Congo, I came across examples in Bosnia, Afghanistan, Chad and the detention centres of migrants in Libya – and heard horrendous stories in refugee camps about prisons in Syria and Iraq.

One early account, which has since been disputed, comes in T. E. Lawrence's *Seven Pillars of Wisdom*, his telling of his swashbuckling role in the Arab Revolt against the Ottoman Empire in the First World War. He graphically describes being captured by the Turkish governor of the Syrian city of Dar'aa in November

---

* Kirsten Johnson et al., 'Association of Sexual Violence and Human Rights Violations with Physical and Mental Health in Territories of the Eastern Democratic Republic of the Congo', *Journal of the American Medical Association*, vol. 304, no. 5 (2010), pp. 553–62.

1917 and being beaten and gang-raped by soldiers – losing at twenty-eight, 'the citadel of my integrity' as he put it.

Almost a century later, in November 2016, I went to Syria, to a war marked by its extreme brutality, its cities now shattered battle-grounds. East Aleppo had been under siege from the forces of President Assad for most of the year and I wandered the streets of the once-fabled Old City, past the derelict Baron Hotel where Lawrence (and Agatha Christie) once stayed, to find a bombed-out ghost town of stray cats wandering amid grey ash. It looked and felt like how I imagined the end of the world. Across each road twisted metal, corrugated iron, concrete slabs and furniture had been piled into makeshift barricades as protection from snipers. I jumped at seeing four naked shop mannequins standing ghost-like among the rubble. Nearby was a filigree cage where songbirds must once have warbled. Now the only sound was the periodic boom of artillery striking into the streets beyond the citadel on the mound where it was said Abraham milked his cows. More than five million Syrians had been forced to flee the country; more than 500,000 killed.

Three waif-like children suddenly appeared with a bucket look-ing for water then melted away in fear. By then, those left were so desperate that they were living on pancakes of fried flour and any greenery they could forage. The Assad regime was about to launch its final assault and a few days later would lay on buses to try and persuade the remaining civilians to leave. Many would remain under fire rather than risk captivity.

Human rights groups believe as many as 90 per cent of male detainees are sexually abused in Syrian custody. A UNHCR report in 2015 entitled *We Keep it in Our Hearts* was based on interviews with refugees and detailed some of the horrors of the Assad pris-ons, particularly sexual abuse of men and boys as young as ten, forced to have sex with family members, tortured with electric shocks to their penis and by anal rape with objects such as sticks, Coke bottles and hoses.

'One of my uncles in Syria was arrested,' said a young man called Ahmed in a camp in Jordan. 'A few months after he was released from detention, he told us – he broke down, crying in front of us – that there was not one spot on his body that had not been abused by an electric drill. He had been raped, they had put the drill in his anus. They tied his penis with a thin nylon string – they tied it hard for three days until it almost exploded. After he was released he stopped eating and became alcoholic. He died from kidney failure.'

As I met survivors, I tried to see what worked in helping them and what didn't. It was clear from what they told me that no one really gets over such an ordeal. Baroness Arminka Helic fled the Bosnian war as a young woman to the UK where she ended up becoming a foreign policy advisor and a member of the House of Lords. She likens the issue to 'a chemical weapons attack in that they have the immediate harm and long-term harm. They don't recover, their husbands don't forget, their children get bullied, they live in the same place and see their rapists in the café.'

The challenge is to find ways for survivors to be able to get on with life. Now, when I look at roses, I think about the raped women of Srebrenica who did not want to cut those they grew because their perfume reminded them of happier times. Bakira, the hunter of war criminals, found solace with her vegetable garden. Aside from gardening, creative activities such as art and music in safe spaces that bring women together seem to be beneficial, as is yoga.

Clearly there needs to be far more support for victims, for what happened to them will be with them for the rest of their lives. Apart from medical care and psychological support, they need economic assistance to help support themselves and rebuild their self-esteem, particularly as survivors are often abandoned by their husbands and families and, in some cases, as with the Nigerian girls taken by Boko Haram, even ostracised by their communities. Faith leaders and community leaders need to be brought onside to explain that the survivors did nothing wrong, rather are heroes for what they endured, and should be welcomed back. Amid the chaos of the DRC, Panzi Hospital and the City of Joy are a model in what can be done, helping repair wounds, offering counselling, skills-training, legal advice and a safe haven.

Above all, in every warzone I went to, I heard the same cry for justice – there must be justice and an end to impunity.

Amal Clooney, the human rights lawyer, who represents Nadia Murad, told the UN Security Council that despite all that the young Yazidi had suffered at the hands of twelve men, and the threats she still received, she had only ever spoken of one fear: 'that when this is all over the ISIS men will just shave off their beards and go back to their lives; that there will be no justice'.*

The brave women of the sleepy Rwandan town of Taba may have had little schooling, and lived in mud huts with no electricity or running water, but by raising their voices they opened the way to the prosecution of Mayor Akayesu.

That ruling seemed like a sea change. However, that was more than twenty years ago and there have been disappointingly few successful prosecutions since. Many of the subsequent cases in Rwanda and Bosnia ended in acquittal, often on the basis of lack of evidence or lack of credibility due to inconsistencies in witness testimony. Only Akayesu was convicted of genocidal rape, and only a handful were found guilty of rape as crime against humanity. No one was convicted for committing rape themselves, rather for supervising others who had.

There has not been a single prosecution for abducting the Yazidi girls nor exhumation of the mass graves of their family

---

* Speech to UN Security Council debate on Women, Peace and Security, New York, 23 April 2019.

members who were killed. Amal Clooney points out that if seventy-nine states can come together as part of the global coalition to fight ISIS on the battlefield, why could they not establish a court?

Nor have there been any prosecutions of the Boko Haram fighters who captured girls in Nigeria. Attempts to bring the Burmese military to justice for its onslaught on the Rohingya were blocked at the UN Security Council by China.

The International Criminal Court (ICC) was set up in 2000 amid great fanfare but only in 2019 did it convict anyone for sexual violence. The one previous conviction, in 2016, of Jean Pierre Bemba, former Vice President of the Democratic Republic of Congo, ended up being reversed, leaving Bemba free to return home and participate in elections.

'Impunity remains the rule and accountability the rare exception,' says Pramila Patten, the UN Special Representative for Sexual Violence, who left a highly successful career in corporate law in her home country of Mauritius to fight for women.

Patricia Sellers, special advisor at the International Criminal Court, who likened the Akayesu ruling to Brown v. Board of Education, argues that this is the start of a process. It was a long time after the earlier case that black children in southern states were attending racially mixed schools.

'Brown comes in 1954 but that didn't stop school desegregation in the United States within the next year or even the next ten years,' she said. 'You still needed the Civil Rights Act in 1964 and Fair Housing Act of 1968, and in fact we are still litigating cases. So these were great pillars and steps but didn't change the comportment of people who committed egregious crimes through discrimination.'

She points out that the Akayesu judgment is now seen as a fundamental pillar of law and widely studied in universities and has been used in cases in Latin America and Africa.

One problem is that the ICC can only try cases from countries which signed up to it – neither Nigeria, Iraq nor Burma are signatories.

Some lawyers, however, are finding innovative alternatives. This can mean using universal jurisdiction – the notion that international crimes are borderless and states have a responsibility to prosecute perpetrators on their soil, regardless of where the crime was committed.

Amal Clooney helped bring the first international case against an ISIS member for war crimes against Yazidis, which opened in a court in Frankfurt in April 2020 under heavy police guard. The twenty-seven year old Iraqi man had been found in a refugee camp in Greece and extradited to Germany. His German wife, who was part of their morality police, was also on trial in a court in Munich. Both were accused of the murder of a five-year-old Yazidi girl who they had enslaved along with her mother. The girl, known as Nora, was repeatedly beaten then left chained up outside their house in the Iraqi city of Fallujah in heat of 122°F until she died of thirst.

In December 2019, I went to the castellated Peace Palace in The Hague, home of the International Court of Justice (ICJ), for a fascinating showdown.

The tiny West African nation of Gambia had taken Burma to court for genocide against the Rohingya and, to widespread surprise, Aung San Suu Kyi had decided to personally defend the very generals who once locked her up for fifteen years.

It was the first time a state had been taken to court by another which had not been directly affected. 'Why not Gambia?' said Abubacarr Tambadou, the Gambian Attorney General, when I asked him. 'This is a stain on the conscience of the world. You don't have to be a military power to stand up for human rights.'

He said he had been shocked by what he had seen on a visit to the Rohingya camps in Bangladesh and added that his own country had just emerged from twenty-two years of brutal dictatorship, which he said had 'taught us we must use our moral voice in condemnation of the oppression of others wherever it occurs so others will not suffer our pain and fate'.

They had turned to the ICJ, the UN's highest court, as the guarantor of the Genocide Convention which was adopted by the UN, seventy-one years earlier in December 1948, amid cries of 'Never Again' following the Holocaust.

The three-day hearing took place inside the Great Hall of Justice, an imposing wood-panelled room with four giant stained-glass windows, a long bench of seventeen black-robed judges, and an audience of diplomats in business suits. It could not have felt further away from the muddy camps in Bangladesh where more than 700,000 Rohingya are still sheltered in makeshift plastic and bamboo shelters on muddy hills.

All focus was on a slight figure on the left-hand bench in a black jacket and long patterned skirt. Hair tied back with pink and yellow flowers, graceful as ever, Aung San Suu Kyi sat rigid as lawyers for the Gambia, led by the British QC Philippe Sands, recounted story after story, each worse than the last – an eight-month-pregnant woman kicked with the boots of Burmese soldiers, hung by her wrists from a banana tree then raped nine times so she lost the baby; a mother forced to watch her baby son beaten to death.

Watching from behind all I could see were the flowers. When she was interviewed for the Radio 4 programme *Desert Island Discs* in 2012, she had chosen as her luxury item a rose bush, the flowers of which would change colour every day.

What could she be thinking, this woman who was once seen as a worldwide symbol of human rights, now apparently throwing her international reputation away for the sake of domestic politics and forthcoming elections? Through it all she betrayed not a flicker of emotion.

Much of the case centred on the horrendous sexual violence, and the lawyers cited the Akayesu judgment in which judges had described it as 'one of the worst ways' of inflicting harm, because it resulted in 'destruction of the spirit, of the will to live and of life itself'.

Each team got to choose an ad hoc judge, and it was no coincidence that the Gambian team had chosen Navi Pillay, the South African whose perceptive questioning at the Rwanda Tribunal led to that ruling and the first definition of rape in international law.

'This case is not just significant for the Rohingya and bringing their plight to the attention of the world, but also how it could be used in future,' said Philippe Sands.

The only other option for legal redress is national courts, where there is often no infrastructure, a shortage of trained judges and prosecutors, little capacity of police to investigate, and a lack of political will, particularly when those on trial are government forces. Courts are intimidating places and often offer no protection for victims; indeed, they may find themselves viewed by the judges through the same stigma as much of society.

In one case in the Rwanda Tribunal in 2001, where a witness called TA testified to being raped sixteen times, defence lawyers asked how she could have been raped as 'she had not bathed and smelled'.* The judges were reported as having 'burst out laughing'. She was repeatedly asked the same questions until on her fourteenth day on the stand she complained, 'Since I came here this matter has been put to me more than 100 times.'

Having already lost her family in the genocide, when she returned home, everyone knew she had testified, her house was

---

* The Prosecutor v. Pauline Nyiramusho, ICTR trial transcript, 6 November 2001.

attacked and her fiancé left her. 'Today I would not accept to testify to be traumatised for a second time,' she said afterwards.*

Often women who do go to court, end up having to tell their story over and over again, despite the re-traumatisation. Baroness Helic told me she heard of Rohingya women in the camps who had to recount what they went through twenty times.

But the incredible courage of a number of victims, prosecutors and judges has seen some progress on the national level in the last few years. In Guatemala, a group of eleven brave Mayan women known as the Grandmothers of Sepur Zarco secured a legal first in 2016 when their testimony resulted in the conviction of a retired army officer and a former paramilitary leader for sexually enslaving them (and four others who had since died) during the country's 36-year-long civil war.

More than 200,000 people were killed in that war, hundreds of villages wiped off the map, and more than 100,000 women raped, mostly Mayans, in an attempt at exterminating the population. Yet, after the war ended in 1996, sexual violence was not included on the agenda of peace deals between government and guerrillas. Negotiators refused to acknowledge it, and a representative for the National Indemnity Programme to compensate victims of the war said he didn't believe it had happened.

It took these women from a small rural village in a valley in northeastern Guatemala to break the silence. They told of how the Guatemalan military had set up a base nearby and how they had come first for the men, snatching them for daring to assert their right to land, during the annual Santa Rosa de Lima festival. Then they came back for the women.

---

* Binaifer Nowrojee, *Your Justice Is Too Slow': Will the ICTR Fail Rwanda's Rape Victims?* United Nations Research Institute for Social Development, Occasional Paper 10, November 2005.

For six years, from 1982 to 1988, they were held by the soldiers in slave-like conditions, made to work as domestic servants and systematically raped, sometimes by up to six men at a time. One described being raped until 'practically lifeless'. Another had been raped in front of her four-year-old son.

For years after they were shunned and referred to as 'the soldiers' women'. Their husbands had never returned and they are still searching for the remains.

Eventually, assisted by a women's organisation which brought them together in a safe space to create art, they started to tell their stories.

They were emboldened by avenging prosecutor Claudia Paz y Paz, who may have appeared soft-spoken and diminutive, but was fearless in tackling impunity when she became the country's first female attorney general in 2010. Inspired by the picture of Bobby Kennedy she kept in her office, she took on everyone from crime bosses to the former dictator Efraín Ríos Montt, who she indicted for genocide in 2012. He was sentenced the following year though this was later overturned after Paz y Paz was removed.

The Sepur grandmothers went to court and bravely spoke in twenty-two hearings despite abuse from pro-military groups who denounced them as liars and prostitutes.

In February 2016, after thirty years of shame, they finally got justice. 'We believe you … it wasn't your fault,' declared the court. 'The army terrorised you in order to destroy your community.'

When the judgment was announced, which sentenced Lieutenant Colonel Reyes Giron to 120 years in jail and Heriberto Valdez Asij to 240 years, the women removed the colourful embroidered shawls with which they had covered themselves through the trial, and smiled.

It was the first time anyone had faced justice for sexual violence during the war – and the first time anywhere in the world that sexual slavery perpetrated during an armed conflict had been prosecuted in the country where the crimes actually took place.

The presiding judge Iris Yassmin Barrios Aguilar, president of the aptly named High Risk Court, had survived threats and assassination attempts, including grenades thrown at her house, as well as attempts to discredit her, which had led to a year-long suspension.

'Rape is an instrument or weapon of war,' she declared. 'It is a way to attack the country, killing or raping the victim, women were seen as a military objective.'

Not only were the perpetrators locked up, but Aguilar ordered reparations from the government in the form of a free health centre in Sepur Zarco, improvements to their primary school and the construction of a secondary school, as well as a provision of scholarships for women, girls and the entire community.

Other women survivors across Latin America have been finding their voices. In Peru, where almost 300,000 women were victims of forced sterilisation during President Alberto Fujimori's rule in the 1990s, and others were raped by both sides during the 1984–95 war between government soldiers and Shining Path rebels, an innovative oral history platform has been created called Quipu. It is named after the knotted cords used by Incas to convey complex messages. Women can record their stories on a free messaging service then upload them onto a website as coloured knots, creating a virtual tapestry.

In Colombia, thousands of cases have gone before a special tribunal created as part of a peace deal between the government and the leftist guerrilla group Revolutionary Armed Forces of Colombia (FARC) to end the 52-year-long civil war in which 260,000 people were killed. There was also widespread sexual violence perpetrated by all sides in the conflict. State-aligned paramilitaries such as the United Self-Defense Forces (AUC) used rape as a weapon of war and to establish control over territory and society, as did FARC, which would force pregnant members to have abortions in order to not encumber the war effort. Between 1985 and 2016 alone, more than 15,000 people were victims of sexual violence in the conflict, according to the National Center for Historical Memory. The Peace Tribunal set up to give survivors their day in court agreed to address this issue and 2000 documented cases were brought before the tribunal in August 2018.

In Argentina, as we have seen, courts investigating the torture and killings of the so-called Dirty War have also recently started addressing the sexual violence that took place under the generals who ruled from 1974–83.

There has been more history made in Africa. In May 2016, not long after the Guatemalan grandmothers secured their historic verdict, the astonishing bravery of a poor illiterate woman from the small central African country of Chad resulted in the first ever conviction of a head of state for rape.

Hissène Habré, who ruled Chad in the 1980s, was a man so vile that he was known as Africa's Pinochet. Forty thousand people were killed during his eight-year rule and many more were raped and tortured by the Directorate of Documentation and Security (DDS), his much-feared secret police. A lot of this torture took place in a notorious underground prison known as La Piscine based in a converted swimming pool. Methods included the horrific 'supplice des baguettes', a technique where two sticks are placed through a piece of rope encircling the victim's head and then turned, slowly tightening the rope until it felt as though their brain was going to explode. Habré had in some cases inflicted the abuse himself.

When Habré was eventually deposed in 1990, he wrote himself a cheque for $150 million, all the money in the Treasury, and fled to neighbouring Senegal to live in luxury.

He was arrested in 2000 and eventually put on trial in Senegal in 2013 after a long campaign by his victims and a brave lawyer called Jacqueline Moudeina who narrowly survived having a grenade thrown at her after filing the first charges against him.

The specially created Extraordinary African Chambers was the first ever trial of a head of state in the court of another country.

Initially there were no charges of rape among those for killing and torture. That changed after dramatic testimony from Khadidja Zidane, who accused him of ordering her to the Presidential Palace where he raped her four times.

She told of how, day after day, in the 1980s, she would be taken to Habré's office in the Palace. There he sat at his desk, smoking and watching, as his agents tortured her, pumping water through a hose down her throat or electrocuting her. Sometimes he would then torture and rape her himself.*

There was nothing she could do. Khadidja's mother and brother were among those murdered in his reign of terror.

She risked her life to testify in the trial which was broadcast in Chad as Habré denounced her as a 'nymphomaniac prostitute'.

After hearing her, the court used the Akayesu precedent to add rape to the charges. Habré was convicted for crimes against humanity, torture and rape, and sentenced to life in May 2016. It was an extraordinary moment, his face hidden behind sunglasses and a white headdress. 'Down with Francafrique,' he muttered.

Once again, the verdict seemed an enormous breakthrough. But it had come at huge cost for Khadidja, who lived alone now her

---

* Ruth Maclean, 'I Told My Story Face to Face with Habré', *Guardian*, 18 September 2016.

husband had left her because of what happened, and who continued to be attacked by strangers who shouted abuse and called her a whore.

Then, a year later in April 2017, the appeal court upheld all convictions against Habré except one. All the sentences for the mass sexual violence committed by his security forces were maintained, but Habré was acquitted of raping Khadidja. The appeals court emphasised that the acquittal was a procedural matter and did not reflect on Khadidja's credibility. It said the new facts she offered in her trial testimony came too late to be included, so they could not serve as the basis for a conviction.

She insisted she was still pleased she testified. 'I had the opportunity to tell the whole world what he did to me,' she said.

'She is very glad she did it,' said her lawyer Reed Brody from Human Rights Watch. 'It was very meaningful. The most important thing for her was that people were told.'

It surely cannot be a coincidence that the judge on the Habré conviction, as well as the judges in Guatemala, Akayesu and the first Bosnian rape conviction, were women, or that the bench comprised three women when Jean-Paul Bemba was convicted.

'Who interprets the law is at least as important as who makes the law,' says Navi Pillay, the judge who asked the vital question on the Akayesu case. 'When there has been a conviction for rape or sexual violence invariably there was a woman on the bench.'

She told me how listening to the Taba women testify had affected her. 'JJ's words caused me to re-examine the law's perception of women's experience of sexual violence in conflict,' she said. 'It seemed to me the traditional practice of law has not paid sufficient attention to the silence of women.'

Some things long hidden in Europe are being brought to light because of another female judge. Women who suffered rape, forced abortion and the theft of their babies in Franco's Spain had never been heard because an amnesty law passed in Spain in 1977 granted immunity. But since 2000, relatives have been taking things into their own hands, digging up mass graves, and in October 2019 finally securing Supreme Court ruling to get Franco's remains exhumed from their vast mausoleum outside Madrid in the Valley of the Fallen. A campaign was also underway to disinter the remains of his chief executioner and advocate of rape in Seville, General Queipo de Llano, from their place of honour in the city's Basilica. Meanwhile, surviving torture victims have come together to demand justice, speaking in townhalls around the country to gather signatures. They may finally get their day in court after a remarkable Argentine judge, eighty-one-year-old Maria Servini de Cubria, launched an investigation using the principle of universal jurisdiction to investigate human rights abuses.

In the same way that having women on the judges' bench seems to result in more convictions of the perpetrators, studies show there is less rape if there are more women in armies. The Israeli–Palestinian conflict is often cited as an example of a war that shows sexual violence is not inevitable where forces are well-disciplined. Israeli men and women must all do national service at eighteen and women make up about a third of Israel's military.

Pramila Patten's office is lobbying for there to be more women among peacekeepers (currently just 4.8 per cent) and mediators so that what happened to women in war is no longer just an afterthought.

31 October 2020 marked the twentieth anniversary of UN Security Council Resolution 1325, which saw every member country vote for greater inclusion of women in peace and security.

However, one only has to look at the mostly male photographs of peace talks between the Taliban and Afghan civil society and government to see there has been little progress. Only 10 per cent of the negotiators are female while there are no women at all in talks to end fighting in Yemen. Not a single peace process going on in the world is led by a woman.

Research by the New York-based Council on Foreign Relations shows that between 1992 and 2019 women only constituted 13 per cent of negotiators, 6 per cent of mediators and 6 per cent of signatories in major peace processes. Less than half of peace agreements signed since the passing of the resolution even make reference to women.

'Male-dominated rooms in the twenty-first century should be embarrassing to us all, not least to the men in those rooms,' actress and playwright Danai Gurira told the UN anniversary meeting.

Yet when belligerents sit down to bargain to end a war, women are overwhelmingly shut out. It is because women are not involved in negotiating the end of conflicts that war rape is not taken seriously.

It's not easy – Baroness Helic recounts how in 2014 she accompanied then Foreign Secretary William Hague to Geneva for international discussions on ending the war in Syria. He had insisted there be women participating. 'When we got into the room, there were fifty men and me. Hague said, "I told you I wanted women negotiators." Then, I kid you not, they drove us twenty minutes away to another much-less-grand hotel where in a dark basement were a group of women.'

Largely as a result of Helic's lobbying and an unlikely alliance with a Hollywood star, the UK has been on the forefront of putting this issue on the international agenda.

'It's all because of a movie,' laughs Helic. 'I was reading in a Bosnian paper about Angelina Jolie making a film there about the rape and I thought, What does this Hollywood woman know about my country? I spent a few months hating her! But when I eventually saw *In the Land of Blood and Honey*, I couldn't believe it: no one had depicted the life and pain of the war like that.'

A highly persuasive woman, she got her boss William Hague to watch it as well as the Prime Minister David Cameron.

Hague had travelled to Darfur in western Sudan when he was Shadow Foreign Secretary in 2006. He had been horrified by the stories of the women he met in camps of war refugees. 'My first knowledge of sexual violence in conflict was meeting women in the camp who had to go out and get firewood and would be raped by government-backed militia trying to make sure they never tried to go back to their homes. Then I went to Bosnia with Arminka and met people who told me they saw their perpetrators walking down the street and there had never been justice despite settlement of the conflict.'

As the biographer of William Wilberforce, the Conservative MP who got the UK to abolish slavery in 1807, Hague knew what could be done by politicians when members of the public rallied behind an issue. 'One of the lessons was: you only achieve your objective when you change the behaviour of those at the end of the chain – people will always find ways of doing something that's illegal until you make it unacceptable.'

The question was how to make people even think about the issue. Helic suggested they invite Jolie to show the film in the Foreign Office and speak about the issue. Officials laughed at the idea that she would be able to pull this off, but she managed to hunt the actress down who sent a message back, asking what they were actually going to do to tackle war rape.

'It was a good point,' said Helic. 'So we suggested forming a rapid-reaction force called the Team of Experts [which included doctors, lawyers, police and forensic experts] to deploy to gather evidence whenever there were reports of sexual violence in war, as there was no body responsible.'

Jolie agreed to come and speak and in 2012 a special team was created inside the Foreign Office for the Prevention of Sexual Violence in Conflict (PSVI). In June 2014 the unlikely double act of the dour, balding Yorkshireman and the glamorous Hollywood star co-hosted a four-day international summit in London to demand an end to sexual violence in conflict, drawing in 1700 delegates, survivors, celebrities and representatives from 100 governments, and gaining widespread media coverage.

'It's not very usual, a foreign secretary and a Hollywood actress, but we needed something unusual to draw world attention,' said Hague. 'Angelina with her global profile and me as Foreign Secretary – what was missing was there had been no major country championing the issue.

'It turned out we could do a lot – the UK for example has presidency of the UN Security Council every fifteen months so I used that to set the agenda. Then we launched a declaration at the UN General Assembly where we got 155 countries to sign up to preventing sexual violence in conflict.'

He also raised it in every bilateral. 'It was a shock to other foreign ministers when they were told the British Foreign Secretary will definitely raise sexual violence in his meetings so they all had to buzz around and get briefings about it.

'Lots of people park it in their minds as a women's issue, and what men do with women's issues is assume women are going to deal with it. So people would ask me, "Why are you as a man involved?"

'My answer was since these crimes are committed almost exclusively by men, how can they be solved without the leadership of men? If you are 99 per cent of the problem you have to be 50 per cent of the solution.

'Others said this is very worthy, but it's as old as humanity and gone on in all wars, so the implication was, Why bother? I told them that sadly this is one of the great mass crimes of the twentieth century and the twenty-first century. If anything, it is getting worse – war-zone rape as a weapon of war, used systematically and deliberately against civilian populations.'

'I think all foreign ministries should have a PSVI unit – it is a fundamental part of peace and security, but still only the Brits have a group of people dedicated to sit and work on it full time. Otherwise it falls between cracks and people think it's hopeless.'

After he stepped down in 2014, subsequent foreign secretaries were less committed. The PSVI department went from thirty-four staff to three and the budget was cut from £15 million in 2014 to £2 million in 2019. 'It's frustrating that it has not become a fixture of British diplomatic efforts to the degree and intensity we had developed,' said Hague.

A report published in January 2020 by the Independent Commission for Aid Impact said the initiative had not delivered and was 'at risk of letting survivors down'. It pointed out the international summit had cost five times the UK's budget for tackling rape in war zones.

Hague had hoped Hillary Clinton would get elected in 2016 as America's first female President, as she shared his passion. Instead the US elected Donald Trump who had been accused of sexual assault and harassment by twenty women.

'In recent years we seem to have gone backwards,' said Hague. 'All recent conflicts still have this on a big scale so we haven't remotely solved the problem.'

Helic and another colleague Chloe Dalton left the Foreign Office and set up a non-profit together with Jolie. Undeterred by the politicians in power having lost interest, they turned to the generals and were met with unexpected enthusiasm.

General Nick Carter, the UK's Chief of Defence Staff, has a small but arresting painting on his dining room wall called *The Boy in Green*. It's of a young Afghan boy in an embroidered prayer cap and oversized camouflage jacket, with what he describes as 'that 1000 yard stare – he has clearly been abused all of his life'.

British soldiers serving in Afghanistan struggled to deal with the predilection of some of their Afghan counterparts, particularly in the police, for what are known euphemistically as 'tea boys'.

'There is a tension between trying to secure your short-term tactical objectives, which is securing the population – and clearly needs to be done by Afghans with us in support – and the longer-term one, which is that much of their behaviour plays into the challenge of the culture of impunity,' said Carter.

He believes that dealing with sexual violence – male and female – is an important part of soldiering, requiring a 'fundamental cultural shift'.

'Our enemies use the abuse of women as a weapon against men – and women. It's effective because of the sense of subjugation about it and brutalisation, and also in the really cynical way it was used in Bosnia it's about long-term ethnic cleansing, and under-mining of national identity, which is deeply distasteful and horri-bly systematic.'

Although Carter served in Bosnia and Kosovo in the 1990s, it was more-recent conflicts that convinced him of the need to act.

'One of the big lessons we've all learnt from campaigns of the last fifteen to twenty years, particularly Iraq and Afghanistan, is that if you're trying to bring stability to these countries, this is a lot less about the enemy and much more about the population at large.

'In order to engage with the population, it's absolutely funda-mental that you can engage both male and female aspects, which means how you secure women, who are often more vulnerable than men, is critical. Then, if you consider the impact the battle-field has on women, you quickly get into sexual violence in combat, because it is a weapon system, and to bring the stability and secu-rity you are trying to achieve in these problem countries, you need to remove the ability for people to use any sort of weapon but particularly that sort of weapon.

'Treating that problem is difficult because armed forces on the whole tend to be manned by men and to have a male culture, and you don't change these things quickly.'

For that reason, one of his priorities in his previous job as head of the army between 2014 and 2018 was to increase the number of women employed – eventually hoping to push it up from 10 per cent to 25 per cent.

'That's one of the reasons I leant into opening all roles in the army to women, particularly ground close-combat roles so I could look people in the eye and say nothing in the British army is excluded from women,' he said.

In autumn 2018 the British army started a two-week course at its Defence Academy in Shrivenham and trained 200 special advisors to help tackle sexual violence in conflict, particularly among troops in nations which they train. It also introduced identifying and responding to sexual violence in conflict into pre-deployment training and annual military tests, and deploying increasing numbers of female-engagement teams.

I witnessed this in action in January 2019 when I went to South Sudan, the world's newest nation, which broke away from Sudan in 2011, only to descend into its own brutal civil war, fuelled by rivalries over oil and ethnicity. Around 400,000 people had died and millions been displaced, and various peace agreements kept collapsing.

I travelled to the northern town of Bentiu where, over a series of ten days, a few weeks earlier, 123 women had been picked off the road by armed militia as they walked twenty miles to an aid-distribution point. The women had been dragged into the forest and raped, sometimes over and over again.

Based in a nearby camp of displaced people was a group of British soldiers known as the Bentiu Engineers, with a female commander Major Alanda Scott. 'The victims were women from eight to eighty, the age of your granddaughter to your grandmother, even pregnant women,' she said. 'It's horrific. No one should have that done to them.'

But she could see a solution. The women were having to walk so far to collect food because the road was impassable for trucks. This was why they were such easy pickings and that was something she could fix.

So she sent thirty of her field engineers out to clear the road, protected by Grenadier Guards and Mongolian peacekeepers. Working non-stop in searing temperatures, within five days they had removed the vegetation, widened the road and flattened the red mud surface.

It was simple – apart from their digging dislodging a nest of killer bees, which meant one soldier ended up with 150 stings – but effective and changed the lives of local women.

For an end to rapists' impunity there must be an end to silence. Shakespeare describes Lavinia as 'seeking to hide herself as doth the deer'. For this is the most personal of violations and is not easy to talk about. Rape is the least reported crime – rape in conflict even less so.

Sometimes this may be for fear of reprisals but mostly it is because of stigma which can be as traumatic as the actual event, so much so that some are driven to suicide. As Pramila Patten says, 'Rape is the only crime in which society is more likely to stigmatise than punish the perpetrator.' After this book was published in Germany in September 2020, a number of women contacted me to say their aunts or great aunts had been raped by Russian soldiers in the war but it was never spoken about.

On 19 June 2018 I went to Geneva for a meeting organised by Dr Mukwege to mark the International Day for Elimination of Sexual Violence.

Eight women from three continents sat nervously on a platform in a basement auditorium in the UN headquarters. They had been brought together by Dr Mukwege as part of the Global Survivor Network he has created, which so far comprises survivors from fourteen countries.

The meeting opened with Meehang Yoon from the Korean Council for the Women Drafted for Military Sexual Slavery by Japan. She showed video testimonies of some of the last surviving comfort women, including the one I had seen before of Kim Bok-dong who was by then ninety-two and suffering cancer so too frail to travel.

'Thanks to their tenacity and courage we are here today,' said Guillaumette Tsongo from Congo. 'They paved the way so that survivors can break shame and obtain justice.'

Among the survivors gathered that day was a serious young woman called Vasfije Krasniqi-Goodman from Kosovo. At the age of just sixteen, in April 1999, she had been abducted from her village by a Serbian policeman who raped her at knifepoint then passed her on to a colleague. 'I begged him to kill me but he said no, you'll suffer more this way,' she said.

'You hurt me,' she later said in a heartbreaking open letter to her rapists she videoed and posted on YouTube. 'I was sixteen, I was a child and had my whole life ahead of me. You stole my youth without a blink of an eye.'

An estimated 20,000 women in Kosovo are believed to have been raped during the war, but Vasfije, who had moved to Canada, was the first to come forward. She said it was only because she was no longer in the country that she had been able to speak out.

Not one of the survivors had received any apology or recognition by the Serbian government, which they blame for the atrocities. In a debate in the Kosovo parliament over whether those eligible for war pensions should include victims of sexual violence, politicians said they should be submitted to gynaecological tests.

Her rapists were indicted at the Basic Prosecution in Pristina in 2012 and the following year she testified in court. Initially the two men were acquitted in April 2014 on a 'technicality', but a month later an appeal court declared them guilty. 'It was the happiest day of my life besides my daughters being born,' said Vasfije. 'It was a vindication, it took away my suffering.'

Then the Supreme Court annulled the verdict. In her video, Vasfije insisted, 'I spoke for eight hours in front of foreign courts without success but I won't stop. I don't want it to happen to my daughter or anyone else's daughter.

'The man was right I would suffer more. Every day my mind goes to what happened. My mother died with a wounded heart from what happened to me.'

She ended with an appeal. 'Us, the 20,000, should unite, speak up, tell our story, find those criminals: our country should punish them.'

Though there has still not been a single conviction, her campaign has raised awareness. In June 2015 the first memorial for the sacrifice of women in the Kosovo War was inaugurated in Pristina. *Heroinat* (the Albanian female plural of heroes) is a striking sculpture of a woman's face made up of 20,000 pins, one to represent each victim.

In the nearby football stadium, an equally striking art installation was opened a few weeks later. Five thousand dresses donated by survivors and others were hung on washing lines on the pitch, all crisply laundered. Entitled *Thinking of You*, the artist was Alketa Xhafa Mripa, who had left Kosovo for London in 1997, just before the war, to study art at Central Saint Martins. 'I wanted to bring this hidden private issue that no one wanted to talk about into a public space and into the man's world to show that there is no shame or stigma,' she told me.

Eventually, in a landmark victory in February 2018, the state agreed to pay the women pensions of 230 euros a month, just as they had been doing for fifteen years for male veterans of the war. However, only 190 were approved in the first year as the process was long and few came forward, not wishing people to know what had happened to them. Many of the victims had not even told their closest family.

In October 2019, a second survivor Shyhrete Tahiri-Sylejmani filed a criminal complaint to Kosovo's Special Prosecution for War Crimes.

Vasfije and the other survivors at the Geneva meeting spoke of the strength they got from meeting others and being together. Dr Mukwege planned to use part of his Nobel Peace Prize to set up a global fund for survivors. 'Suffering is the same whether women are in Colombia or Central African Republic, Congo or Iraq,' he said. He also wanted to set up global centres of excellence where people could be trained, and to help women who have suffered transform pain to power.

Can women ever recover? I asked him.

'I have talked to so many and the answer is you can't,' he replied. 'When a woman decides to speak out, it's not to say I have recovered but to be an agent of change – to say it happened to me but shouldn't happen to my children or others.'

It is easy to despair that for every step forward there is one backward. A few months after that inspirational gathering in Geneva, *The Japan Times*, the country's oldest English language newspaper, appeared to cave in to those who would rewrite its wartime history. Apparently provoked by a decision by South Korea's Supreme Court to order Mitsubishi to compensate ten wartime forced labourers, which infuriated the Japanese government, the paper announced in November 2018 that it had previously used terms 'that could have been potentially misleading' and that it would henceforth alter its description of comfort women. In an editor's note, the newspaper noted that it had previously described the victims as 'women who were forced to provide sex for Japanese troops before and during the

Second World War'. But it added: 'Because the experiences of comfort women in different areas throughout the course of the war varied widely, from today we will refer to "comfort women" as "women who worked in wartime brothels, including those who did so against their will, to provide sex to Japanese soldiers".'

That's not all. The overturning of the Bemba case in June 2018 on a technicality sent a worrying signal that could endanger further convictions.

Professor Christine Chinkin, law professor and founding director of the recently created Centre for Women, Peace and Security at the London School of Economics, where Angelina Jolie is a visiting professor, said that what had been achieved in Guatemala and elsewhere was impressive but warned, 'This is a handful of cases. Compared with the level of sexual violence in conflict, even when there are successes it's a minute number. The great majority are not subject to prosecution.'

Perhaps this is not surprising, she added. 'Think about the appalling level of rape convictions in the UK where only 9 to 10 per cent of rape cases that get to court get a conviction.'

Indeed in 2018 more women came forward than ever before to report rape to the police – 57,882 – yet the number of convictions was at a record low, just 1925 – only 3.3 per cent.* An investigation by the Law Society found that between 2016 and 2018 rape prosecutors had been given a target conviction rate of 60 per cent, deterring them from charging cases they considered weaker.†

We still have a long way to go in the West. Astonishingly, all too often there is a tendency for men to think 'she was asking for it'.

There was outcry among women in Portugal in September 2017 when two men, a nightclub barman and a bouncer, were

---

* Crown Prosecution Service, *Violence Against Women*, 2018–19.

† Melanie Newman, '"Perverse Incentive" Contributed to Slump in Rape Charges', *Law Society Gazette*, 13 November 2019.

allowed free after raping a twenty-six-year-old woman in the club's toilets who had passed out from drink. The men were convicted and sentenced to four years in prison but the court then suspended the sentence on appeal on the basis of 'mitigating circumstances' of 'mutual flirting' and 'alcohol abuse'. One of the deciding judges was the President of the Judges' Union.

Women came out on the streets of Spain in 2018 after the so-called Wolf Pack case saw five men cleared of gang-raping an eighteen-year-old girl during the annual bull-running festival in Pamplona. The men belonged to a WhatsApp group called La manada or 'wolf pack' in which they boasted of their sexual exploits. One exchange mentioned the need for rope and date-rape drugs 'because when we get there, we'll want to rape everything we set eyes on'. The men had videoed their victim who they raped nine times – orally, anally and through the vagina – then left lying there, having stolen her phone. Somehow, the judges ruled this was not rape but the much lighter offence of sexual abuse.

In November 2018, there was a similar case in Ireland where a man was acquitted of raping a seventeen-year-old in an alleyway in Cork after the defence lawyer told the jury 'you have to look at the way she was dressed. She was wearing a thong with a lace front.'

The #MeToo movement which took the world by storm in autumn 2017 was of course a massive step in the right direction. Yet, as Eve Ensler pointed out, 'Women seem to be finding their voice at the same time as many misogynist leaders are coming to power.' Among them was Jair Bolsonaro elected president in Brazil in 2018, who a few years earlier had told a woman politician on the floor of Congress that she was 'too ugly to rape'.

Trump still got elected despite the emergence of what became known as the 'Grab 'em by the pussy' videotape, in which he is seen bragging about sexually assaulting women. Indeed, he got 47 per cent of the white female vote, more than for Hillary Clinton (though he claimed 52 per cent, a figure based on exit polls). And exit polling for the 2020 election indicate that Trump's support had *increased* among white women to 55 per cent.

No fan of the UN, the Trump administration withdrew all support for the International Criminal Court. In late 2018, his then National Security Advisor John Bolton declared 'for all intents and purposes the ICC is already dead to us'.

Spring 2019 saw a wave of state-led campaigns to bring in the most restrictive limits on abortions in decades. Alabama passed the most extreme abortion law in US history to ban abortion at all stages of pregnancy with no exception for rape or incest. Though these were blocked at least temporarily by federal courts, Ohio introduced a bill in November which would create a new crime called 'abortion murder', making people who undergo or perform abortions subject to life in prison.

This did not just affect women within the US. The Trump administration's opposition to abortion forced a watering down of language in a United Nations resolution in April 2019 that condemned sexual violence in conflicts, the US vehemently objecting to any reference to reproductive health care for victims. They insisted on removing the phrase which stated that the UN, 'recognising the importance of providing timely assistance to survivors of sexual violence, urges United Nations entities and donors to provide non-discriminatory and comprehensive health services including sexual and reproductive health, psychosocial, legal and livelihood support'.

France, the UK and Belgium all expressed regret. François Delattre, the French ambassador to the UN, described it as 'going against twenty-five years of gains for women's rights in situations of armed conflict'.*

---

* Liz Ford, 'UN Waters Down Rape Resolution to Appease US Hardline Abortion Stance', *Guardian*, 23 April 2019.

The awarding of the Nobel Peace Prize to Nadia Murad and Dr Mukwege in late 2018 for their work against sexual violence in conflict sent a strong message worldwide that women's bodies can no longer be seen as battlefields.

Just as the #MeToo movement has emboldened women all over the world to come forward about sexual harassment, there is much more awareness of rape in war. The two things are of course linked. It seems no coincidence that in countries such as Guatemala, where there had long been impunity for rape in war, we find the world's highest rates of violence against women, with 700 murders a year.

Similarly, in Sierra Leone, where rape was rampant in its ten-year civil war, sexual violence is so high, much of it against minors, that in February 2019 its government declared a national emergency. Of 8505 cases reported last year only 26 were prosecuted. In one case, a fifty-six-year-old man who raped a six-year-old girl was sentenced by a court in Freetown to just one year.

Christine Schuler, at the City of Joy in DRC, said she worried that so many children had witnessed rape that they thought it normal to carry it out.

Yet for all the lasting damage we have seen it cause, there is still a tendency to think of sexual violence in war as secondary to the killing. 'People think war authorises to kill, so raping women is nothing,' says Judge Pillay.

'There has been no trajectory of development since Akayesu,' she adds. 'It made legal history but hasn't helped much women in conflict situations.'

The South African admits it is frustrating but shrugs. 'Well, you know we learnt a lot of patience under apartheid. Every step counts.'

'Of course, we're disappointed,' agrees Patricia Sellers. 'War hasn't been outlawed and the question of impunity remains. But things have changed. One of the things that is different now is when we talk about Yazidis no one would dare not mention sexual violence.'

One of the challenges, apart from overcoming stigma so that women can come forward, is the importance of collecting evidence, not easy in such cases.

'If you don't have good evidence you don't have a case,' says Danaé van der Straten Ponthoz, an international lawyer who helped draft an international protocol on best practice for documenting and investigating sexual violence in conflict, which was launched in 2014 by the UK Foreign Office and since translated into a number of languages.

With no official international body, sometimes there are too many people taking statements, and every time survivors tell their story it changes, making it easy for defence lawyers to challenge in a court of law. Ironically, this is the case with Nadia Murad.

In an office with no name in a European capital is a locked vault monitored by security cameras, lined with shelves of numbered brown cardboard boxes, 265 of them. Their contents are chilling – inside more than a million documents gathered from Syria and Iraq, often at great risk, some bearing the signature of President Assad.

The documents are part of a secret project set up by war-crimes investigators to amass evidence on Assad, ready for potential prosecution for war crimes, after frustration that the international courts are too slow.

In 2018 the group also started collecting evidence on ISIS and its abduction of Yazidis as sex slaves. Like the Assad regime, the terrorist organisation documented many of its activities, and the paper trail makes clear that the slave trade was a system directed from the top and which the women kept track of.

Military records of fighters document how many *sabaya* or slaves each had while court records reveal the trade between them. Investigators have identified hundreds of slave owners, and four dozen slave traders who organised the system and ran the markets, as well as Shariat judges who presided over sales.

The keeping of slaves went to the very top – ISIS leader Abu Bakr al-Baghdadi held slaves whom he raped repeatedly, including a twenty-six-year-old American aid worker, Kayla Mueller, who was captured in Aleppo and kept along with two Yazidis by an ISIS fighter Abu Sayyaf and his wife Umm Sayyaf. Mueller was tragically killed in a 2015 raid by US Special Forces meant to rescue her.

The gruesome archive also includes articles from the group's glossy monthly magazine *Dabiq*. One in October 2014 is entitled 'The Renewal of Slavery Before the Hour'. This describes sexual slavery as 'a firmly established aspect of the Sharia' and clarifies that Yazidis should be treated as *mushrikin* – devil worshippers.

The documents have all been digitalised and in the 'sexual violence room' one of the investigators calls up one on her screen to show me. It is a certificate of ownership with two thumbprints of seller and buyer with date and place of where the purchase took place – Mosul – and price – $1500 in cash. The document is signed by a judge and witness.

It's the same way you would sell a car. The only details to describe the product are: 'age 20, with hazel green eyes, thin and short, height 1.3m.'

'It's awful, like cattle,' says the investigator. 'We're war-crimes investigators so used to shocking things but these documents are horrific, for they are about the ownership of human beings.'

I don't think I will ever finish this journey. War rape may never be eradicated completely but we must stop marginalising it and thinking of it as spoils of war that has gone on since time immemorial. As Angelina Jolie says, 'It is a preventable war crime that should be confronted with the same determination as the use of cluster bombs and chemical weapons', and we must do better to ensure that perpetrators don't get away with it. That takes political will and public pressure. Yet at the moment, justice is very much the exception not the rule. If anything, there seems to be less international appetite than ever to act against atrocities such as those against the Rohingya and the Yazidis as well as in Syria and Yemen.

We can start by listening to women's voices. These women who told me their stories did this so we can't say we didn't know. I will never forget Rojian, the sixteen-year-old Yazidi girl in Germany, with the word *Hope* in sparkly letters on her mobile phone, as she struggled to tell me what it was like hearing her fat captor rape a ten-year-old in the room next door as she cried for her mum. 'It is', she said, 'hard to tell, but even harder for people not to know.'

Maybe, reading this in our safe homes, this seems like a faraway problem. But many of these women thought it could never happen to them. This is not a local issue but a global one – as one of the women in Congo said, like a fire which starts in a forest and keeps burning. As long as we keep silent, we are complicit in saying this is acceptable.

During the protracted count for the 2020 US elections, I was struck by all the messages of hope I received from women I had met around the world. Not just at the change of occupant in the White House to Joe Biden but that he brings with him the first female Vice President Kamala Harris, a former prosecutor who has spoken about the importance of justice for sexual violence.

I never stopped being humbled by the women I met or being haunted by their feeling that those in the graves were the lucky ones. To me they are as much heroines of war as the fighters and should be recognised as such.

Things are changing. 'Military history is what was written in the past, purely by men and about men, but now we have started to write the proper history of war which of course includes the experiences of women and children,' said Antony Beevor. 'I have always been struck that the best diaries of war were written by women.'

Meanwhile, every time I walk past a war memorial, I wonder why the women's names are not on it.

The Hague, December 2019

Acknowledgements

I wrote this book because I was angry at coming across more and more brutality against women in the conflicts I reported on and wanted to know why it was happening and why no one was doing anything.

My reporting on Yazidis and girls abducted by Boko Haram started with articles for the *Sunday Times Magazine* and I cannot thank enough my brilliant editor Eleanor Mills and her deputy Krissi Murison for their support, for never being afraid to tackle difficult subjects, and motivating me with the occasional Casse-Croûte lunch!

What had become a personal obsession began to take shape as a book following encouragement from my friends Bettany Hughes and Aminatta Forna over dinner in the spectacular setting of Traquair, Scotland's oldest inhabited house, at Beyond Borders Festival.

Thank you as always to my wonderful agent David Godwin for believing in the project and shepherding it into the wide world, along with his colleague Lisette Verhagen, and to my amazing editor Arabella Pike and her fantastic team at HarperCollins. In particular thanks to Julian Humphries for designing the eye-catching cover and Katherine Patrick for spreading the word.

This book would not have been possible without so many incredible women agreeing to share their stories and I am immensely grateful to them for talking about the most painful and sensitive experiences anyone can endure.

I am a great believer in breaking the silence as the first step towards changing things. But these are the hardest of stories to tell. We talked over time in the way they wanted and where possible in safe spaces in the presence of psychiatrists. Everything was recorded and their accounts recounted in their own words. In some cases, names were changed; in others the women wanted their names told.

Some of the women are campaigners who have bravely told their stories many times in the hope of changing things, though it is no easy thing to be best known for enduring the worst experiences of your life.

This might have been a very dark book but I hope you will find, as I did, the strength and heroism of many of the women inspiring.

A note on language: in general, I use the expression 'survivors' to emphasise the resilience of these women, as after all they have survived, rather than 'victim' which has a more helpless connotation and some see as a dirty word. Meeting all these women, the last word I would use about them is passive. However, while I do not want to make 'victims' their identity, at the same time they are victims of an appalling brutality and injustice, so I do think the word has some validity. In some languages, such as Spanish, the word 'survivor' means survivor of a natural disaster. Colombian and Argentinian women I met told me it made no sense to refer to them as survivors. So I have used both where appropriate. In the same way, Yazidis told me they did not object to being described as kept as sex slaves, as long as that was not seen as their identity.

Many, many people helped me along the way. Starting with the Yazidis, I would like to thank Dr Khabat Kedir for putting me in touch with the Yazidis in Germany, Dr Michael Blume for enabling my visit and Shaker Jeffrey for translating. Anne Norona, an NHS nurse from Penzance who gives Botox injections on the side to raise money to help, was a great travelling companion both in Germany and Iraq. In Khanke camp, thanks to Pari Ibrahim and Silav Ibrahim from the Free Yazidi Foundation, trauma psychologists Ginny Dobson and Yesim Arikut-Treece, and the lovely Khairi for her interpreting. Shilan Dosky provided invaluable help in Kurdistan.

In Nigeria, thanks to the Bring Back Our Girls campaign, Barrister Mustapha and local NGOs working in the IDP camps who prefer to remain nameless.

In the Rohingya camps, thanks to Save the Children and my interpreters Reza and Sonali. Dr Azeem Ibrahim was a great sounding board back in London.

In Bangladesh, I am very grateful to Aziz Zaeed who helped set up meetings with *birangonas* and interpreted, and to Safina Lohani and Mofidul Hoque.

Thank you to James Hill and Remembering Srebrenica for arranging my visit to Bosnia and my amazing guides Resad Trbonja and Aida, as well as the staff of Medica Zenit.

In Rwanda, thanks to Samuel Munderere at Survivors Fund (Surf), Felix Manzi and my friend Michele Mitchell whose film *The Uncondemned* on the fight for justice is a must-watch. Her Californian wine supply and adorable brother Matt provided much-needed light relief in dark moments.

In Argentina, thanks to Lorena Balardini and Miriam Lewin, as well as the staff at ESMA.

My visit to DRC and Panzi Hospital and City of Joy would not have been possible without the help of Elizabeth Blackney, Esther Dingemans, Apolline Pierson and Crispin Kashale. Thanks also to Rodha, psychiatrist and interpreter, Daniele Perissi and the staff of TRIAL International, and Simon O' Connell, executive director of Mercy Corps and his assistant Amy Fairbairn, as well as Jean-

Philippe Marcoux in Goma who was a fount of knowledge about the militias of eastern Congo.

In the Philippines, thanks to Sharon Cabusao-Silva from Lila Pilipina for organising my meetings and to Joan Salvador from Gabriela and Oscar Atadero for translating.

Many other people who are experts in this field were immensely helpful and generous with their time. Huge thanks to Antony Beevor, Eve Ensler, Baroness Arminka Helic, Lord William Hague, Peter Frankopan and Leslie Thomas.

The photographers I worked with on some of the assignments made the job much more enjoyable – and they took some wonderful pictures, some of which are in the book. Georgios Makkas in Leros and Germany, Justin Sutcliffe on one of my trips to Maiduguri, Nichole Sobecki in Rwanda, Paula Bronstein in the Rohingya camps and DRC.

Huge thanks to David Campbell for providing, in Casa Ecco on the shores of Lake Como, a stunning place to think, and the Two Ms – Margherita and Marilena – for plying me with delicious pasta and fish to fuel the writing.

I know many of these stories were not easy to read. Thank you for reading and caring and hopefully spreading the word, for nothing will change without justice.

This was not an easy book to write – or live with. Thanks to my wonderful son Lourenco for putting up with a distracted mother, and my own amazing mum who brought me up to care about right and wrong. Above all thanks to Paulo. *Até o fim do mundo.*

Select Bibliography

Alexievich, Svetlana, *The Unwomanly Face of War* (London: Penguin Classics, 2017)

Bourke, Joanna, *Rape: A History from 1860 to the Present Day* (London: Virago, 2007)

Brownmiller, Susan, *Against Our Will: Men, Women and Rape* (New York: Simon & Schuster, 1975)

Chang, Iris, *The Rape of Nanking: The Forgotten Holocaust of World War II* (New York: Basic Books, 1997)

Herzog, Dagmar (ed.), *Brutality and Desire: War and Sexuality in Europe's Twentieth Century* (Basingstoke: Palgrave Macmillan, 2009)

Jesch, Judith, *Women in the Viking Age* (Woodbridge: Boydell Press, 2003)

Sanyal, Mithu, *Rape: From Lucretia to #MeToo* (London: Verso, 2019)

Shakespeare, William, *Titus Andronicus* (London: Penguin Classics, 2015)

Vikman, Elisabeth, 'Ancient Origins: Sexual Violence in Warfare, Part I' (London: *Anthropology & Medicine*, vol. 12, no. 1, pages 21–31, 2005)

Vikman, Elisabeth, 'Modern Combat: Sexual Violence in Warfare, Part II' (London: *Anthropology & Medicine*, vol. 12, no. 1, pages 33–46, 2005)

Argentina

Balardini, Lorena, Sobredo, Laura and Oberlin, Ana, *Gender Violence and Sexual Abuse in Clandestine Detention Centers: A Contribution to Understanding the Experience of Argentina* (Buenos Aires: CELS/ICTJ, 2010)

Lewin, Miriam and Wornat, Olga, *Putas y guerrilleras* (Buenos Aires: Planeta, 2014)

Sutton, Barbara, *Surviving State Terror: Women's Testimonies of Repression and Resistance in Argentina* (New York: New York University Press, 2018)

Bangladesh

Bass, Gary Jonathan, *The Blood Telegram: Nixon, Kissinger, and a Forgotten Genocide* (London: Hurst, 2014)

Mookherjee, Nayanika, *The Spectral Wound: Sexual Violence, Public Memories and the Bangladesh War of 1971* (Durham, NC: Duke University Press, 2015)

Raja, Khadim Hussain, *A Stranger in My Own Country: East Pakistan, 1969–1971* (Dhaka: University Press, 2012)

Berlin

Anonymous, *A Woman in Berlin: Diary 20 April 1945 to 22 June 1945* (London: Virago, 2005)

Beevor, Antony, *Berlin: The Downfall, 1945* (London: Viking, 2002)

Djilas, Milovan, *Conversations with Stalin* (London: Rupert Hart-Davis, 1962)

Huber, Florian, *Promise Me You'll Shoot Yourself: The Downfall of Ordinary Germans, 1945* (London: Allen Lane, 2019)

Köpp, Gabriele, *Warum war ich bloß ein Mädchen?: Das Trauma einer Flucht 1945* (Herbig Verlag, 2010)

Merridale, Catherine, *Ivan's War: Life and Death in the Red Army, 1939–1945* (New York: Metropolitan Books, 2006)

Bosnia

Andric, Ivo, *The Bridge over the Drina* (London: Harvill, 1994)

Borger, Julian, *The Butcher's Trail: How the Search for Balkan War Criminals Became the World's Most Successful Manhunt* (New York: Other Press, 2016)

Butcher, Tim, *The Trigger: The Hunt for Gavrilo Princip – The Assassin Who Brought the World to War* (London: Vintage Digital, 2014)

Glenny, Misha, *The Fall of Yugoslavia: The Third Balkan War* (London: Penguin, 1992)

Warburton, Ann, *EC Investigative Mission into the Treatment of Muslim Women in the Former Yugoslavia, Summary of Report to EC Foreign Ministers* (Copenhagen: WomenAid International, 1993)

Burma-Rohingya

Human Rights Council, *Report of the Independent International Fact-finding Mission on Myanmar* (Geneva: United Nations Human Rights Council A/HRC/39/64, 2018)

Ibrahim, Azeem, *The Rohingyas: Inside Myanmar's Hidden Genocide* (London: Hurst & Company, 2016)

Orwell, George, *Burmese Days* (New York: Harper & Brothers, 1934)

DRC

Guevara, Ernesto 'Che', *The African Dream: The Diaries of the Revolutionary War in the Congo* (London: Harvill, 2000)

Hochschild, Adam, *King Leopold's Ghost: A Story of Greed, Terror, and Heroism in Colonial Africa* (Boston, Houghton Mifflin, 1998)

Johnson, Kirsten et al., 'Association of Sexual Violence and Human Rights Violations with Physical and Mental Health in Territories of the Eastern Democratic Republic of the Congo'

(Chicago: *Journal of the American Medical Association*, vol. 304, no. 5, pages 553–562, 2010)

SáCouto, Susana, *The Impact of the Appeals Chamber Decision in Bemba: Impunity for Sexual and Gender-Based Crimes?* (New York: Open Society Justice Initiative, International Justice Monitor, 22 June 2018)

United Nations Security Council, *Final Report of the Panel of Experts on the Illegal Exploitation of Natural Resources and Other Forms of Wealth of the Democratic Republic of the Congo* (New York: UNSC S/2002/1146, 2002)

van Reybrouck, David, *Congo: The Epic History of a People* (London: 4th Estate, 2014)

Nigeria

Habila, Helon, *The Chibok Girls: the Boko Haram Kidnappings and Islamist Militancy in Nigeria* (London: Penguin, 2017)

O'Brien, Edna, *Girl* (London: Faber & Faber, 2019)

Thurston, Alex, *'The Disease Is Unbelief': Boko Haram's Religious and Political Worldview* (Washington DC: The Brookings Institution, Center for Middle East Policy, Analysis Paper no. 22, 2016)

Walker, Andrew, *'Eat the Heart of the Infidel': The Harrowing of Nigeria and the Rise of Boko Haram* (London: Hurst, 2016)

Nineveh

Brereton, Gareth (ed.), *I Am Ashurbanipal: King of the World, King of Assyria* (London: Thames & Hudson, 2018)

Perpetrators

Ensler, Eve, *The Apology* (London: Bloomsbury, 2019)

Human Rights Center, *The Long Road – Accountability for Sexual Violence in Conflict and Post-Conflict Settings* (Berkeley: UC Berkeley School of Law, 2015)

Human Rights Watch, *Kurdistan Region of Iraq: Detained Children Tortured – Beatings, Electric Shock to Coerce ISIS Confessions* (New York: Human Rights Watch, 2019)

Skjelsbæk, Inger, *Preventing Perpetrators: How to Go from Protection to Prevention of Sexual Violence in War?* (Oslo: Peace Research Institute Oslo, PRIO Policy Brief 3, 2013)

Slahi, Mohamedou Ould, *Guantánamo Diary* (New York: Little, Brown & Company, 2015)

Wilén, Nina and Ingelaere, Bert, 'The Civilised Self and the Barbaric Other: Ex-Rebels Making Sense of Sexual Violence in the DR Congo' (*Journal of Contemporary African Studies*, vol. 35, no. 2, pages 221–239, 2017)

Wood, Elisabeth Jean, 'Rape during War Is Not Inevitable', in *Understanding and Proving International Sex Crimes* (Beijing: Torkel Opsahl Academic EPublisher, 2012)

Rwanda

Durham, Helen and Gurd, Tracey (eds), *Listening to the Silences: Women and War* (Leiden: Martinus Nijhoff Publishers, 2005)

Gourevitch, Philip, *We Wish to Inform You That Tomorrow We Will Be Killed with Our Families: Stories from Rwanda* (New York: Farrar, Straus & Giroux, 1998)

Hatzfeld, Jean, *A Time for Machetes: The Rwandan Genocide – The Killers Speak* (London: Serpent's Tail, 2005)

Human Rights Watch, *Shattered Lives: Sexual Violence during the Rwandan Genocide and its Aftermath* (New York: Human Rights Watch, 1996)

Nowrojee, Binaifer, *'Your Justice is Too Slow': Will the ICTR Fail Rwanda's Rape Victims?* (Geneva: United Nations Research Institute for Social Development, UNRISD Occasional Paper 10, 2005)

Sundaram, Anjan, *Bad News: Last Journalists in a Dictatorship* (London: Bloomsbury, 2016)

Van Schaack, Beth, *Engendering Genocide: The Akayesu Case Before the International Criminal Tribunal for Rwanda* (Human Rights Advocacy Stories, New York: Foundation Press, 2009)

Spain

Beevor, Antony, *The Battle for Spain: The Spanish Civil War 1936–1939* (London: Weidenfeld & Nicolson, 2006)

Preston, Paul, *The Spanish Holocaust: Inquisition and Extermination in Twentieth-century Spain* (London: HarperPress, 2013)

Sender Barayón, Ramón, *A Death in Zamora* (San Francisco: Calm Unity Press, 2019)

Syria

Human Rights Council, *'I Lost my Dignity': Sexual and Gender-based Violence in the Syrian Arab Republic* – Conference Room Paper of the Independent International Commission of Inquiry on the Syrian Arab Republic (Geneva: United Nations Human Rights Council A/HRC/37/CRP.3, 2018)

United Nations High Commissioner for Refugees, *'We Keep It in Our Heart': Sexual Violence Against Men and Boys in the Syria Crisis* (Geneva: UNHCR, 2017)

US Civil War

Carr, Matthew, *Sherman's Ghosts: Soldiers, Civilians, and the American Way of War* (New York: New Press, 2015)

Feimster, Crystal Nicole, *Southern Horrors: Women and the Politics of Rape and Lynching* (London: Harvard University Press, 2009)

Vietnam

Hastings, Max, *Vietnam: An Epic Tragedy, 1945–1975* (London: William Collins, 2018)

Yazidi

Jeffrey, Shaker and Holstein, Katharine, *Shadow on the Mountain: A Yazidi Memoir of Terror, Resistance and Hope* (New York: Da Capo Press, 2020)

Murad, Nadia and Krajeski, Jenna, *The Last Girl: A Memoir* (London: Virago, 2017)

Otten, Cathy, *With Ash on Their Faces: Yezidi Women and the Islamic State* (New York: OR Books, 2017)

Films

Blood in the Mobile. Directed by Frank Piasecki Poulsen, Koncern TV, 2010

City of Joy. Directed by Madeleine Gavin, Netflix, 2016

In the Land of Blood and Honey. Directed by Angelina Jolie, GK Films, 2011

The Prosecutors. Directed by Leslie Thomas, Art Works Projects, 2018

The Silence of Others. Directed by Almudena Carracedo and Robert Bahar, Semilla Verde Productions, 2019

The Uncondemned. Directed by Michele Mitchell, Film at Eleven Media, 2015

Image Credits